S0-AZQ-682

SPOTLIGHT™ on MUSIC

Authors

Judy Bond
René Boyer
Margaret Campbelle-Holman
Emily Crocker
Marilyn C. Davidson
Robert de Frece
Virginia Ebinger
Mary Goetze
Betsy M. Henderson
John Jacobson
Michael Jothen
Chris Judah-Lauder
Carol King
Vincent P. Lawrence
Ellen McCullough-Brabson
Janet McMillion
Nancy L. T. Miller
Ivy Rawlins
Susan Snyder
Gilberto D. Soto

Kodály Contributing Consultant
Sr. Lorna Zemke

MACMILLAN
McGRAW-HILL

ACKNOWLEDGMENTS

Creative Direction and Delivery: The Quarasan Group, Inc.

From the Top—On National Radio! selections are adapted from the nationally distributed public radio program *From the Top.* CEOs/Executive Producers: Jennifer Hurley-Wales and Gerald Slavet. Authors: Ann Gregg and Joanne Robinson. © 2000, 2002, 2003 From the Top, Inc.

The Broadway Junior® logo and MTI® logo are trademarks of Music Theatre International. All rights reserved.

Grateful acknowledgment is given to the following authors, composers, and publishers. Every effort has been made to trace the ownership of all copyrighted material and to secure the necessary permissions to reprint these selections. In the case of some selections for which acknowledgment is not given, extensive research has failed to locate the copyright holders.

Atlantic City, From MTI's Broadway Junior Broadway for Kids RAGTIME Junior. Music by Stephen Flaherty. Lyrics by Lynn Ahrens. Copyright © 1996, 1997 WB Music Corp., Pen and Perseverance and Hillsdale Music, Inc. All Rights Reserved. Used by Permission.

Autumn Fires by Robert Louis Stevenson, from *A Child's Garden of Verses*. Copyright © 1905, by CHARLES SCRIBNER'S SONS. All Rights Reserved. Reset March 1955. Used by Permission.

Be Yours, Words and Music by Mary Unobsky. Copyright © by Unobsky Songs. International Copyright Secured. All Rights Reserved.

Castle on a Cloud from LES MISÉRABLES, Music by Claude-Michel Schönberg, Lyrics by Alain Boublil, Jean-Marc Natel and Herbert Kretzmer. Music and Lyrics Copyright © 1980 by Editions Musicales Alain Boublil. English Lyrics Copyright © 1986 by Alain Boublil Music Ltd. (ASCAP). Mechanical and Publication Rights for the U.S.A. Administered by Alain Boublil Music Ltd. (ASCAP) c/o Stephen Tenenbaum & Co., Inc., 1775 Broadway, Suite 708, New York, NY 10019, Tel. (212) 246-7204, Fax (212) 246-7217. International Copyright Secured. All Rights Reserved. This music is copyright. Photocopying is illegal. All Performance Rights Restricted.

Circle of Life from Walt Disney Pictures' THE LION KING, Music by Elton John, Lyrics by Tim Rice. © 1994 Wonderland Music Company, Inc. All Rights Reserved. Used by Permission.

Come On-A My House, Words and Music by Ross Bagdasarian and William Saroyan. Copyright © 1957 Ross Bagdasarian Music, Adam Bagdasarian Music and Carol Bagdasarian Music. Copyright Renewed. All Rights on behalf of Ross Bagdasarian Music Administered by Sony/ATV Music Publishing, 8 Music Square West, Nashville, TN 37203. International Copyright Secured. All Rights Reserved.

Don't Laugh at Me, Words and Music by Steve Seskin and Allen Shamblin. Copyright © 1998 Sony/ATV Tunes LLC, David Aaron Music and Built On Rock Music. All Rights on behalf of Sony/ATV Tunes LLC and David Aaron Music Administered by Sony/ATV Music Publishing, 8 Music Square West, Nashville, TN 37203. International Copyright Secured. All Rights Reserved.

Down at the Twist and Shout, Words and Music by Mary Chapin Carpenter. © 1990 EMI APRIL MUSIC INC. and GETAREALJOB MUSIC. All Rights Controlled and Administered by EMI APRIL MUSIC INC. All Rights Reserved. International Copyright Secured. Used by Permission.

El cóndor pasa (If I Could), English Lyric by Paul Simon. Musical Arrangement Written by Jorge Milchberg and Daniel Robles. Copyright © 1933, 1963, 1970 Edward B. Marks Music Company and Jorge Milchberg. English lyrics Copyright © 1970 Paul Simon (BMI). International Copyright Secured. All Rights Reserved. Used by Permission.

Emergency, Words and Music by Evelyn Maria Harris. Copyright © 1985 by Hazel Eyes Music. International Copyright Secured. All Rights Reserved.

Follow Your Dream, Words and Music by Janet McMahan-Wilson and Ted Wilson. Copyright © by Janet McMahan-Wilson and Ted Wilson. International Copyright Secured. All Rights Reserved.

Freedom Is a Constant Struggle, Words and Music by Roberta Slavit. Copyright © 1965 (Renewed 1993) by Stormking Music, Inc. International Copyright Secured. All Rights Reserved.

Give a Little Love, Words and Music by Albert Hammond and Diane Warren. © 1986 ALBERT HAMMOND MUSIC and REALSONGS. All Rights Reserved. Used by Permission.

God Bless the U.S.A., Words and Music by Lee Greenwood. Copyright © 1984 SONGS OF UNIVERSAL, INC. and UNIVERSAL-SONGS OF POLYGRAM INTERNATIONAL, INC. All Rights Controlled and Administered by SONGS OF UNIVERSAL, INC. All Rights Reserved. Used by Permission.

Hang on Sloopy, Words and Music by Wes Farrell and Bert Russell. Copyright © 1964, 1965 by Morris Music, Inc., Sony/ATV Songs LLC and Sloopy II, Inc. in the U.S. Copyright Renewed. All Rights on behalf of Sony/ATV Songs LLC Administered by Sony/ATV Music Publishing, 8 Music Square West, Nashville, TN 37203. All Rights outside the U.S. Administered by Morris Music, Inc. International Copyright Secured. All Rights Reserved.

Henry Ford, From MTI's Broadway Junior Broadway for Kids RAGTIME Junior. Music by Stephen Flaherty. Lyrics by Lynn Ahrens. Copyright © 1996, 1997 WB Music Corp., Pen and Perseverance and Hillsdale Music, Inc. All Rights Reserved. Used by Permission.

continued on page 275

The McGraw·Hill Companies

Published by Macmillan/McGraw-Hill, of McGraw-Hill Education, a division of The McGraw-Hill Companies, Inc., Two Penn Plaza, New York, New York 10121.

Printed in the United States of America
ISBN 0-02-296047-3 / 7
7 8 9 006/043 10 09 08 07 06

CONTRIBUTORS

Consultants

Brian Burnett,
Movement

Stephen Gabriel,
Technology

Magali Iglesias,
English Language Learners

Roberta Newcomer,
Special Learners/Assessment

Frank Rodríguez,
English Language Learners

Jacque Schrader,
Movement

Kathy B. Sorensen,
International Phonetic Alphabet

Patti Windes-Bridges,
Listening Maps

Linda Worsley,
Listening/Singable English Translations

Sr. Lorna Zemke,
Kodály Contributing Consultant

Contributing Writers

Allison Abucewicz
Sharon Berndt
Rhona Brink
Ann Burbridge
Debbie Helm Daniel
Katherine Domingo
Kari Gilbertson
Janet Graham
Hilree Hamilton
Linda Harley
Judy Henneberger
Carol Huffman
Bernie Hynson, Jr.
Sheila A. Kerley
Ellen Mendelsohn
Cristi Cary Miller
Leigh Ann Mock
Patricia O'Rourke
Barbara Resch
Isabel Romero
Carl B. Schmidt
Debra Shearer
Ellen Mundy Shuler
Rebecca Treadway
Carol Wheeler
Sheila Woodward

Recordings

Executive Producer
John Higgins

Senior Music Editor/Producer
Emily Crocker

Senior Recording Producer
Mark Brymer

Recording Producers
Steve Millikan
Andy Waterman

Associate Recording Producers
Alan Billingsley, Darrell Bledsoe, Stacy Carson, Emily Crocker, Rosanna Eckert, John Egan, Chad Evans, Darlene Koldenhoven, Chris Koszuta, Don Markese, Matthew McGregor, Steve Potts, Edwin Schupman, Michael Spresser, Frank Stegall, David Vartanian, Mike Wilson, Ted Wilson

Project/Mastering Engineer
Mark Aspinall

Post Production Engineer
Don Sternecker

Multicultural Consultants

William Anderson, Chet-Yeng Loong, Edwin Schupman, Kathy B. Sorensen, Gilberto D. Soto, Judith Cook Tucker, Dennis Waring

In the Spotlight Consultant

Willa Dunleavy

Multicultural Advisors

Brad Ahawanrathe Bonaparte (Mohawk), Emmanuel Akakpo (Ewe), Earlene Albano (Hawaiian), Luana Au (Maori), Ruby Beeston (Mandarin), Latif Bolat (Turkey), Estella Christensen (Spanish), Oussama Davis (Arabic), Mia Delguardo (Minahasa), Nolutho Ndengane Diko (Xhosa), Angela Fields (Hopi, Chemehuevi), Gary Fields (Lakota, Cree), Gilad Harel (Hebrew), Josephine Hetarihon (Bahasa Indonesian, Minahasa, and Maluko dialect), Judy Hirt-Manheimer (Hebrew), Rose Jakub (Navajo), Elizabeth Jarema (Fijian), Rita Jensen (Swedish), Malou Jewett (Visayan), Alejandro Jimenez (Hispanic), Chris Jones (Hungarian), Wendy Jyang Shamo (Mandarin), Amir Kalay (Hebrew), Michael Katsan (Greek), Silvi Madarajan (Tamil), Georgia Magpie (Comanche), Nona Mardi (Malay), Aida Mattingly (Tagalog), Mike Kanathohare McDonald (Mohawk), Vasana de Mel (Sinhala), Marion Miller (Czech), Etsuko Miskin (Japanese), Mogens Mogenson (Danish), Kenny Tahawisoren Perkins (Mohawk), Pradeep Nayyar (Punjabi, Hindi), Renu Nayyar (Punjabi), Mfanego Ngwenya (Zulu), Wil Numkena (Hopi), Samuel Owuru (Akan), Nina Padukone (Konkani), Hung Yong Park (Korean), James Parker (Finnish), Jose Pereira (Konkani), Berrit Price (Norwegian), John Rainer (Taos Pueblo, Creek), Lillian Rainer (Taos Pueblo, Creek, Apache), Arnold Richardson (Haliwa-Saponi), Ken Runnacles (German), Trudy Shenk (German), Ron Singer (Navajo), Ernest Siva (Cahuilla, Serrano [Maringa']), Bonnie Slade (Swedish), Cristina Sorrentino (Portuguese), Diane Thram (Xhosa), Elena Todorov (Bulgarian), Zlatina Todorov (Russian), Tom Toronto (Lao, Thai), Rebecca Wilberg (French, Italian), Sheila Woodward (Zulu), Keith Yackeyonny (Comanche)

Contents

Music in My WORLD

MUSIC in My SCHOOL

MUSIC in Our CITIES

Our Musical Legacy

The Many MOODS of Music

Expressing with Music

Celebrating with MUSIC

Connecting Through Music

Broadway For Kids

ADMIT ONE 0596033

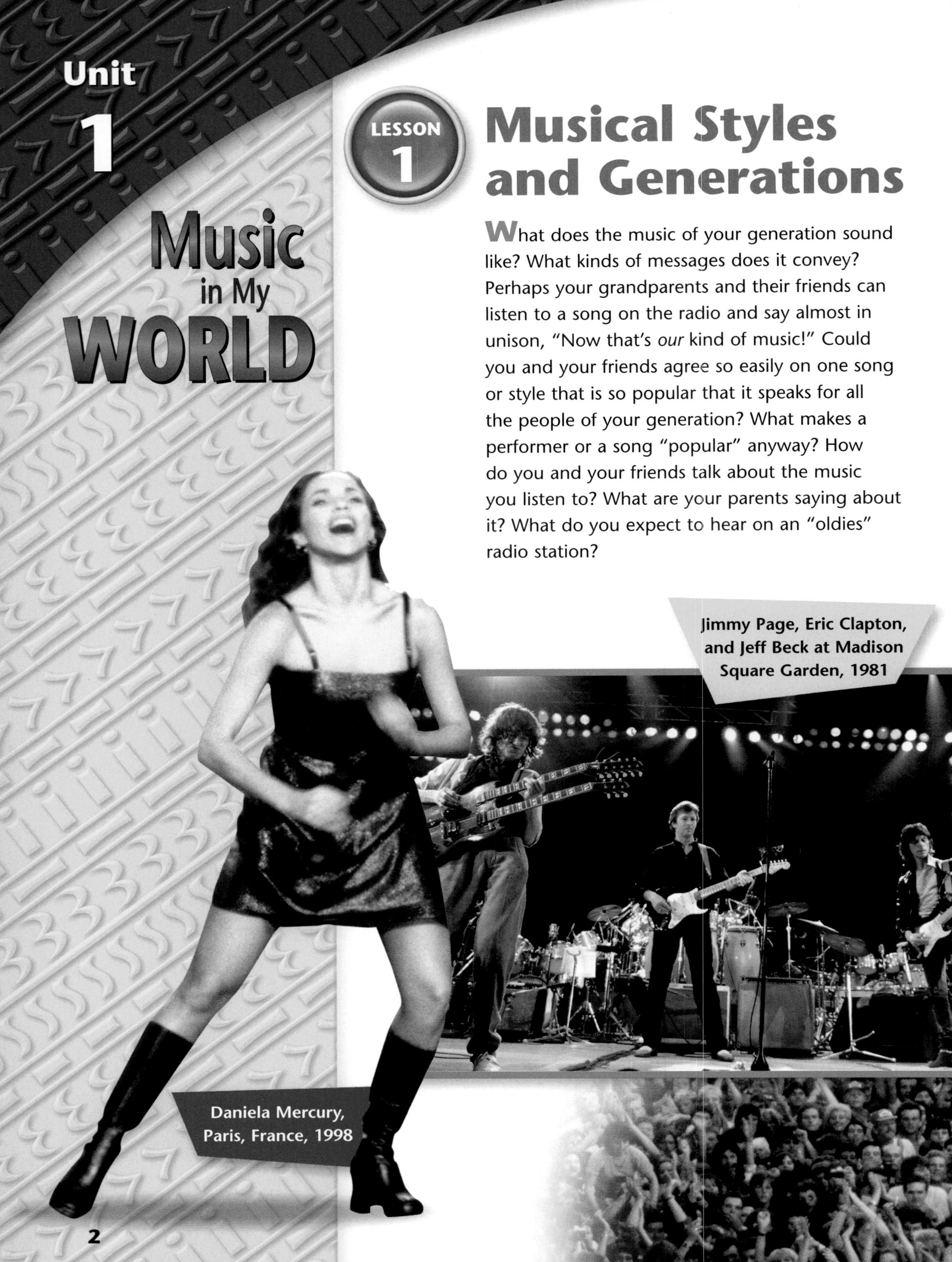

Unit 1

Music in My WORLD

LESSON 1 Musical Styles and Generations

What does the music of your generation sound like? What kinds of messages does it convey? Perhaps your grandparents and their friends can listen to a song on the radio and say almost in unison, "Now that's *our* kind of music!" Could you and your friends agree so easily on one song or style that is so popular that it speaks for all the people of your generation? What makes a performer or a song "popular" anyway? How do you and your friends talk about the music you listen to? What are your parents saying about it? What do you expect to hear on an "oldies" radio station?

Jimmy Page, Eric Clapton, and Jeff Beck at Madison Square Garden, 1981

Daniela Mercury, Paris, France, 1998

LISTENING CD 1:1

Music of the Generations (montage)

Look at the titles in "Music of the Generations." Before you listen to these excerpts, predict whether or not you will recognize the piece by its title, the performer, or the songwriter. Predict as well whether or not it will be in a style that you enjoy listening to, dancing to, or performing.

Listen to "Music of the Generations." For each excerpt, try to identify the decade, generation, or century that you think it comes from. Comment on the **style** in light of your own preferences and, when appropriate, identify the culture that you think the excerpt may come from. *Style* refers to musical qualities that are characteristic of a particular person, culture, or time period.

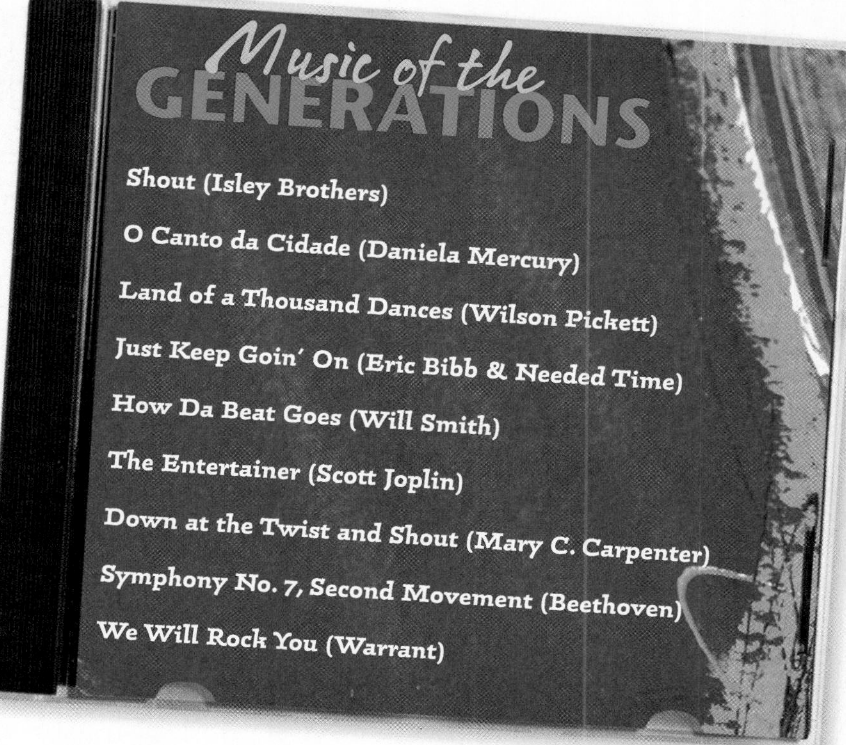

Music of the GENERATIONS
Shout (Isley Brothers)
O Canto da Cidade (Daniela Mercury)
Land of a Thousand Dances (Wilson Pickett)
Just Keep Goin' On (Eric Bibb & Needed Time)
How Da Beat Goes (Will Smith)
The Entertainer (Scott Joplin)
Down at the Twist and Shout (Mary C. Carpenter)
Symphony No. 7, Second Movement (Beethoven)
We Will Rock You (Warrant)

Music Journal

What helped me decide whether or not I would recognize musical selections and styles of different generations? How can I describe some characteristics of the different styles I think I will hear?

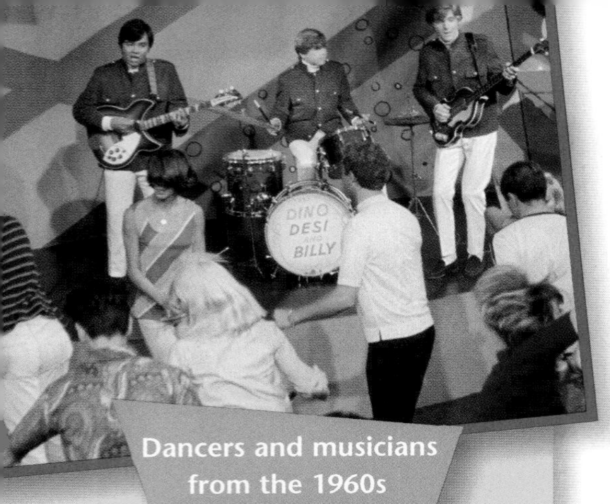

Dancers and musicians from the 1960s

Music Across the Generations

Look at the photographs throughout this lesson. Determine which ones are from your own generation, your parents' generation, or your grandparents' generation. Describe similarities and differences among the people and activities in the photographs.

Which generation (or generations) would you associate with each item?

1. They know a lot about technology.
2. They care nothing about current fashion.
3. They are optimistic about the future.
4. They usually share their parents' opinions.
5. They fear the future.
6. They question authority.
7. They love to dance.
8. They are hard workers.
9. Culture is very important to them.
10. They like to do their own thing.

The word *generation* describes a group of people born at about the same time. What have you heard about the Silent Generation, the Baby Boomers or Boom Generation, Generation X, Generation Y, or the Millennial Generation? What would you like people to say about *your* generation?

Rapper Will Smith

LOG ON

music.mmhschool.com
Research Baby Boomers, Generation X, and other generations on the Web.

Although it may be challenging to identify a single musical style as dominant in any one generation, each generation surely finds its own distinct way of expressing itself musically. Whatever the style, the basic musical elements remain the same. Most music, for example, has a steady silent pulse underlying it. This underlying pulse, or beat, is called the **steady beat**. It is hard to imagine how anyone could move or dance to music without a steady beat!

LISTENING **CD 1:2**

Respect (two versions)
by Otis Redding

The two performances of "Respect" highlighted in this recording are by the Seattle Men's Chorus and a mixed choir.

Snap, clap, or pat the steady beat as you listen to "Respect (two versions)."

Clap or pat the patterns below with your hands while tapping the steady beat with one foot.

Play drumsticks or other percussion instruments to accompany "Respect (two versions)" with the rhythm pattern or patterns you think are most appropriate.

Listen once more to "Respect (two versions)." Notice the different vocal and instrumental sounds. The unique sound of each instrument and voice is called **tone color**.

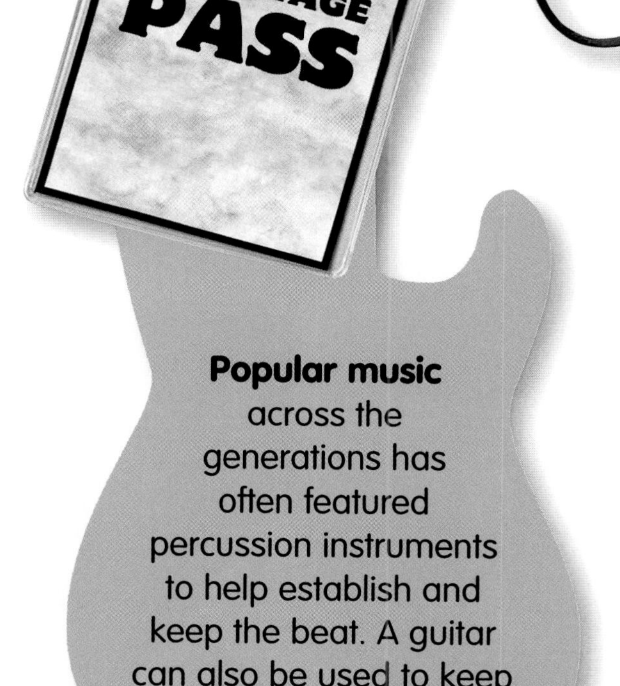

Popular music across the generations has often featured percussion instruments to help establish and keep the beat. A guitar can also be used to keep the beat going.

Music Journal

Which rhythm patterns, movements, or dance steps were most challenging to perform? Why?

Generational Differences

The **popular music** of a generation is the music that is most liked and accepted by the people of that generation. It is the music that people spend the most time listening to, performing, and watching. The music we call **contemporary** is the music that is currently most popular in a particular place and time.

The musical style of a generation has unique characteristics that can tell us about where and when the music was performed. We can *listen* for these characteristics—the quality of a recording can provide some hints about when the music was recorded. The choice of instruments or rhythmic styles used to accompany a melody might also help us determine when or where a song was performed and can change the sound of a song altogether.

LOG ON

music.mmhschool.com
Find Grammy winners on the Web.

1950s

Duke Ellington, Ella Fitzgerald, Frank Sinatra, Perry Como, Judy Garland, Ethel Merman, Nat "King" Cole, The Kingston Trio, Bobby Darin

1960s

Ray Charles, Miles Davis, Chubby Checker, Barbra Streisand, The Beatles, Peter, Paul & Mary, Joni Mitchell, Aretha Franklin, Glen Campbell

1970s

Simon & Garfunkel, Carole King, James Taylor, Carly Simon, Ike & Tina Turner, Bette Midler, The Eagles, Stevie Wonder, Linda Ronstadt, Billy Joel

We can also *look* for distinctive characteristics of a generation's musical style. A popular performing group in one generation may include 20 musicians in a swing band, all dressed alike and playing in an orchestral setting.

Sometimes there is a featured vocalist. A popular group in another generation may have several singers and musicians wearing headphones and cordless microphones while moving around a laser-lit stage.

music.mmhschool.com
Hear the progress in recording technology throughout the 20th century.

Improvise on the following rhythm patterns on percussion instruments. Express something unique about your own preference when it comes to musical style.

The Glenn Miller Orchestra performing in the movie *Sun Valley Serenade*

Music Journal

How would I arrange "Respect" for a performance in my school? What instruments and voices would I highlight? Why?

1980s

Willie Nelson, Michael Jackson, Whitney Houston, Metallica, Bruce Springsteen, U2, Randy Travis, Bobby McFerrin, Bonnie Raitt

1990s

Mariah Carey, Eric Clapton, Alanis Morissette, Sting, Barry White, Shania Twain, Celine Dion, Lauryn Hill, Madonna, Santana

2000s

Britney Spears, Eminem, Norah Jones, 'N Sync, Alan Jackson, Ashanti, Dixie Chicks, Radiohead, Faith Hill

Classics of Yesterday and Today

What do you think of when you hear the word *classics?* Do you think of cars, comedians, TV shows, movies, songs? Some of the selections you heard in "Music of the Generations" are considered classics.

"Shout" is a good example of a classic. People have been dancing to it at wedding receptions and parties for more than four decades. Some of Elvis Presley's songs have become classics as well. Who could ever have imagined that some of Elvis's songs would reappear at the top of the charts more than twenty-five years after Elvis died?

Classics in music are songs that continue to have appeal generation after generation. They never completely disappear into the past. In the most "classic" sense, they are works of enduring excellence! They are the kinds of songs that define a generation and capture a particular period of time, yet they also have staying power. Each generation passes them on to the next. Like a magnet, these songs keep drawing people together to sing, dance, or listen to them year after year, generation after generation.

LISTENING **CD 1:3**

Blue Suede Shoes

(excerpt) by Carl Perkins

Composer Carl Perkins performs on this recording of what is considered the first true rock and roll hit. It sold well in three different markets: blues, country, and pop. In 1955, singer Johnny Cash suggested that Perkins write a song based on a saying he heard once while waiting on a food line in the army. Elvis's 1956 recording of "Blue Suede Shoes" was a top Billboard single and one of Elvis's first hit singles.

Listen to "Blue Suede Shoes" and describe some reasons some people consider it a classic.

Elvis Presley (1935–1977), often referred to as the "King of Rock 'n' Roll"

Elvis's Album Sales

81 Gold Albums

43 Platinum Albums

19 Multi-Platinum Albums

Look back on page 3 at the track list for "Music of the Generations." Are any of these songs still being played on the radio? In music videos? Movie soundtracks? TV commercials? At wedding receptions? Can you think of at least one song that both you and your parents know *and* like?

"It seems to me that classics are a thing of the past. Nobody these days stays in the limelight long enough to be considered a classic!"

—Kate Lawrence,
Music Editor

Your Creative Unit Project

Start a "time capsule" to capture for future generations your own experience and understanding of music in *your* world today. The time capsule can take the form of an online journal, a video, a documentary script, or an original song or other work of art. Include your thoughts and feelings about the music of previous generations. Interview people of different generations to find out how their musical tastes and experiences compare with your own. Continue to prepare your time capsule as you work through the other lessons in this unit. Present your final project to the class.

Think about your favorite music and what is popular right now. What do you think future generations will say about the music of *your* generation? Are there any new classics on the horizon?

Music Journal

How similar are my experiences and personal music tastes to those of my peers? Of previous generations? What have I learned in the interviews that helps me better appreciate musical tastes that are different from mine?

Dance Styles

One important way that people enjoy and learn about music is to move or dance to it. How many different kinds of dance steps have you tried? The photographs in this lesson show some of the dance movements named in the song "Land of a Thousand Dances." Do you recognize any of them?

LISTENING **CD 1:4**

Land of a Thousand Dances (Wilson Pickett version)

by Chris Kenner

This song was first recorded by the composer in 1962. In 1966, singer Wilson Pickett, featured on this recording, took it to Number 6 on the pop music charts.

Listen to "Land of a Thousand Dances" and write down the names of the dances as you hear them in the lyrics. Be sure to list them in the correct order.

Perform the dance movements you are familiar with as you hear them mentioned in the song.

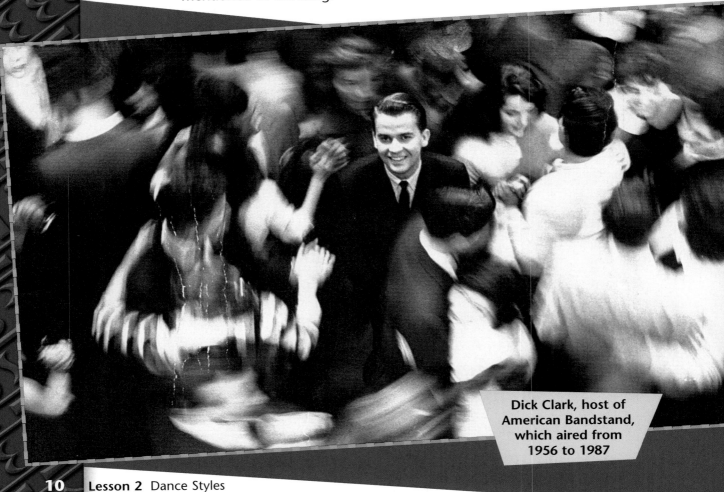

Dick Clark, host of American Bandstand, which aired from 1956 to 1987

The Twist

Dance the Twist. Stand on the balls of your feet while twisting your heels and lower body, with knees together, in the opposite direction of your arms and upper body. Variations include: (a) raising the right knee across the front and to the left of your upper body and then the left knee across the front and to the right of your upper body; (b) twisting for eight counts while bending your knees and lowering your body and squatting to the floor, then twisting back up for eight counts until you are standing up straight again; and (c) doing the twist while leaning slowly to the left for a certain number of beats, then leaning to the right for the same number of beats.

Chubby Checker dancing the Twist

LISTENING CD 1:5

Let's Twist Again by David Appell and Kal Mann

Chubby Checker, called "King of the Twist," sings this hit that actually rose higher on the charts than "The Twist" which started the dance craze.

Perform the dance movements of the Twist.

Chubby Checker's "The Twist" remained at the top of the charts in 1960 for 15 weeks and in 1961 for another 18 weeks! Still, Chubby Checker thinks the Pony was the biggest dance of the 20th century!

The Watusi

Dance the Watusi. With bent elbows and both hands clenched in fists, alternate your right and left arms up and down in front of you. With knees slightly bent, bounce in place to the beat of the music.

The Watusi

Music Journal

If I were to write a new lyric about the dance styles of my generation, what dance names and movements might I include?

Musical Form

The order and repetition of sections or phrases in a song determine a song's overall structure, design, or **form**. The form in "Land of a Thousand Dances" can be outlined as ABAB.

Identify the two sections of the song that name dance steps. Although the words change, the melody for these sections is the same. We call each section that has this melody section A.

Identify the section with nonsense syllables sung to a different melody. This is section B. Each time section A is sung, it is followed by section B.

Sing the song with the recording, noticing the A and B sections. Notice changes in the accompanying instruments with each repetition.

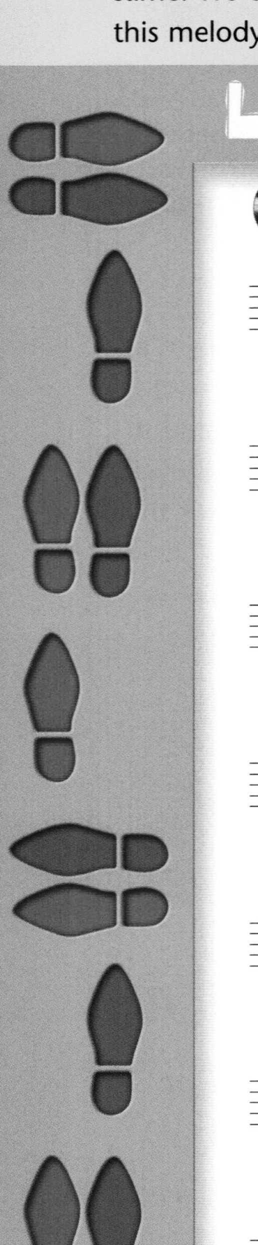

Land of a Thousand Dances

CD 1:6

Words and Music by Chris Kenner

F7
You got - ta know how to po - ny___ like

F7
Bo - ny Mar - o - nie, Mashed Po - ta - to,

F7
do the Al - li - ga - tor. Put your

F7
hands on your hips, let your back - bone slip.

F7
Do the Wa - tu - si like my lit - tle Lu - cy.

N.C.
Clap
continue clapping
Uh! Na, na na na na,___ na na na na,___

___ na na na, na na na, na na na na.___

F7

Na, na na na na, na na na na,

F7 (2nd time) Fine

na na na, na na na, na na na na.

N.C. *end clapping* F7

Dance with me hon - ey like

F7

Long Tall Sal - ly, twist-in' with Lu - cy,

F7

do - in' the Wa - tu - si, got - ta hold of your back, I

F7

like it like that. Do the Jerk,

F7 *Clap* D.S. al Fine

watch me work. Uh!

Garage Bands

In the 1960s, many American teens began forming small rock bands. They often practiced and performed in the garages of their parents' homes. These groups became known as **garage bands**. Band members sometimes wrote their own music. But they also played their own versions of popular songs. "Land of a Thousand Dances" quickly became a favorite garage band song because it was so easy to play and sing.

Garage bands usually included two or three guitars and a drum. They transformed the American popular music scene in the early 1960s.

CD 1:9

Land of a Thousand Dances (Garage Band version) by Chris Kenner

Many garage bands perform both original music and music that has already enjoyed a great deal of airtime. This recording gives you an insider's listen to one band hard at work.

Listen to the garage band version of "Land of a Thousand Dances" and discuss how it is different from the first two versions you heard in this lesson.

Perform the hand claps as you listen to the song recording again.

A tradition continues . . . While some people think "garage rock" reached its peak in the mid-sixties, teens around the country continue the tradition into the 21st century.

music.mmhschool.com Garage bands share the spotlight—online at least!

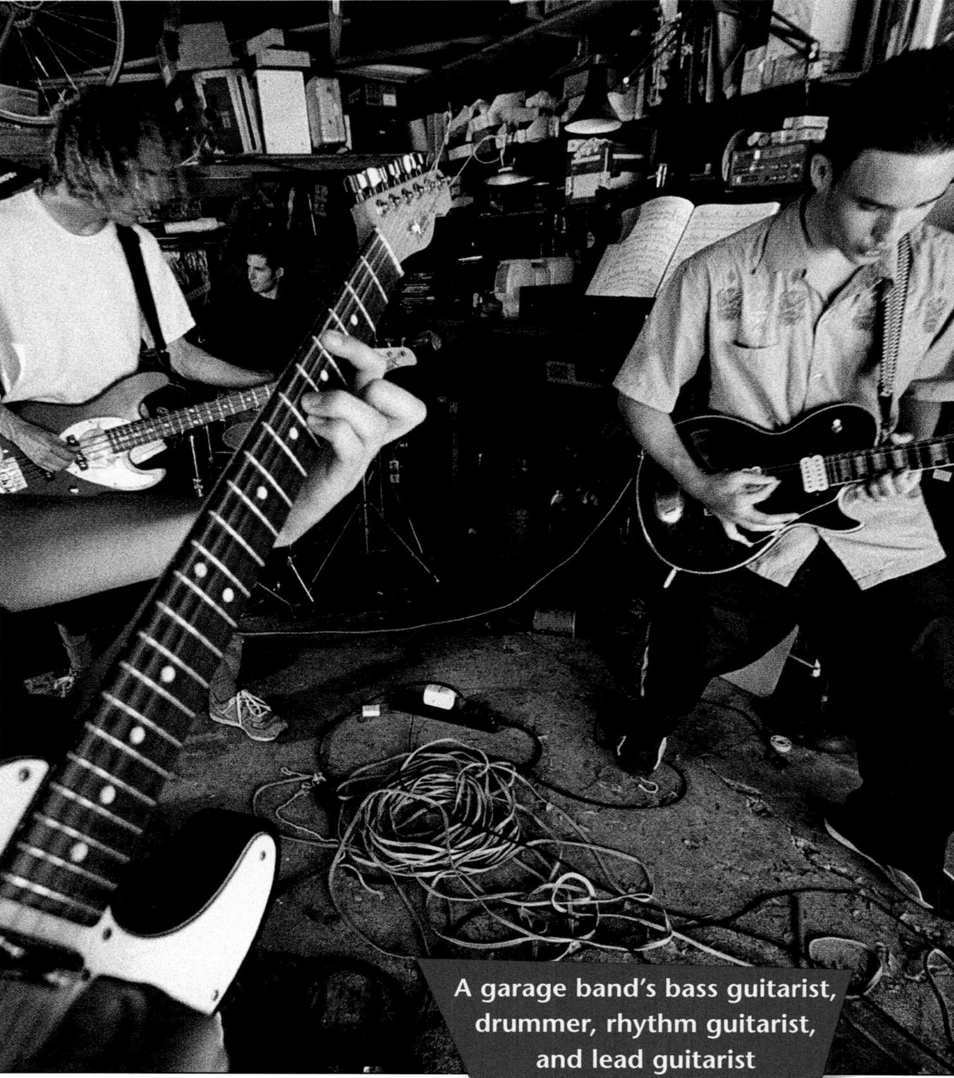

A garage band's bass guitarist, drummer, rhythm guitarist, and lead guitarist

Playing the Guitar

In "Land of a Thousand Dances," a single **chord** is repeated throughout the entire song. You can see why this song was so popular with garage bands! A chord is a combination of three or more pitches sounding together. On pages 12 and 13, the one chord indicated in "Land of a Thousand Dances" is **F7**. In the recorded garage band version, the **G7** chord is used, raising the song a whole step higher in pitch. Here's your chance to test your own potential as a garage band guitarist!

For an activity on creating music with an Afro-Cuban dance beat, see ***Spotlight on Music.***

Hold the guitar as shown above.

Strum rhythms 1, 2, and 3 with your right hand on open strings as shown. Your fingernails should brush the strings with a downward motion. The symbol ⊓ means to strum downward. The symbol V indicates an upward strum with the fingers of your right hand.

Play the **G7** chord as shown. Make sure the fingers of your left hand are not touching any open strings.

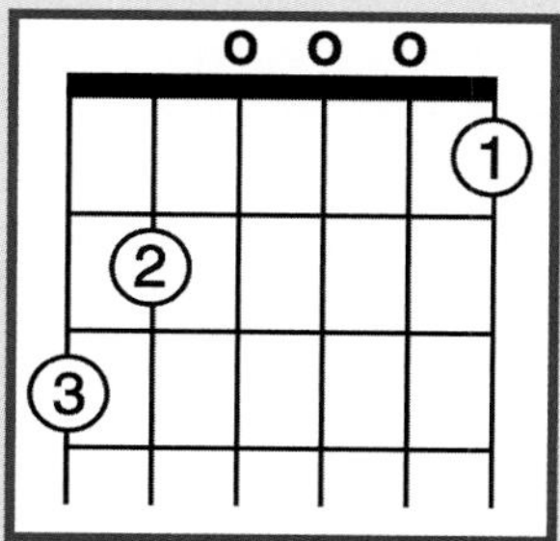

Practice rhythms 1 through 3 using the G7 chord.

Accompany "Land of a Thousand Dances (Garage Band version)," using one of the given rhythm patterns. You may also create your own rhythmic accompaniment.

Music Journal

What other instruments can I use to accompany "Land of a Thousand Dances"? What makes them appropriate?

Creating and Performing

More than anything else, what makes a work of art unique and different is the person who creates it. Each artist's experiences in life are his or her very own. Events in the artist's life, where and when the artist lives, and the artist's personal style all contribute in some way to the artistic work. A person's creative work can often reveal a great deal about the person.

A song is as much a work of art as an oil painting. Composing or performing a song requires the use of one's musical knowledge, imagination, and skill. The kinds of songs a performer chooses and the style of the performance often reflect not only a performer's abilities and musical tastes but also his or her cultural influences.

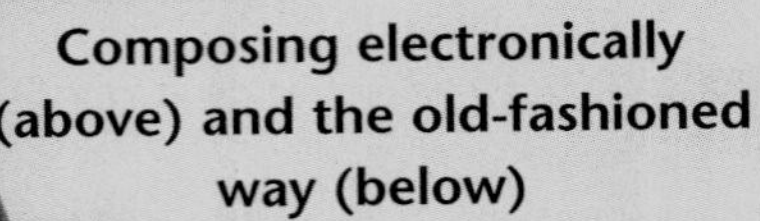

Composing electronically (above) and the old-fashioned way (below)

LISTENING **CD 1:10**

Just Keep Goin' On by Dan J. Smith

Eric Bibb's performance style is influenced by legendary folksingers such as Woody Guthrie, Joan Baez, Bob Dylan, and Judy Collins.

Listen to "Just Keep Goin' On." Discuss characteristics of the song and performance that give you some hints about the background of singer Eric Bibb.

Art Gallery

Untitled
by Romare Bearden
1914–1988,
mixed media,
ca. 1985

The Story Unfolds

The lyrics in the refrain of "Just Keep Goin' On" express the belief that even when things are not going your way, you should keep thinking positively because, in the long run, everything will work out alright. Read through the words of Refrain 1 on page 18.

This message is common to many work songs from the African American experience. Even while enslaved, people held onto hope for a better future. Work songs and spirituals often inspired or reinforced this hope. The musical style of "Just Keep Goin' On" has hints of a **blues** influence. A blues style often sounds more melancholy than this. This uniquely American musical style is characterized by flatted notes and a slow jazz rhythm that is sometimes **syncopated**. In syncopated melodies, the rhythm pattern places emphasis on beats that are not normally accented, giving a catchy, uneven sound. The gospel-style roots of the blues are especially evident in the foot-stomping that this song invites.

Tap the steady quarter-note beat as you listen to "Just Keep Goin' On." Then, as you listen again, tap or pat the patterns below each time you hear the refrain. For each quarter rest, make a palms-up, silent motion. For each whole note (𝅝), perform a pat-slide-slide-slide motion. For each half note (𝅗𝅥), perform a pat-slide motion.

1. 4/4 Tap T T T
2. 4/4 (rest) (rest) Tap T
3. 4/4 Pat–Slide Pat–Slide
4. 4/4 Pat–Slide (rest) (rest)
5. 4/4 Pat–Slide Tap T
6. 4/4 Pat–Slide–Slide–Slide

Meet the Musician

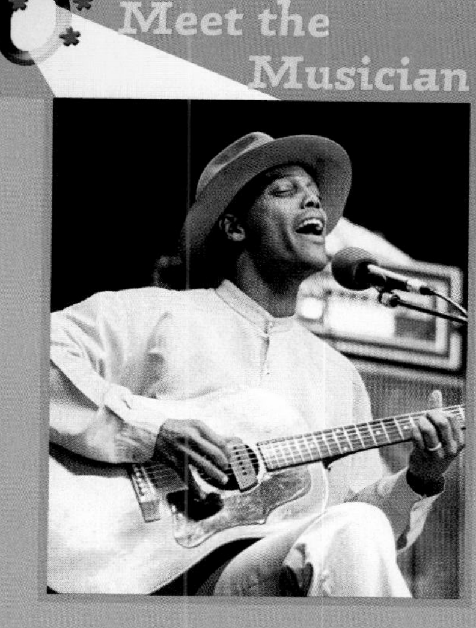

Eric Bibb (b.1951) Born in New York City, folk-blues singer Eric Bibb was playing steel guitar at age 7. He won "Best Newcomer" in the British Blues Awards in 2000. His band is mostly Swedish. His simple style has generated worldwide interest in a new generation of African American acoustic blues players.

music.mmhschool.com
Learn more about Eric Bibb.

Music Journal

What are some other ways I can add my own personal style to a performance of this song? What does my musical interpretation say about who I am?

Singing Away the Blues

Sing "Just Keep Goin' On" with the recording or with guitar accompaniment. Read and sing the rhythms as accurately as you can.

G6 C D G
times you get dis - cour-aged, don't stop and wring your hands. Your
G C D G
priv - i - lege can - not be tak - en, your rights can - not be banned. If
G6 C G
some - one like me can make it, I know you can!
Refrain 2 (6 times) (On recording, harmonica solo 3rd time, mandolin solo 6th time)
G6 C
Just keep go - in' on, just keep go - in' on,
G6 C G C D G
just keep go - in' on just keep go - in' on, a - take
G C
ev-'ry knock as a boost, and ev-'ry stum-blin' block as a step-pin' stone, lift
G6 G C G
Last time to Coda
up your head, hold your own, just keep go - in' on.
CODA
G6 C
Just keep go - in' on, just keep go - in' on,
G C G C G
just keep go - in' on, just keep go - in' on, a - take
G C
ev-'ry knock as a boost and ev - 'ry stum-blin' block as a step-pin' stone, lift
G6 G C
Repeat and fade
up your head, hold your own, just keep go, a - take

Performing on Recorder

Play pitches G, A, B, and C on recorder, keyboard, bells, or other instruments.

Play each pitch, using all quarter notes as below, then all half notes, and then all whole notes.

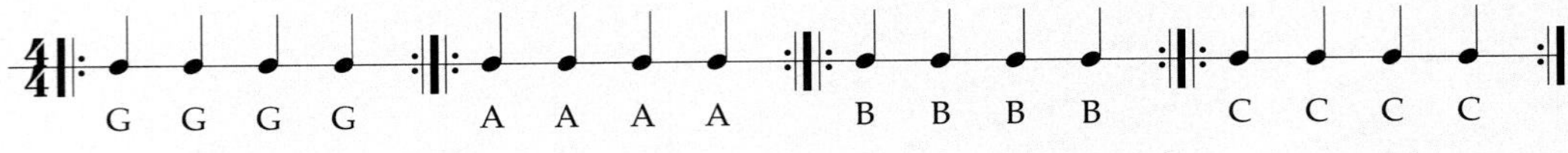

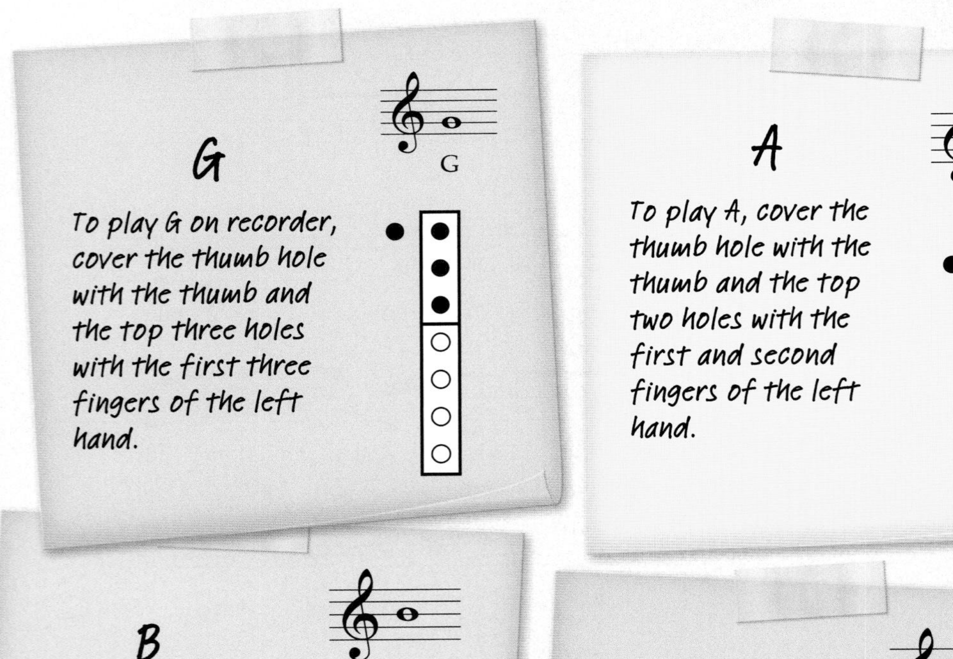

G
G
To play G on recorder, cover the thumb hole with the thumb and the top three holes with the first three fingers of the left hand.
A
A
To play A, cover the thumb hole with the thumb and the top two holes with the first and second fingers of the left hand.

B

B

To play B, cover the thumb hole with the thumb and the first (top) hole with the first (index) finger of the left hand.

C

C'

To play C, cover the thumb hole with the thumb and the second hole with the second finger of the left hand.

Play each pattern below. The $\frac{4}{4}$ time signature indicates that there are four beats in each **measure**. A set of beats is organized into a measure when the notes are placed between two bar lines.

Performing on Keyboard

Play on keyboard the melodic accompaniment below each time the refrain is repeated as you listen to "Just Keep Goin' On." Notice that you should rest for ten measures before the melodic accompaniment begins.

Playalong

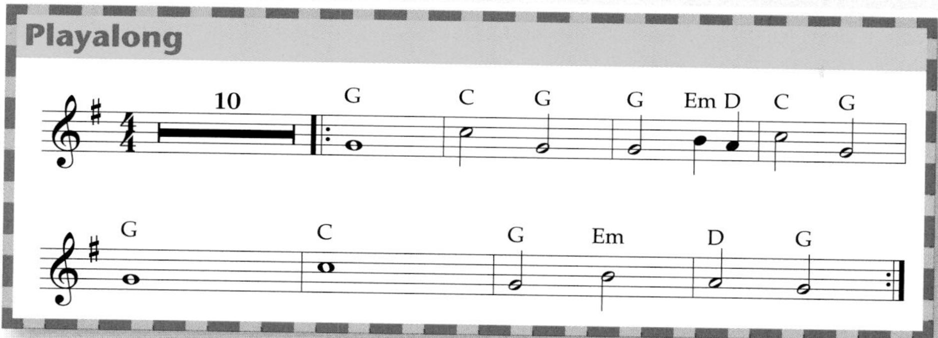

Play the chords on guitar or with the left hand on keyboard as an alternative to the recorded accompaniment for the refrain.

Creating and performing music is individual and personal. It is a way for you to share yourself with the world. The opportunity to celebrate your uniqueness as a person can come through in your music.

Create your own accompaniment to the song on pitched or unpitched instruments. Try to honor the simplicity of both the composition and Eric Bibb's performance.

By Popular Demand

One of the first truly American styles of popular music was created during the late 1800s. Musicians living in African American communities in St. Louis and Sedalia, Missouri, began to join different musical styles together. One result was a new form of music called **ragtime**. Usually performed on piano, ragtime has rhythmically complex and syncopated melodies performed over a steady beat. By the late 1890s, ragtime had become America's favorite form of popular music. Its popularity continued for about 30 years.

LISTENING **CD 1:11**

The Entertainer (piano version) by Scott Joplin

Written in 1901, "The Entertainer" was Joplin's second ragtime composition. Joplin's goal was to create a new style that was on the same level as the great European classics.

Tap each of the following rhythm patterns and then determine which patterns can be heard in "The Entertainer."

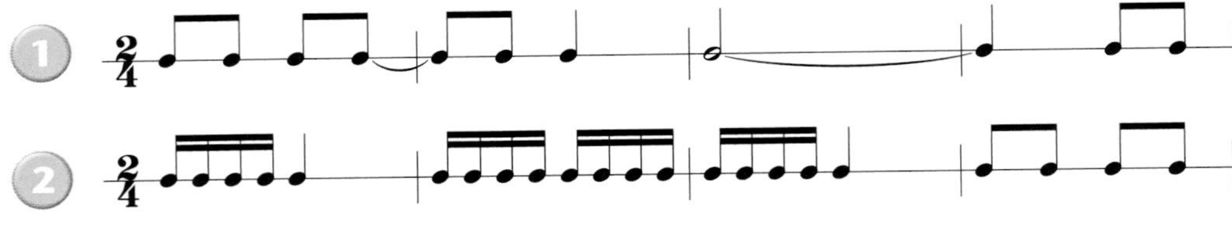

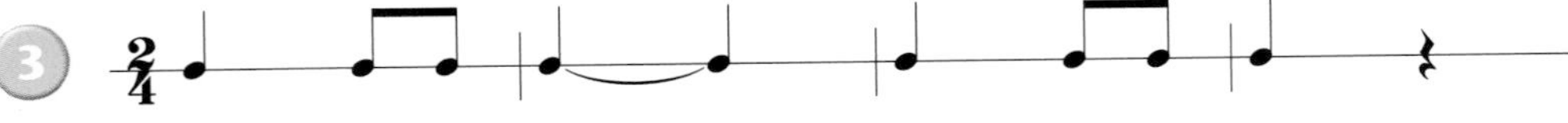

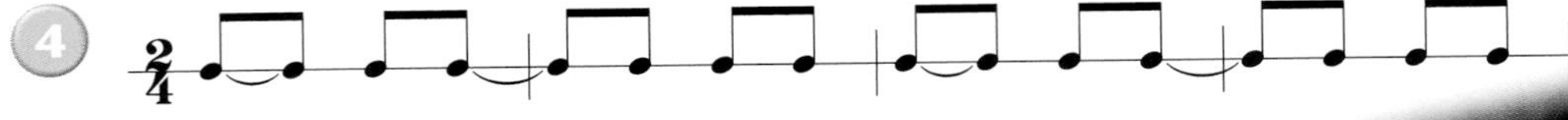

Scott Joplin (1868–1917)

Play the following melodic accompaniment to the beginning section of "The Entertainer" on keyboard, piano, or recorder.

By the 1920s, ragtime's popularity was fading. With new inventions such as the radio and cylinder recordings, people were listening to a much greater variety of music from near and far. The media was beginning to influence what music people listened to.

In 1973 "The Entertainer" was used in the soundtrack for the movie *The Sting*. Due to the movie's popularity, the soundtrack got a lot of airtime on the radio. Ragtime was soon enjoying popularity again.

LISTENING **CD 1:12**

The Entertainer (orchestra version)

by Scott Joplin

This arrangement of "The Entertainer" earned composer/arranger Marvin Hamlisch an Oscar in 1973 for best adaptation of a musical score.

Identify the various instruments you hear and recognize in this version.

Meet the Musician

Careers

Bob Milne, composer of over 40 piano rags, gives more than 200 performances a year, keeping ragtime music alive across America today. Performing for more than 25 years, he has been called "the busiest pianist in America." Also a French horn virtuoso, Milne is regarded by many as the finest ragtime pianist on the planet!

music.mmhschool.com Learn more about Bob Milne's "concerto in ragged time."

Music Journal

How can I best describe the differences in instrumentation and style between the two versions of "The Entertainer"? What helps keep a particular style or performer "popular" across the decades, or even centuries?

The Latest Scoop

Music has certainly grown to be a huge industry in today's world. Opportunities for the creative and talented among us seem almost limitless. But how do we get the word out about the latest up-and-coming "star"? And once we do, how do we keep the music on the airwaves and on the music store shelves? In an age of instant downloads of everything from songs to book excerpts, what brings us to a particular Web site or venue in the first place? Is it a firsthand recommendation from a friend? An online review by a professional critic, or even an amateur one? Many local newspapers around the country now have regular columns written by teens that review and help promote the latest local talent. Just as the media influenced the 1970s return to popularity of ragtime music, the media continues to influence our musical choices today.

Media Journal

Take time to stop and think about the many ways you encounter and experience music each day for a week. Keep a log of how much time you spend each day listening to music in various environments and through various media. Here are just a few possibilities to help get you started.

	Headphones in Transit	Online at Home	The Car Radio	Live Concerts	PA System at School	Watching Music on TV
SUNDAY		2 hours				
MONDAY	30 minutes					2 hours
TUESDAY		1 hour				30 minutes
WEDNESDAY			1 hour			
THURSDAY	30 minutes					1 hour
FRIDAY					30 minutes	
SATURDAY				2 hours		

Who has the power to make decisions about the music you hear in all these different environments? **Music critics** often enjoy this kind of power. Critics share their opinions through published reviews online, in newspapers and magazines, and on television and radio. They review live performances as well as recordings, new talent along with well-known artists. Critics can get very creative and flagrant in expressing their opinions, but they also need to do their homework. To write or talk about the music in an interesting and sometimes personal way, critics need to research the background about both the music and the artist.

Listen to our interview with Sarah Zupko to find out how "powerful" she really thinks she is—or isn't!

Write your own review of a favorite recording or a live or recorded performance you've recently experienced!

m u

BEST MUSIC OF 2002
[31 December 2002]

by Sarah Zupko
PopMatters Editor & Publisher

e-mail this article

4. The Coral, *The Coral* (Deltas
This merry crew of psychedelic Liver
debuts of the year in their native Eng
influences such as Captain Beefheart
La's, these very young 20-something
sophisticated stew of ambitious musi
intentions. It's frankly very refreshin
see young bands trying to hard to create a classic and expl
potential. Ranging from sea shanty-like tunes to '60s Briti
Coral is an addicting listen and a fabulous introduction to
music for a very long time. These guys are hotly tipped for U
shores come spring.

Meet the Critic

Sarah Zupko writes a syndicated music column online that not only takes her around the globe but also has her spending hours in music stores on a regular basis. She makes a point of seeking out "fresh" material that has made it into the recording studio and onto the shelves, but which might not be getting the attention it deserves.

music.mmhschool.com
Read reviews by Sarah Zupko and other critics.

RECORDED INTERVIEW **CD 1:13**

Listen to Sarah Zupko talk about how music critics help newer performers get "noticed" and what role critics play in shaping people's opinions about popular music.

Your Musical Influence

Can you imagine watching your favorite movie, TV show, or commercial without any background or theme music? It just wouldn't be the same, would it? Music goes a long way in helping set the mood, anticipating the next action scene, or influencing how you feel about a certain character or product.

Create a dramatic reading presentation with background music for a poem, short script, or reflection of your choice. The reading selection as well as the background music can be original compositions. You may also use something that has been previously written or recorded, such as the poem below. Consider including movement and gestures in your presentation.

Autumn Fires

In the other gardens
And all up the vale,
From the autumn bonfires
See the smoke trail!

Pleasant summer over
And all the summer flowers,
The red fire blazes,
The grey smoke towers.

Sing a song of seasons!
Something bright in all!
Flowers in the summer,
Fires in the fall!

—Robert Louis Stevenson

Looking Back

Just as you have started to explore the music of your world in this unit, you might continue to explore ways that you can influence the music of your world. The story that your "time capsule" tells can be your very own. Even as the popular music scene changes throughout your own lifetime, your musical tastes and the decisions you make today about the kinds of music you listen to and the ways you are involved in music may well last for a very long time. Chances are, the music you love today will be the same music you love twenty or thirty years from now. Just ask your parents how old they were when they first began to discover the musical styles that they still love today!

Music Journal

What is the single most important thing that I would want future generations of my own family to know about the music that I enjoyed most in my lifetime? How would I describe the people who most influenced my experience of and participation in the music of my time and my world?

Unit 2

MUSIC in My SCHOOL

Something for Everyone

Think about some songs that both faculty and students are familiar with in your school. How difficult do you think it would be to decide on an official song for your school?

Hillside, Ohio USA • Volume 43 No. 2

An amazing faculty-student rock combo debut!

Talent Abounds at HMS!

HMS students and teachers took the term "Good sports!" to a new level at last week's pep rally! Our gymnasium was really "rocking" as the whole student body, along with faculty and staff, joined in an unforgettable performance of "Hang on Sloopy."

Gazette sports reporter Sue Fallon asked Principal McCoy who chose *this* song for the occasion. "Well, for starters, it happens to be the official rock song of the state of Ohio, and Mr. Haber said it would be really easy for everyone to pick up quickly." Mr. Haber, of course, is our fantastic band director! History teacher Ms. Beach added, "We wanted to find a song that students *and* faculty would like. As you know, our faculty members alone span a few decades. Most of *us* knew the song already, and even some of the students were familiar with it. It's a really fun song that gives us all a chance to let our hair down a little."

Mr. Haber wanted to be sure we didn't miss out on a little music lesson here, too. He explained that many popular songs have a **motive** that is easy to learn. He defined a motive as a musical hook or motif; a short musical phrase that is repeated throughout the song. Sometimes, as in the case of "Hang on Sloopy," this hook phrase serves as the song's refrain.

LISTENING **CD 1:14**

Hang on Sloopy (The McCoys) by Wes Farrell and Bert Russell

The McCoys of Union City, Indiana, recorded the hit song "Hang on Sloopy" in the mid-1960s. Rock guitar legend Rick Derringer was the group's leader. In 1975, a remake of the song made the Top 100.

Clap the following pattern each time you hear the motive, or repeated refrain, as you listen to the recording of "Hang on Sloopy."

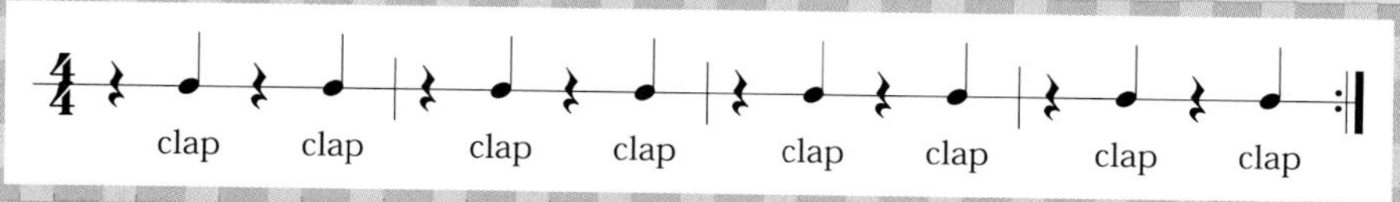

The chords D, G, and A are used in the refrain of the second version of "Hang on Sloopy" found on pages 30 and 31. Each chord takes its name from its **root**, the pitch on which the chord is built.

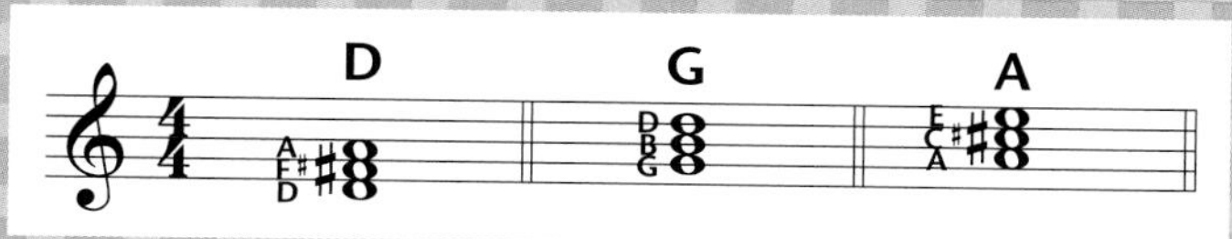

Respond to each chord change as you listen to the second version of "Hang on Sloopy" by touching the chord name on the chart below.

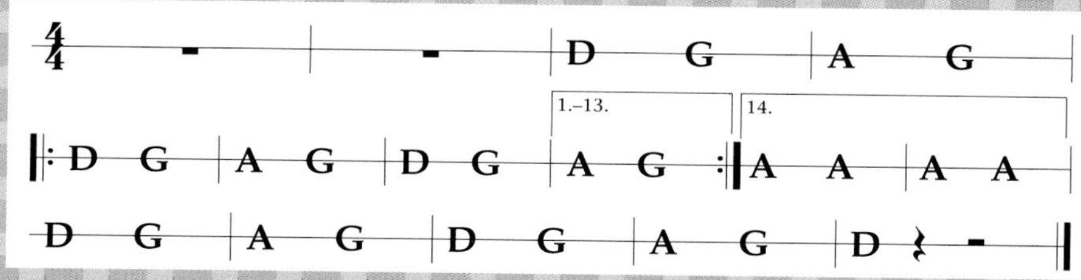

Play the root of each chord on keyboard or bells.

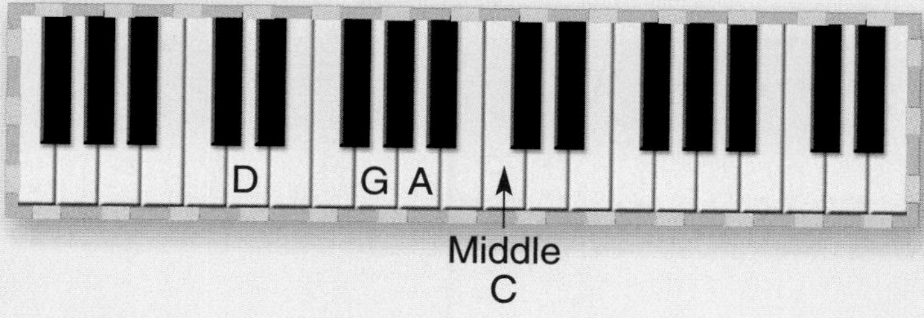

Music Journal

If I were on the committee for a student-faculty talent show, what songs might I suggest for everyone to perform that would be both appealing and easy to learn? How could I convince the committee that my suggestions would work?

One Section at a Time

Even a simple song like "Hang on Sloopy" has an identifiable form, or overall structure and design with a specific order of phrases or sections. *Introduction, refrain, verse,* and *coda* are examples of such phrases or sections.

Identify the form in "Hang on Sloopy" by looking at the sections labeled in the notation.

Sing the refrain through several times until everyone is singing with precision.

Tap the rhythm to the verses several times until everyone is tapping precisely and confidently. Keep the steady beat with your foot.

Describe some similarities and differences among the sections.

HANG ON SLOOPY

CD 1:15

Words and Music by
Wes Farrell and Bert Russell

Introduction

D G A G

Refrain

D G A G D G A G

Hang on Sloo - py, Sloo - py hang on!

Verse

D G A G D G A G

D G A G D G A G

Refrain

D G A G D G A G

Hang on Sloo - py, Sloo - py hang on!

Mr. Haber and friends in rare *FORM!*

The McCoys' recording of "Hang on Sloopy" rose to the top of the Billboard charts in 1965. That same year, the song was performed at an Ohio State football game. It became so popular with fans that it has been closely identified with the team ever since.

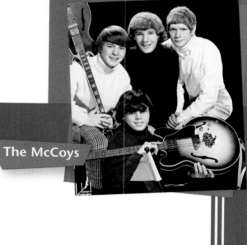

The McCoys

Interlude *(Guitar solo, improvised)*

D G | A G | D G | A G

Verse *(Guitar solo, freely)*

D G | A G | D G | A G

D G | A G | D G | 1. A G | 2. A A | A A

Refrain

D G | A G | D G | A G

Hang on Sloo-py, Sloo-py hang on!

Coda

D G | A G | D G | A G | D

Strike Up the Band!

LISTENING **CD 1:18**

Hang on Sloopy (The Ohio State Glee Club and Marching Band)
by W. Farrell and B. Russell

"Hang on Sloopy" is one of those songs that enjoys success in a variety of very different arrangements. In this arrangement, voices imitate instrumental sounds. And then the marching band itself helps you experience the song in a whole new way!

Listen to the voices imitating band instruments and imagine what instruments you will hear next.

Identify when the key changes in both the vocal and instrumental parts of the recording.

Identify the form of the marching band segment of the recording using the listening map below. Notice the two different versions of the refrain, each of which is repeated several times.

Listening Map for *Hang on Sloopy*

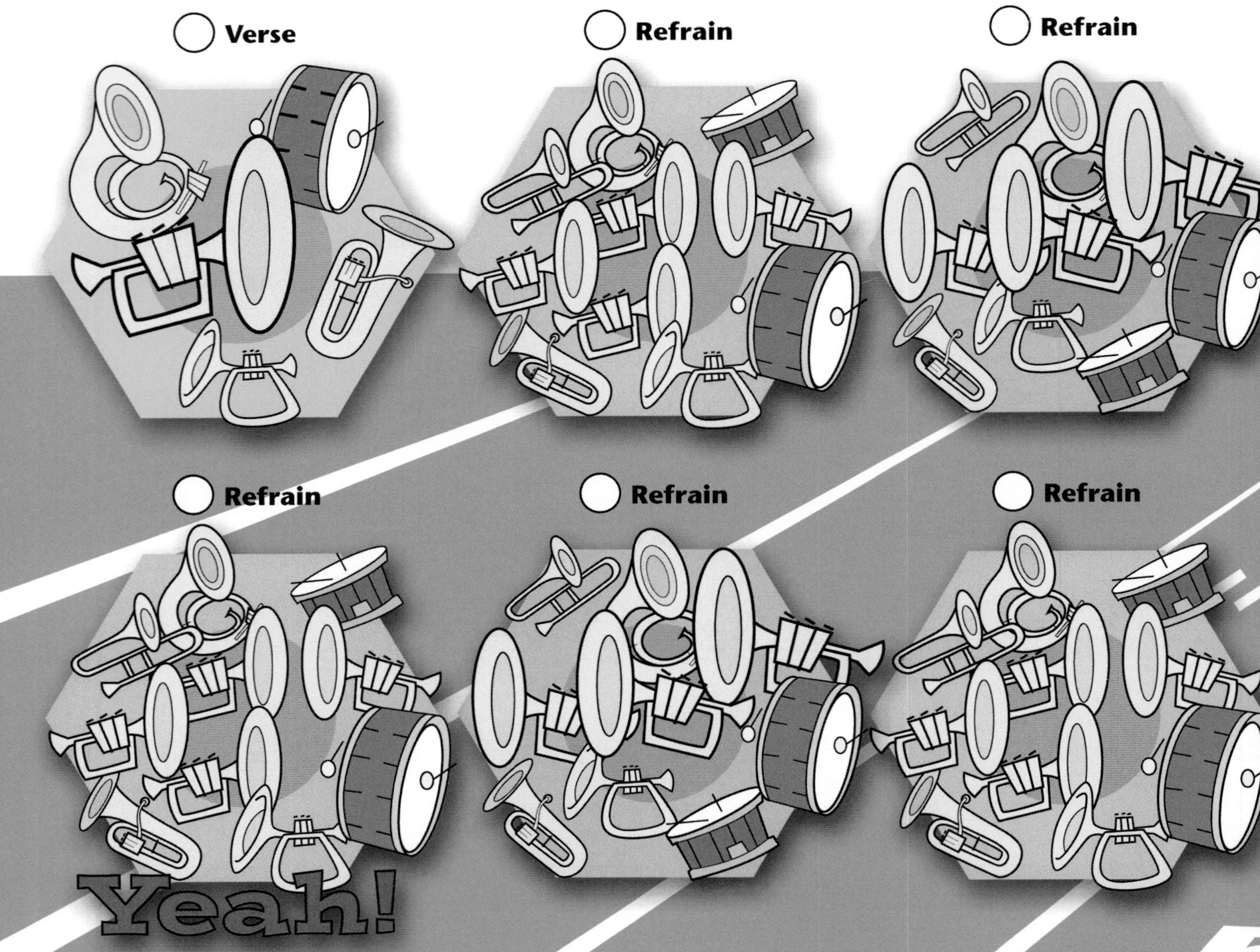

The rhythmic accompaniment to "Hang on Sloopy" uses a combination of the rhythms below.

Tap the steady beat with your foot as you clap or speak each rhythm with the recording.

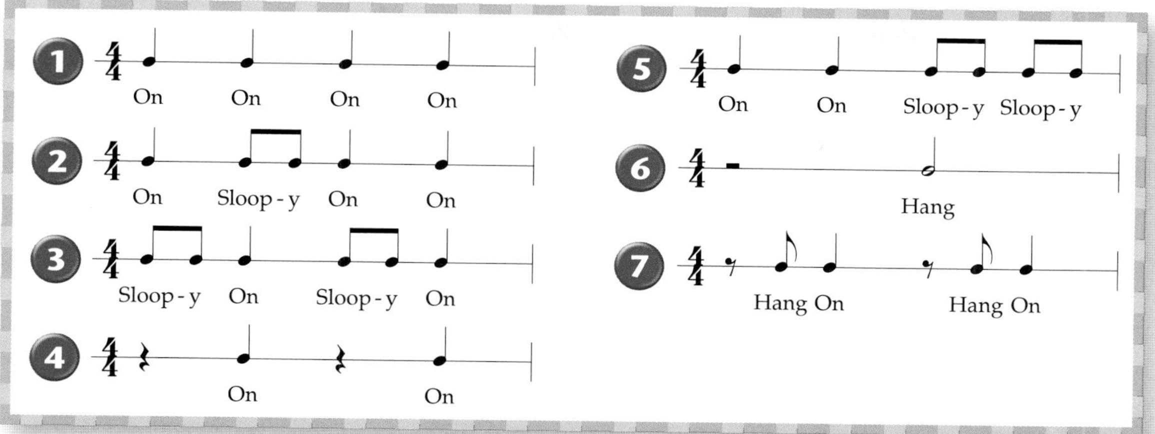

Play the rhythmic accompaniment below along with the marching band recording of "Hang on Sloopy." Use the percussion matched grip. Use your right and left hands as indicated in the notation.

Pep Rally Finale

Even if you think you have no sense of rhythm, chances are that you have at least joined in a cheering rhythm at a school sporting event or a concert. You don't have to be a great musician to perform this cheer. Try it! You may surprise yourself!

Clap a steady quarter-note beat in a clockwise circular motion as you listen to "Cheers."

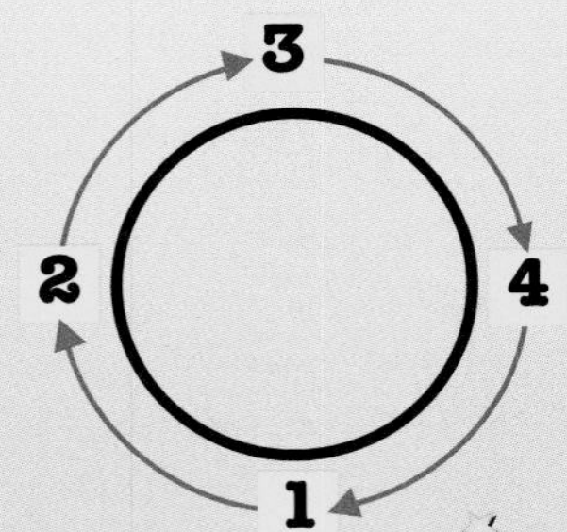

CHEERS

CD 2:1

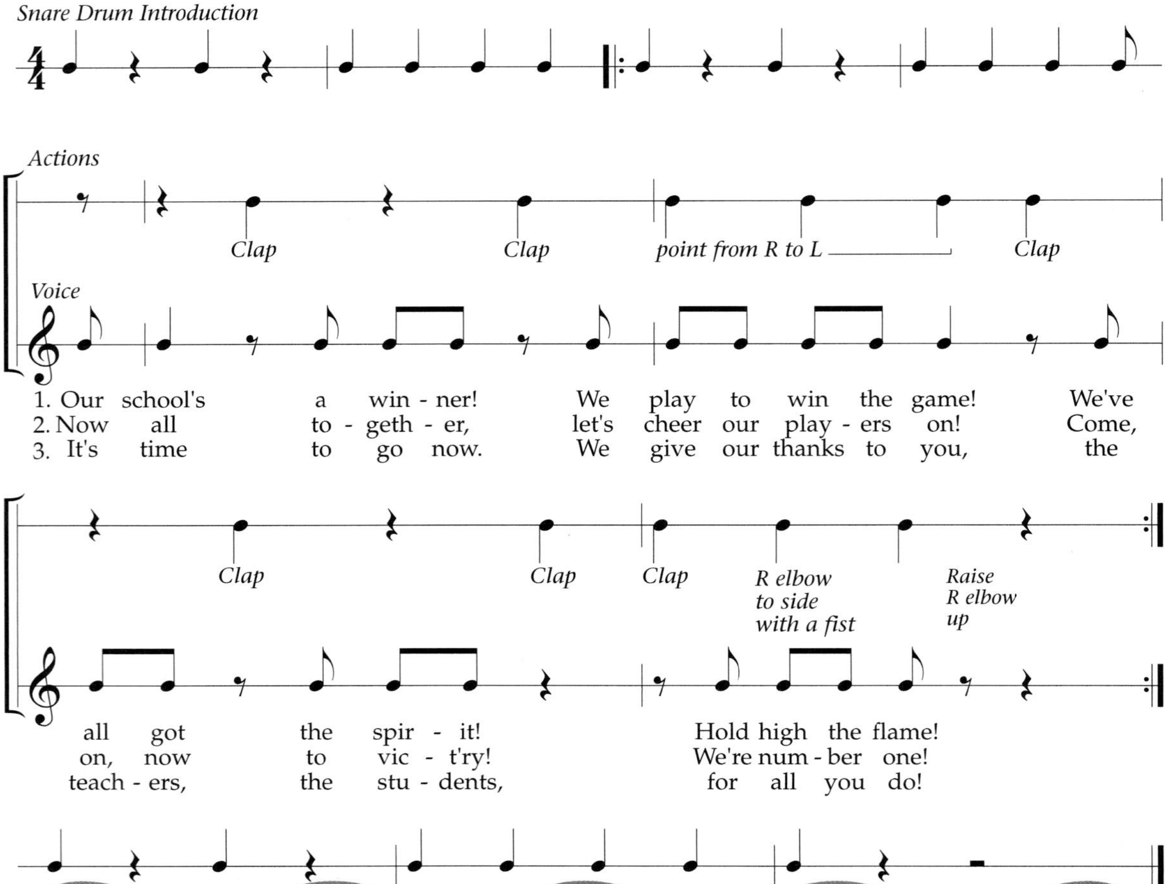

Snare Drum Introduction

Actions

Clap *Clap* *point from R to L* *Clap*

Voice

1. Our school's a win - ner! We play to win the game! We've
2. Now all to - geth - er, let's cheer our play - ers on! Come,
3. It's time to go now. We give our thanks to you, the

Clap *Clap* *Clap* *R elbow to side with a fist* *Raise R elbow up*

all got the spir - it! Hold high the flame!
on, now to vic - t'ry! We're num - ber one!
teach - ers, the stu - dents, for all you do!

Clap the rhythm pattern in the action part of the notation for "Cheers" as you tap your foot to the steady beat.

Speak the voice part in rhythm for all three verses of "Cheers."

Perform the action part and the voice part of "Cheers" together.

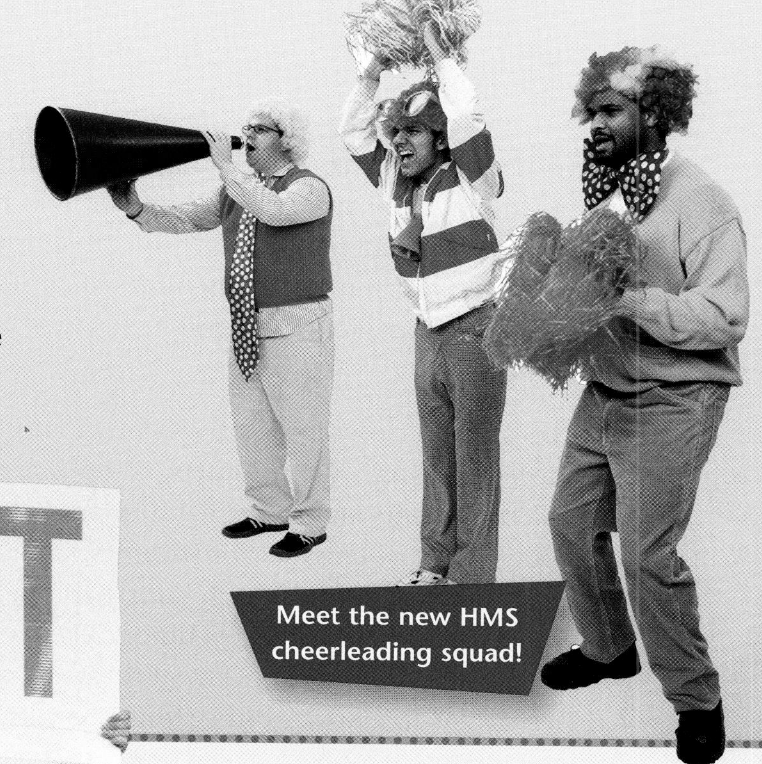

Meet the new HMS cheerleading squad!

FIGHT

TEXAS

Your Creative Unit Project

Plan an assembly for your school that highlights the variety of talent among your classmates and teachers. Start by brainstorming a theme that will be interesting for both students and faculty. Identify possible faculty or student performers and consider what music and other various media forms you might use.

If you choose a dramatic presentation, think about stage props and scenery or decorations. Music can play an important "out front" role or it can be used as background. It can be a live performance or a recording. Make sure everyone has a valuable role in implementing your plan, whether they are onstage or behind the scenes. Sound and lighting control, recording, and creating sets are just as important as performing onstage.

LESSON 2

Sounds of Our Band and Chorus

When you think about music in your school, what comes to mind? Many schools have a band, a chorus, and an orchestra. Some may even have a mariachi band, a steel drum band, or a jazz ensemble. For more than a century, musical ensembles of all kinds have been an important part of school life. What ensemble opportunities are offered in *your* school?

Let's take a closer look at the band. A concert band includes three sections: **brass**, **woodwinds**, and **percussion**. Together, these families of instruments enable the band to produce sounds that are stirring and powerful. The *brass* section includes musical instruments such as the trumpet, trombone, French horn, baritone, and tuba. The *woodwind* family includes instruments historically made of wood. Woodwinds include the flute, oboe, clarinet, bassoon, and saxophone. The *percussion* family includes instruments such as the drum, cymbal, xylophone, tambourine, and piano that are struck to produce a sound.

LISTENING CD 2:2

School Band Rondo by Michael Jothen

Band music often includes musical themes that feature individual instruments and sections. This allows the band to create musical **contrast** in its performances, or musical ideas that are new or different from those already heard. **Rondo** is a musical form that uses alternating repetitions of the main theme with two or more contrasting sections, such as A B A C A.

Identify each of the instrument families in "School Band Rondo" as you listen, and follow the written notation for the four themes on pages 36, 37, 38, and 39.

The Brass Section

The sound of brass instruments is produced when players buzz their lips against the mouthpiece and blow air through metal tubing. The tone color of brass instruments is determined by the length and diameter of their metal tubing. Sometimes the length of the tubing can be changed by the use of valves. The size of the mouthpiece also varies.

Respond by singing along with a vocal tone that imitates a brass sound each time you hear the brass instruments. Listen for the brass especially in the B section of "School Band Rondo."

Can you name each instrument pictured on pages 37, 38, and 39?

Meet the Musician

Meet **John Philip Sousa** (1854–1932). Brass sections sometimes include an instrument called the *sousaphone*, named after the famous band director and composer. At the age of 13, Sousa left home to join a circus band. Sousa's father later encouraged him to join the Marine Band. Sousa's father was a member of this band during the Civil War. By age 26, John Philip was the Marine Corps Band's conductor. Ten years later, he formed his own band and composed so many marches that he became known as the "March King." A **march** is characterized by a strong steady beat, the use of accents, and repeated and contrasting sections, and is usually performed by a band. Sousa's most famous march is "Stars and Stripes Forever."

The Woodwind Section

Woodwind instruments produce sound in several ways. The vibration of a single wooden reed, fastened to the mouthpiece, produces sound for the clarinet and saxophone. The oboe and bassoon produce sounds through the use of two vibrating reeds. The flute produces sound simply by air flowing over an edge on the mouthpiece, without a reed. The player changes pitch on a woodwind instrument by covering various holes.

Describe the similarities and differences in how woodwind instruments produce sound.

Respond by singing along with a vocal tone that imitates a woodwind sound each time you hear the woodwind instruments. Listen for the woodwinds especially in the C section of "School Band Rondo."

Music Journal

What differences did I notice between the tone color of the brass instruments and the tone color of the woodwind instruments?

The Percussion Section

Percussion instruments require the performer to strike the instrument with mallets, sticks, the hands, or in the case of the cymbal, with another cymbal. When a drum is struck, the head or skin of the drum vibrates to produce sound. Sometimes a set of wires or a snare is stretched across the head to produce a louder sound. On the timpani, the pitch can be changed by tightening or loosening the tension on the drum head.

Respond by singing along with sounds that imitate percussion sounds each time you hear the percussion instruments playing. Listen for them especially in the D section of "School Band Rondo."

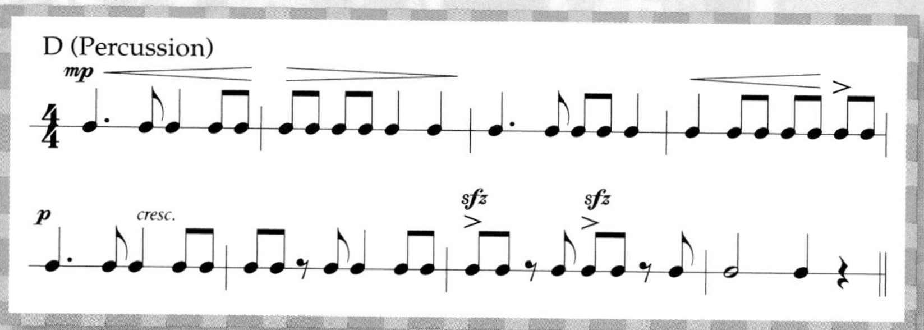

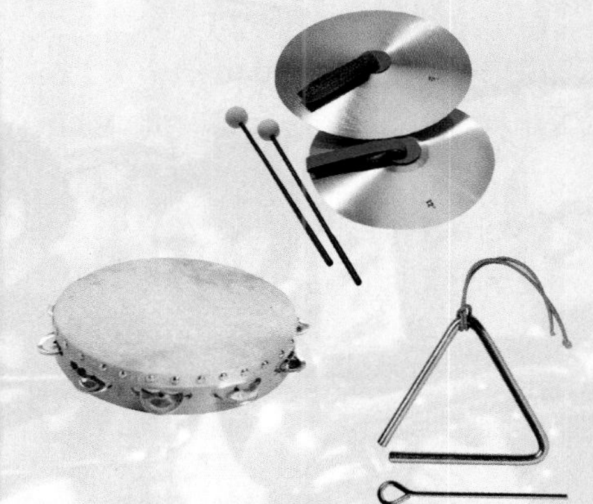

Music Journal

How might an experience of playing percussion instruments in an ensemble differ from playing percussion instruments alone?

Changing Voices

Singing has been a part of every generation since the beginning of human history. It has been an important way for people to express feelings such as joy and sorrow. Singing has given people of all times and places a sense of hope and has inspired patriotism. What performing or listening experiences of vocal music have been especially memorable for you?

Each person's voice has a unique tone quality. Still, everyone's voice usually falls into a specific **vocal range**, which is the pitch distance between the lowest and highest notes a person can sing without straining. The chart below shows the approximate singing ranges for young adults.

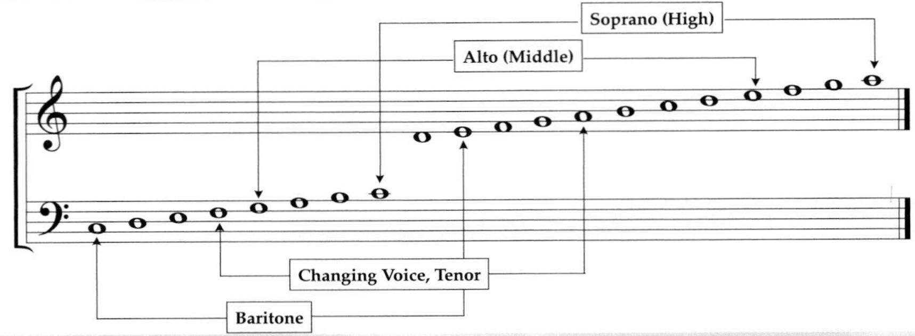

CIRCLE OF LIFE

from *The Lion King*

"Circle of Life" is from the 1994 film (and 1997 Broadway musical) *The Lion King* which won an Academy Award for best original music score. The song is about how we are all connected, even as we find our own place in the world.

Sing along with the recording of "Circle of Life" and identify the parts you can easily sing.

Read the notation to see which passages are designated for the various vocal ranges.

Determine your own vocal range classification.

As we mature, our voices often change. Male voices often become deeper, enabling them to sing in a lower range. They eventually become tenors, baritones, or basses.

Female voices also change, but this change is usually one of tone quality rather than range. Female voices usually fall into the soprano or alto range. However, some females sing tenor. And some males sing alto or soprano. We call these males countertenors.

LESSON 3

Coming Together

Have you ever been inspired by a great speaker to get involved in an activity or to support a good cause? There's nothing like meeting someone in person or learning about something firsthand, rather than through print or electronic media, to capture your interest. Public gatherings are a good way for people who live, work, or learn together to get involved with important issues and to celebrate accomplishments and milestones. School assemblies, political rallies, baseball games, and birthday parties are just a few examples. What are some of the occasions for which *your* school or community has gathered together? However formal or informal the occasion, what role did music play? Did it help set the mood? What kinds of gatherings just wouldn't be the same without music?

School Auditorium Transformed into a Planetarium

LISTENING CD 2:6

Assembly Memories (montage)

This selection includes a medley of college fight songs and our national anthem. At what kinds of gatherings or school assemblies might you hear these selections?

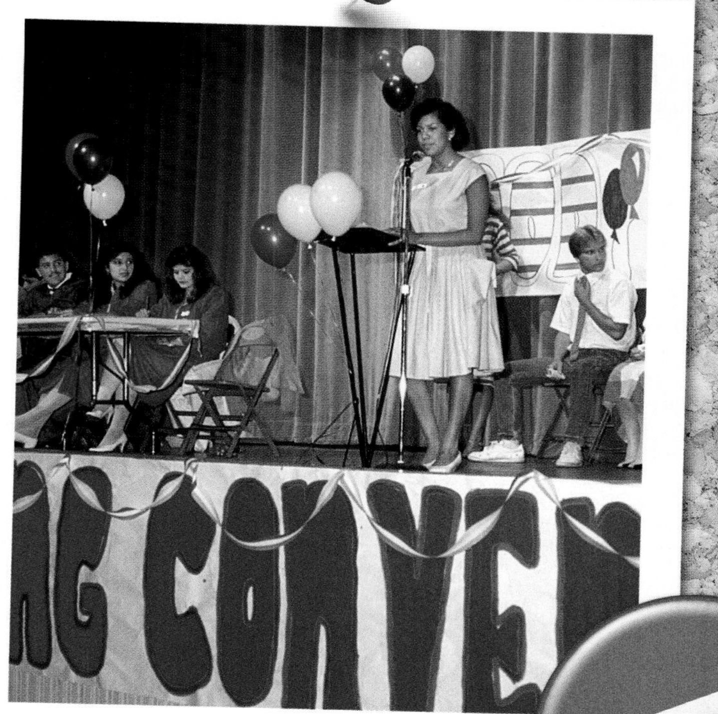

Student Council Election Time!

VOTE

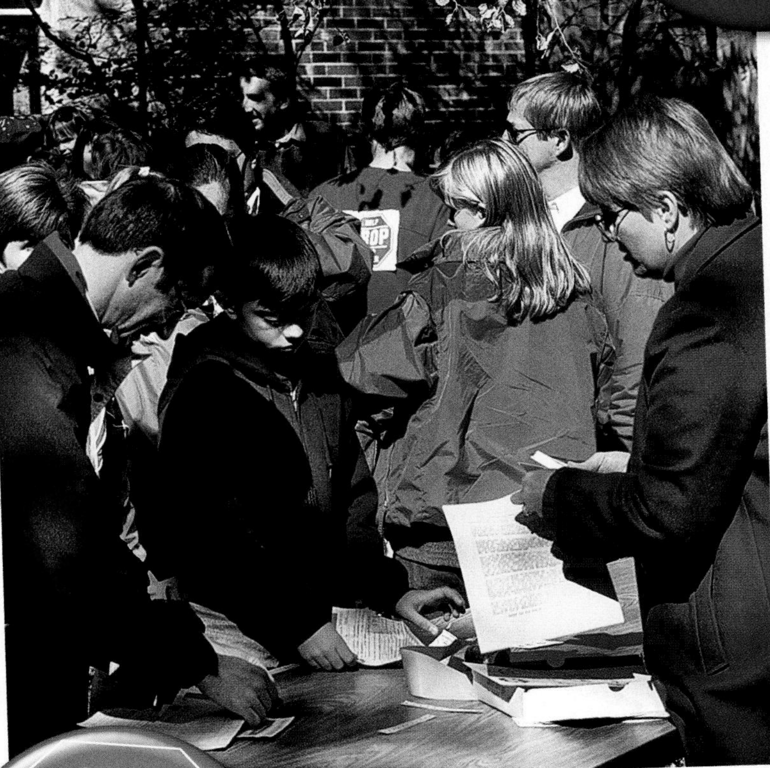
Fall CROP Walk Registration!

HELP CROP STOP HUNGER

Fireworks and music go hand in hand in many communities across the United States each Fourth of July. These communities use computers to coordinate everything from thrilling patriotic music to American popular standards with their annual fireworks display. Can you even remember a time when music was *not* a part of such a celebration?

Music Journal

If I could suggest some music for an assembly, what popular compositions would I suggest? What classical compositions? What folk material?

Cadences in Percussion Ensembles

When was the last time you were at a parade or watched one on television? Chances are, you couldn't just stand or sit still without tapping your feet, bouncing to the rhythm, or finding some way to move to the music. It is often the percussion section that plays the biggest role in getting you moving, whether you want to or not.

In marching band performances, it is the percussion section that keeps the band moving and playing together. When the whole band is marching and not playing, the percussion section performs a drum cadence. Usually sixteen beats long, drum cadences feature a strong, steady beat.

LISTENING CD 2:7

Rhythm Review Warm-Up

Rhythm patterns can be combined in an endless variety of ways. This recording presents some of the basic patterns from which you can create your own combinations.

Practice playing the basic rhythms with the recording on percussion instruments or by tapping the rhythms.

Create your own rhythm patterns by combining two or more connecting squares in the chart below.

Notate your new rhythm patterns on staff paper.

1	2	3	4
5	6	7	8
9	10	11	13
13	14	15	16

The Nicolet High School band from Milwaukee, WI, marches through downtown Moscow on Sept. 7, 1997, during celebrations marking Moscow's 850th anniversary.

Identify the percussion cadences in "Spirit Medley Rondo" as you listen to the recording.

Play the following rhythmic accompaniment to "Spirit Medley Rondo" on drumsticks. Alternate your right and left hands as marked in the notation.

LISTENING CD 2:8

Spirit Medley Rondo

This medley includes "The Notre Dame Victory March," "Fight On" (USC), and "The Eyes of Texas."

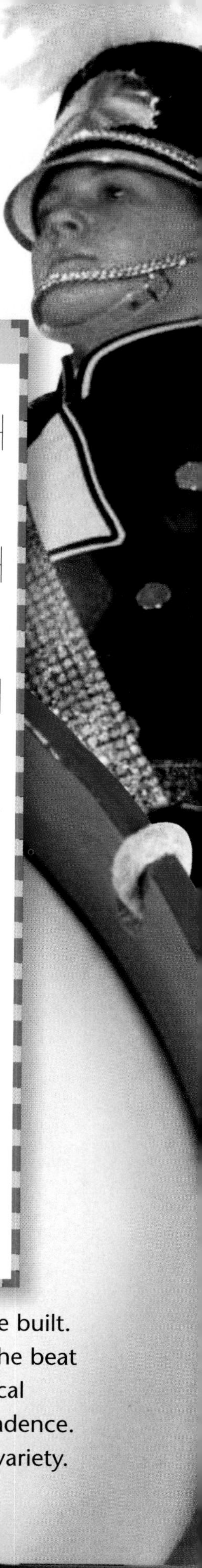

Playalong

Percussion Cadence 1

R L R L RLRLRLR R L R L RLRLR R L R RLR

Notre Dame Victory March

16

Percussion Cadence 2

RLR RLR R RL R L RLR RLR RL R L RL RL RL R L

Fight On (USC)

20

Percussion Cadence 3

R L R R L R L R R L R L R L R L R RL RL R L R

The Eyes of Texas

16

Percussion Cadence - Coda

R RLR RL R RLRLRLR R RLR L RLRLRLR R RLRLRLRL R L R

A given cadence can help percussionists compose and arrange new musical cadences. Each of the cadences you played in "Spirit Medley Rondo" is the same length. This consistency allows percussionists a musical structure upon which new music can be built. As long as the length is the same and the beat remains steady, new rhythms and musical timbres or sounds can be added to a cadence. This creates more musical interest and variety.

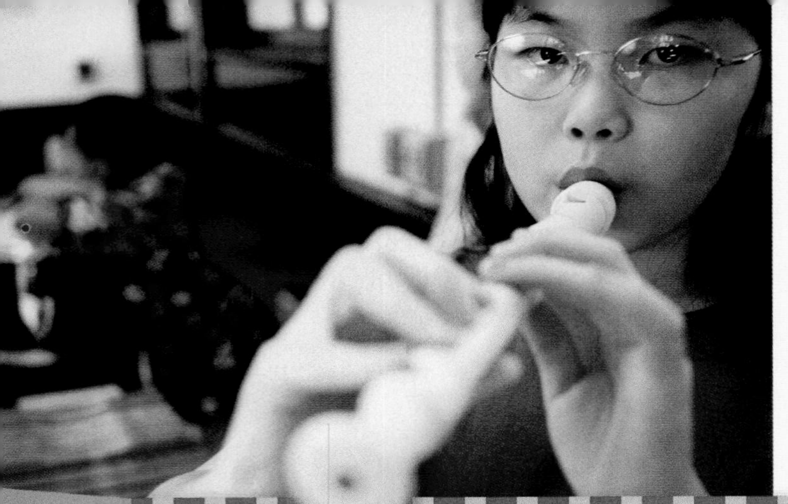

Melodic Patterns

Play the following melodic accompaniment to each fight song in "Spirit Medley Rondo." Each song begins after a six-measure percussion cadence.

Playalong

LISTENING CD 2:9

Pitch Review Warm-Up

Like rhythm patterns, melodic patterns can also be combined in a variety of ways. This recording reviews some of the basic patterns from which you can create your own combinations.

Create your own melodic patterns by using any of the pitches illustrated below.

Notate your melodic patterns on staff paper.

Perform your melodic patterns using keyboard, bells, or recorder. When you feel comfortable with some of your new melodic patterns, accompany them with some of your rhythm patterns.

Onstage with Our Strings

The **string** family typically includes violin, viola, cello, and bass. However, it also includes all musical instruments that are made of wood and have strings that are bowed or plucked. So instruments from the sitar to the guitar and from the harp to the electric bass are all part of the string family. The bass guitar used in many jazz and rock bands is actually an electronic version of the double bass.

The **orchestra** is a traditional musical ensemble that has four sections: strings, brass, woodwinds, and percussion. While orchestral music is usually performed in formal concert settings, stringed instruments are used in informal music-making scenarios as well. Jazz violinists, those who play electric violins in pop music groups, and country fiddle players can all be quite lively.

LISTENING CD 2:10

String Instruments in the Orchestra (montage)

Excerpts from Handel, Mozart, and Vivaldi highlight the string section. Individual string instruments are highlighted in excerpts from Sibelius, Berlioz, Bach, Beethoven, and Glazunov.

Listen to "String Instruments in the Orchestra" and identify the order in which the string instruments are heard.

Describe how the tone color of strings is different from that of the other instrument families.

The school and concert hall are just two places you may have heard an orchestra perform. But there are many other ways you have probably experienced orchestral or string music. Think about some of the movies you have seen recently. Or think about television shows or commercials. Now that you know what strings sound like, in what other settings have you heard music performed by an orchestra or individual stringed instruments?

LISTENING **CD 2:11**

Strings in the Media (montage)

This montage includes excerpts from "Hoe Down," "The Aquarium," "Night on Bald Mountain," "Adagio for Strings," and "St. Crispin's Day." Where in the media might you hear these selections?

Use the ***Orchestral Instruments* CD-ROM** to further explore the tone colors of string instruments.

Listen to "Strings in the Media" as you follow the listening map below.

Listening Map for *Strings in the Media* (montage)

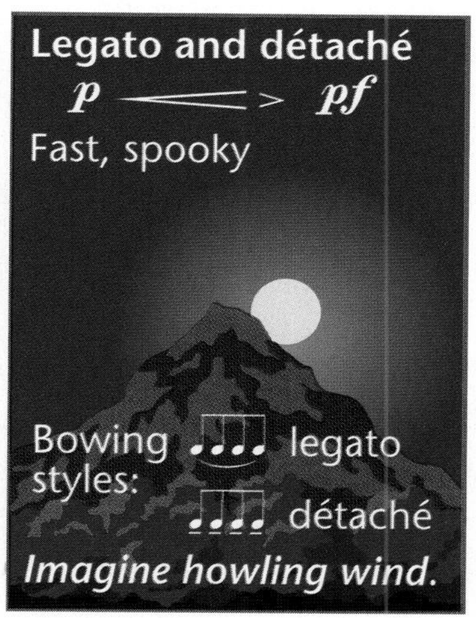

Music Journal

In what settings and media have I heard stringed instruments perform? What feelings can I associate with these experiences?

Processional Music

Have you ever been to a graduation ceremony? While some graduations are more formal than others, there is usually some music performed at the ceremony. Many schools, from elementary schools to colleges and universities, continue a longstanding tradition.

Processional music is played as the graduates enter the auditorium or lawn where the ceremony is going to take place. Like many other kinds of rituals, a graduation ceremony marks the end of something and the beginning of something new.

LISTENING CD 2:12

Pomp and Circumstance by Sir Edward Elgar

One of the most famous compositions used in ceremonies around the world is the Trio section from "Pomp and Circumstance March No. 1" by English composer Edward Elgar. The strong, steady pulse and majestic quality of the music make this composition a favorite for graduation processions.

Listening Map for *Pomp and Circumstance*

strings
woodwinds
brass
p *mp*

Read through the listening map as you listen to "Pomp and Circumstance." Move to the next square every four pulses.

Identify the different sections and form of "Pomp and Circumstance."

Describe how the string instruments help create musical unity and variety.

Describe some musical characteristics that might contribute to the popularity of "Pomp and Circumstance" as a processional for graduations and other ceremonies.

Music Journal

What are some musical compositions I am familiar with that are appropriate for graduation or other school ceremonies or processions? What performance ensembles in my school are best suited to perform them?

Meet the Musician

ON NATIONAL RADIO!

Name: Karla Donehew
Age: 17
Instrument: Violin
Hometown: Albany, CA

Karla Donehew moved with her family from Puerto Rico to California when she was twelve. Most of her relatives still live in Puerto Rico. She misses going to her grandparents' home in the little village of Cidra, where many of her relatives still get together for holidays. "It's very friendly there, and we have such a large, close family," Karla says.

Since both of Karla's parents are musicians, Karla feels she was destined to play music too. "In many ways it helps to have parents who are musicians because they are very supportive and know what I'm going through," Karla comments. "On the other hand, they always want to tell me what to do and how to practice; and although they're usually right, I still don't want to listen!"

Karla definitely wants to be a professional violinist, but admits that thinking about what it takes to be a great violinist can be daunting. "There are just so many things to think about," she says. "Not only does your technique have to be solid, there are so many other things to consider, such as the ideas you want to put into your music. You don't ever stop working on something."

RECORDED INTERVIEW

Listen to Karla's performance of Violin Concerto, First Movement (Andante Tranquillo) by William Walton **(CD 2:13)** and her interview **(CD 2:14)** on the national radio program From the Top.

Meet the Musician

Careers

Cellist Beatrice Harrison makes a recording with composer Sir Edward Elgar, November 5, 1920.

Sir Edward Elgar (1857–1934) Born in Worcester, England, Sir Edward Elgar was one of the most celebrated British composers of his time. Having received little formal training in music, Elgar drew on the heritage of folk music when composing.

"Pomp and Circumstance" was performed at the 1905 Yale University graduation ceremony. Other American universities soon adopted this tradition. Sounding both triumphant and melancholy, this piece strikes a perfect chord for graduations. It reflects mixed feelings about leaving friends behind while moving on to meet new ones.

Looking Back

From impromptu faculty-student performances at pep rallies to formal holiday concerts and graduation ceremonies, music plays an important role in the life of your school. Students who participate in band, chorus, orchestra, and other ensembles as well as those who work behind the scenes help bring the music to life! Now that you are more familiar with some of the talented singers and insrumentalists in your school, what "performance" opportunities can you suggest to highlight the best talent that your school has to offer?

Unit 3

LESSON 1 Heritage Festivals

Much of the music you hear in your community has its origins in the musical and cultural heritage of other countries. These countries usually represent the ancestry of people living and working in your community. Some communities celebrate ethnic festivals where people can experience a variety of cultures in a single event. The festivals often include everything from music

Parade participants beat drums and gongs to celebrate Chinese New Year in Beijing, China.

A brass band marches to the Oktoberfest grounds during the morning procession in Munich, Germany.

Country musicians perform bluegrass for an audience in Mountainview, Arkansas.

and dancing to ethnic foods and crafts. To hear, see, and participate in the music and culture of different people's backgrounds helps create a sense of community that you just can't get from reading the news or watching TV.

LISTENING **CD 2:15**

Heritage Festival Music (montage)

Many communities also celebrate specific heritage festivals throughout the year. You might enjoy Oktoberfest in October. Perhaps you'll hear Chinese music at a New Year's Lantern Parade in January or Mexican music at a Cinco de Mayo celebration in May.

Listen to "Heritage Festival Music" and identify which musical excerpts might be associated with the three celebrations mentioned.

The word *culture* also refers to the beliefs and customs of a specific group of people that are passed on from generation to generation. Music is just one aspect of a group's culture, but an important one! It often conveys ideas and feelings that are unique to the group. Can you think of an example? Thinking of your own generation as a cultural group may help!

Music Journal

What musical characteristics helped me associate the musical excerpts with specific celebrations? What other musical characteristics can I think of that would convey certain celebrations?

Chinese New Year Music

The new year is celebrated at different times around the world. The Jewish New Year is celebrated in the fall, and the Hindu New Year is celebrated in the spring. Both of these traditions use calendars that are different from the Roman calendar system used in the United States. In China and the United States, the new year begins in winter.

New Year's Lantern Festival, Beijing, China

The Chinese New Year begins with the first new moon of the year and ends with the full moon fifteen days later. On the fifteenth night of the year, the Lantern Festival is celebrated. Lanterns are displayed under the full moon, and children carry lanterns in parades. Groups of people dress up and perform as dancing lions, dragons, or horses. Chinese communities throughout the United States share in this tradition.

music.mmhschool.com Learn more about New Year celebrations around the world.

LISTENING **CD 2:16**

Bo Hai Huan Ten Chinese Folk Music

Traditional music for a Chinese New Year celebration includes "Bo Hai Huan Ten." The English translation of this title is "Jubilation All Around." Performed by a Chinese orchestra, this selection features several Chinese folk instruments.

Listen to "Bo Hai Huan Ten" and identify the families of instruments in the Chinese orchestra.

Chinese ensemble that includes *gaohu, erhu, pipa, zhonghu, guanzi,* and *sanxian* (L to R)

Read and clap the rhythm pattern.

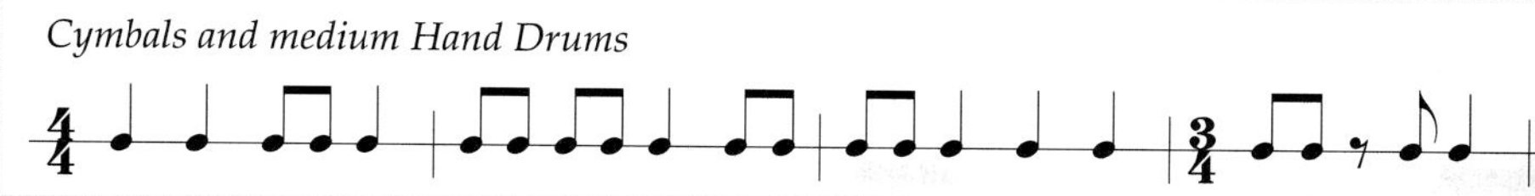

Clap the rhythm pattern each time it occurs as you listen again to "Bo Hai Huan Ten."

Play the rhythm pattern on cymbals and hand drums along with the recording.

You should have played five repetitions of the rhythm pattern. When there are repetitions after more than one contrasting section, the form is called return form, or rondo form. The form of "Bo Hai Huan Ten" can be outlined as: A B A C A D A E A. The rhythm pattern you played is represented by the letter A.

Create and notate a simple hand drum accompaniment to play along with the recording. This is a **mixed meter** song, or a song in which the meter or time signature changes. The last measure is completed for you.

A group of children play various traditional Chinese instruments, including the pear-shaped pipa and the round yue-qin. Two boys on flute accompany them at the Children's Palace, in Shanghai, China.

Yuanxiao is one of the traditional foods enjoyed at the Lantern Festival. It is a sweet, sticky, round dumpling made with rice flour. Its round shape symbolizes family unity, completeness, and happiness.

Music Journal

In my opinion, what musical characteristics of "Bo Hai Huan Ten" help to portray a sense of celebration?

Cinco de Mayo

Ballet Folklorico dancers at State Capitol in Austin, Texas

A national holiday in Mexico, Cinco de Mayo is also celebrated in Mexican-American communities in the southern United States. This "Fifth of May" celebration marks the victory of the small Mexican army over the huge French army at the Battle of Puebla in 1862. While the United States was embroiled in its own Civil War, those few but brave Mexicans helped defend more than their own land. The French had their eyes on many lands throughout the southern United States. Traditionally, Americans of Hispanic heritage along with many other Americans join in the celebration.

In addition to feasts of traditional foods, sporting events, and fireworks displays, Cinco de Mayo festivals also feature mariachi bands that accompany traditional dancers. Three of the most popular native Mexican dances are the Mexican Hat Dance, La raspa, and El jarabe tapatío.

LISTENING **CD 2:17**

El jarabe tapatío Mexican Folk Dance

Mariachi bands, often referred to as street bands, traditionally included the *vihuela* (a small five-stringed guitar), *guitarrón* (bass guitar), guitar, and violin. They first appeared in the late 1700s in small towns such as Jalisco, Mexico. Since the 1930s, trumpets have also been accepted as a traditional instrument in these bands.

Identify the instruments or families of instruments used in a mariachi band as you listen to the recording.

Identify the three sections of the piece that can help you determine the form.

Describe how contrast is achieved among the three sections.

Tap on the first beat of each measure of the harmonic accompaniment on page 59 to experience the contrasts of meter and tempo.

Play the harmonic accompaniment for "El jarabe tapatío" on guitar, keyboard, or bells.

Musicians perform at the famous Hofbrauhaus Hall during the annual Oktoberfest celebration in Munich, Germany.

The Chicken Dance is often performed at Oktoberfests. The Guinness Book of World Records reports that the biggest Chicken Dance ever was held at the Cincinnati, Ohio, Oktoberfest in 1996, which boasted 48,000 participants.

music.mmhschool.com
Discover various ways to perform the Chicken Dance.

Oktoberfest

The tradition of Oktoberfest originated in Germany in 1810. It began as the wedding feast for the Crown Prince Ludwig of Bavaria and his bride, Theresa von Sachsen-Hildburghausen. To this day, the world's largest Oktoberfest draws seven million people to Munich, Germany, each fall.

Communities throughout the United States enjoy their own imitations of this celebration, including the best of German foods and music. Traditional dancers and singers performing to the music of Bavarian bands can be found in nearly every state in the nation!

In the United States, the Chicken Dance is popular with all age groups. It is performed at dances, weddings, and football games.

LISTENING **CD 2:18**

The Chicken Dance Traditional

Although usually associated with German folk festivals, this song may have originated in Switzerland. Its original title *Der Ententanz* means "The Duck Dance." It is also known by the title "Dance Little Bird."

Perform the following movements to the Chicken Dance. Notice that the movements help you experience the contrasting sections of the music.

On the Verse:

1. *With hands raised, forming bird beaks, open and close beaks four times.*
2. *With thumbs tucked under armpits forming wings, flap wings four times.*
3. *With clenched fists at shoulder level, wiggle body, and bend knees up and down four times.*
4. *Clap 4 times.*

On the Refrain:

1. *All join hands and skip counterclockwise for 16 steps.*
2. *All join hands and skip clockwise 16 steps. OR*

1 2 *With a partner, hook elbows and turn 16 beats one way, then turn 16 beats the other way.*

The form of the Chicken Dance is created by alternating verse and refrain. This can be described as **AB Form**, or **Binary Form**.

Your Creative Unit Project

Explore the cultural heritage of your own community or surrounding communities. You might start with your family and closest friends. Find out what their favorite ways are of celebrating their cultural heritage. Contact the Chamber of Commerce to find out about special events your community offers that people from outside the community are invited to participate in. As you work through the lessons in this unit, continue to talk to people in your community about music's role in heritage festivals, ceremonies, parades, and other recreational offerings. Then work together with classmates to create a brochure, a television ad, or a school assembly presentation that promotes your community's cultural events. In your promotion, make an extra effort to encourage other young people to contribute to and participate in these events.

FREE music concert in the Park this Friday at 8 sharp! Don't be late!

This concert is sponsored by our neighborhood park district.

Ceremonial Music

LESSON 2

From the music heard in your community's houses of worship to our nation's military bands, there is a large body of music that could be called ceremonial. Time-honored traditions such as greeting the President of the United States with a rousing rendition of "Hail to the Chief" and the drumming ceremony that calls Native Americans together for a powwow are two examples. Ceremonies often have an established form or ritual with prescribed music and readings. Can you think of some examples of ceremonies that you have participated in or attended?

The choir at Tabernacle Baptist Church sings for the Easter morning service (left). The United States Air Force Academy Band marches together (right).

Ceremonies play an important role in all kinds of communities. They help create unity within communities, and they help to celebrate and strengthen this unity. The survival of communities and cultures throughout history and around the world can often be attributed to their faithful observance of traditions and ceremonies.

The Cahuilla

The Cahuilla people live in the Sonoran and Mojave Desert regions of Southern California. They have lived there for centuries.

"Powama," which can be translated "these feathers move when you dance," is from the body of Cahuilla songs known as "Bird Songs." Imagine the costumes and movements that might be a part of a ceremonial dance to this song! Most Native American music highlights the use of percussion instruments. The rattle is used with this selection.

music.mmhschool.com
Explore the music of other Native American communities.

Cahuilla woman in rabbit robe and feather hat

Read the notation as you listen to "Powama." Notice how the lyrics are pronounced.

Perform the voice and rattle parts for "Powama," paying careful attention to the rhythm patterns.

Cahuilla dew claw rattle

CD 2:19

Powama

Traditional Cahuilla Indian Song

To Coda

Voice

po wa mə po wə mai_ yə we po wa mə po wə mai_ yə we

Rattle

po wa mə po wə mai_ yə we - e po wa mə po wə mai_ yə we

po wa mə po wə mai_ yə we - e po - o wa mə po wə mai_ yə we - e

D.C. al Coda

po - o wa mə po wə mai_ yə we - e po - o wa mə po wə mai_ yə we

Coda

po wa mə po wə mai_ yə we - e po wa mə po wə mai_ yə we

Music and Movement in Ceremonies

One of the formal movements in many ceremonies is the processional. Olympic ceremonies feature this kind of movement. All the participants enter the arena to the Olympic theme music as well as the national anthems of the participating athletes.

Olympic torch

Processionals are also common in worship settings around the world. In Cameroon, a country in West Africa, the original French version of "Oh, Come Sing a Song" was traditionally used on special Sundays. While it is not uncommon for songs from other cultures to be arranged for use in new settings, respect for the original context is important.

Listen to "Oh, Come Sing a Song" as you follow the notation. This arrangement uses the claves, the calabash, double bells, and congas. These percussion instruments reflect the use of both traditional and modern instruments in Cameroon.

Improvise a rhythmic accompaniment with drumsticks or other percussion instruments.

Welcoming ceremonies are a familiar scene in Cameroon when a bus arrives in the community. A common mode of transportation, buses in Cameroon often transport chickens, sacks of grain, and other goods along with people. At these ceremonies, visitors as well as returning friends are invited to listen to and play native percussion instruments such as drums, shakers, string instruments, and whistles.

modern rattle ▶

◀ Drum from Cameroon

Traditional central African processional

Music Journal

What role does music play in the ceremonies that I have participated in, observed, or attended?

Perform the processional step as you listen to the recording again, starting with both feet together.

- **Beat 1** ***tap right foot out to side***
- **Beat 2** ***feet together***
- **Beat 3** ***tap right foot back***
- **Beat 4** ***step forward with right foot***

Then repeat this pattern starting with the left foot. Beat 1: tap left foot out to side; Beat 2: feet together; Beat 3: tap left foot back; Beat 4: step forward with left foot.

Sing the song in four parts as on the recording.

MAP
NIGERIA
CAMEROON
CENTRAL AFRICAN REPUBLIC
EQUATORIAL GUINEA
GABON
CONGO

Oh, Come Sing a Song

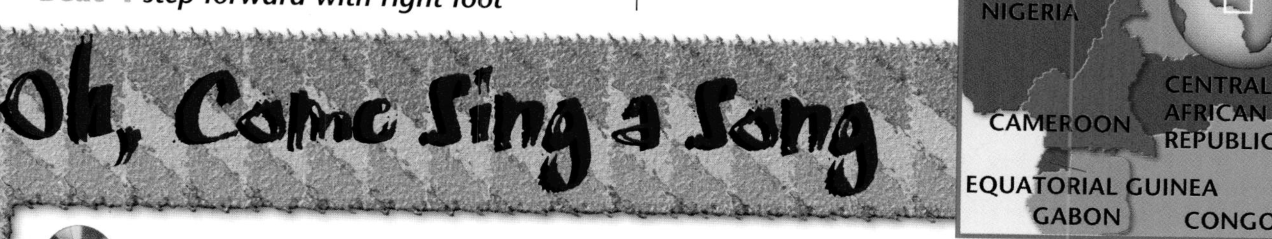

CD 3:1

Traditional Cameroon Processional Melody
Arranged by MMH

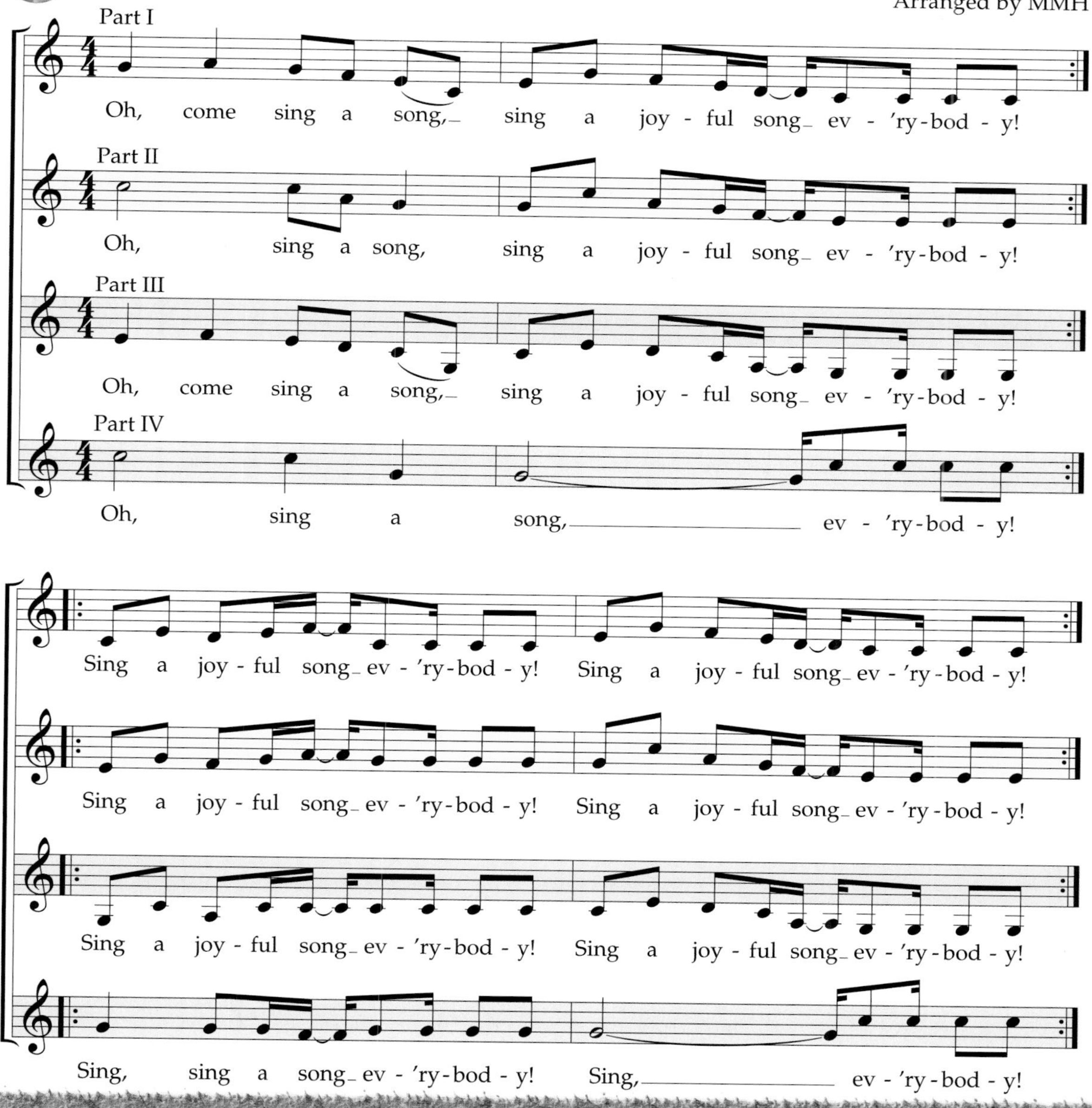

Part I
Oh, come sing a song,_ sing a joy - ful song_ ev - 'ry-bod - y!
Part II
Oh, sing a song, sing a joy - ful song_ ev - 'ry-bod - y!
Part III
Oh, come sing a song,_ sing a joy - ful song_ ev - 'ry-bod - y!
Part IV
Oh, sing a song,______ ev - 'ry-bod - y!
Sing a joy - ful song_ ev - 'ry-bod - y! Sing a joy - ful song_ ev - 'ry-bod - y!
Sing a joy - ful song_ ev - 'ry-bod - y! Sing a joy - ful song_ ev - 'ry-bod - y!
Sing a joy - ful song_ ev - 'ry-bod - y! Sing a joy - ful song_ ev - 'ry-bod - y!
Sing, sing a song_ ev - 'ry-bod - y! Sing,______ ev - 'ry-bod - y!

Shona children perform traditional dance at Chapunga.

Syncopation in a Ceremonial Song

The Shona people in the African country of Zimbabwe also use processional music in religious ceremonies. "Uyai Mose" has its origins there but is also familiar in many worship communities in the United States.

Syncopation is one of the musical characteristics that helps make "Uyai Mose" engaging processional music. Each vocal part is syncopated.

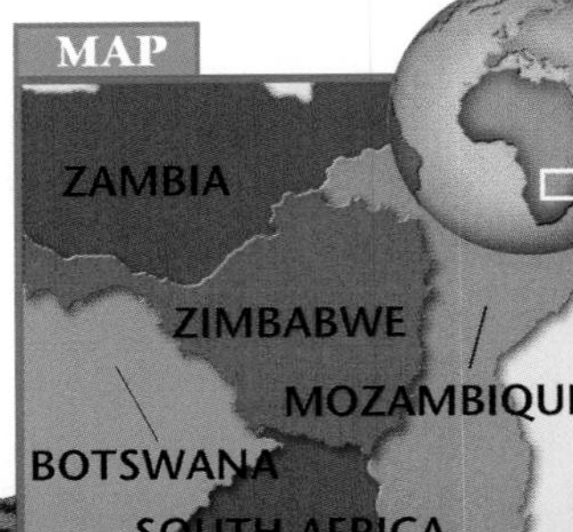
MAP
ZAMBIA
ZIMBABWE
MOZAMBIQUE
BOTSWANA
SOUTH AFRICA

Uyai Mose

CD 3:7
Come All You People
Words and Music by Alexander Gondo
Descant:
Shona: U - ya - i mo - se, ti - na - ma - te Mwa - ri.
Pronunciation: u ya i mo se ti na ma te mwa ɾi
English: Come, all you peo - ple, come and praise your Mak - er.
D G
Shona: U - ya - i mo - se, ti - na - ma - te Mwa - ri.
Pronunciation: u ya i mo se ti na ma te mwa ɾi
English: Come, all you peo - ple, come and praise your Mak - er.
U - ya - i mo - se, ti - na - ma - te Mwa - ri.
u ya i mo se ti na ma te mwa ɾi
Come, all you peo - ple, come and praise your Mak - er.
D D A D A7
U - ya - i mo - se, ti - na - ma - te Mwa - ri.
u ya i mo se ti na ma te mwa ɾi
Come, all you peo - ple, come and praise your Mak - er.

Identify the lyrics that match the following syncopated rhythm patterns as you listen to the recording. **Clap** each pattern as you speak the lyrics.

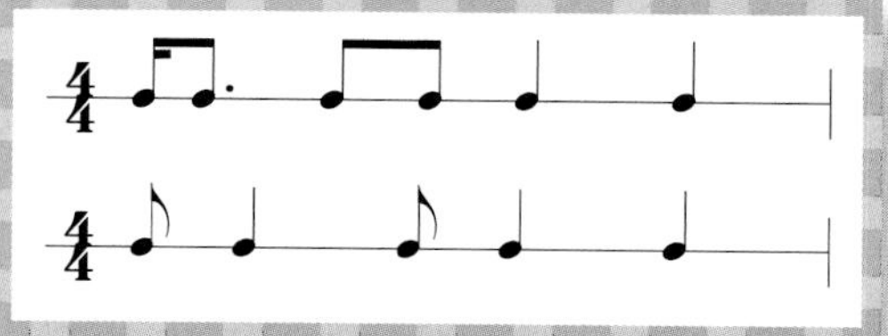

Notate on staff paper at least two measures of other syncopated patterns in the song. **Play** the percussion part on claves and maracas as you sing along with the recording.

The Iona Community, founded in 1938, is a monastic community on the island of Iona off Scotland's west coast. The community works for social and political change and believes that music can be a big part of this effort. They collect songs from around the globe, such as "Uyai Mose."

U - ya - i mo - se, ti - na - ma - te Mwa - ri.
u ya i mo se ti na ma te mwa ɾi
Come, all you peo - ple, come and praise your Mak - er.

D G

U - ya - i mo - se, ti - na - ma - te Mwa - ri.
u ya i mo se ti na ma te mwa ɾi
Come, all you peo - ple, come and praise your Mak - er.

3 *Last time*

U - ya - i mo - se zvi - no. Ti - na - ma - te Mwa - ri.
u ya i mo se ʒi no ti na ma te mwa ɾi
Come now and wor - ship the Lord. Come and praise your Mak - er.

D Em7 D D Em A7 D

U - ya - i mo - se zvi - no.
u ya i mo se ʒi no
Come now and wor - ship the Lord.

Music in the Parks

LESSON 3

Does your community have an outdoor summer concert series? If so, perhaps it's every Thursday night in front of the town library or town hall. Maybe it's in your neighbor's barn or on a big stage in a city park. Or it could include the carousel's music at an amusement park or county fair.

Many music venues feature local musicians alongside more widely recognized performers. No matter where you live, these venues might feature performing styles ranging from country line dancing to Latin jazz. When was the last time you heard music in a park? What do you remember enjoying most (or least) about the music?

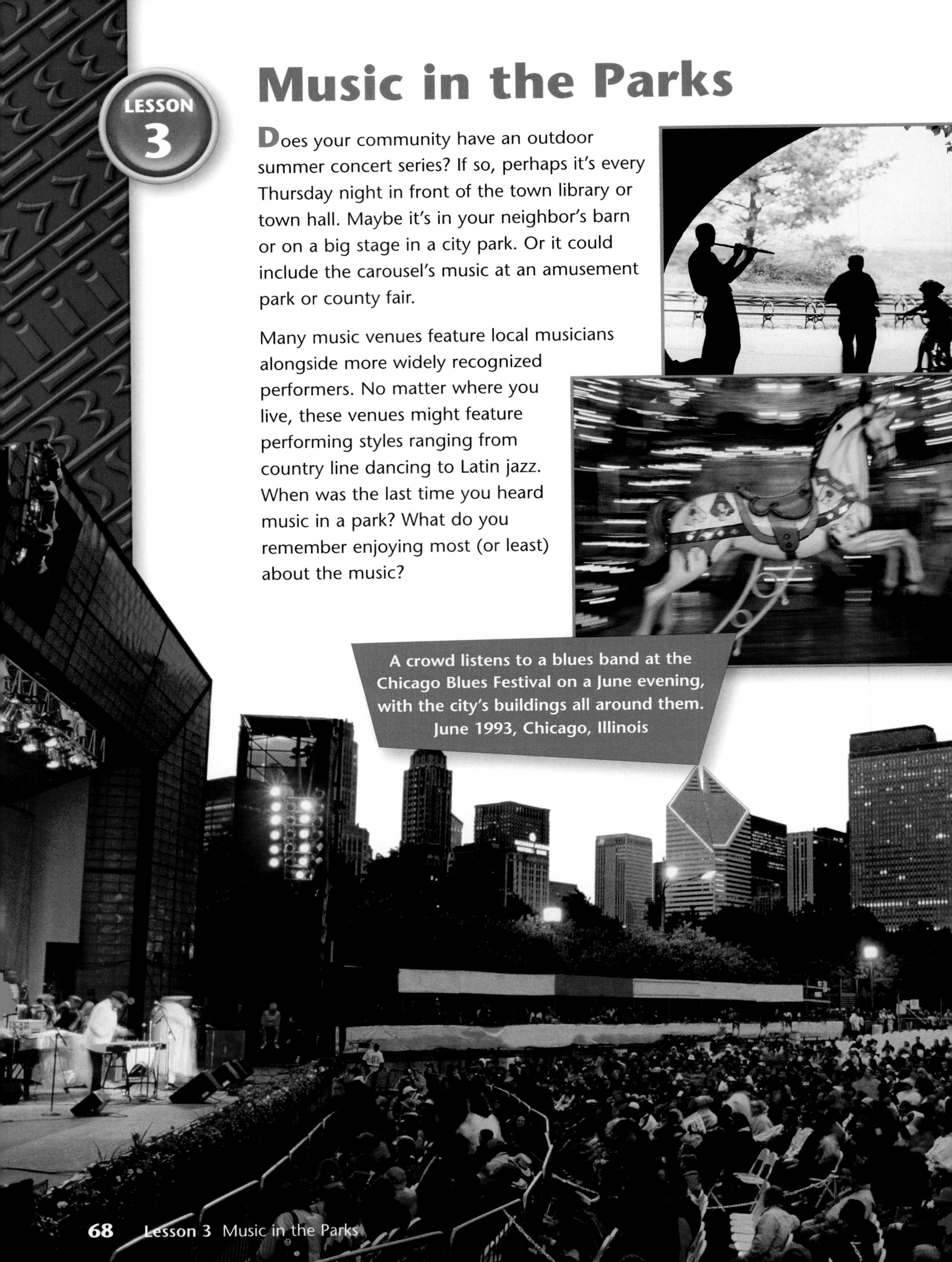

A crowd listens to a blues band at the Chicago Blues Festival on a June evening, with the city's buildings all around them. June 1993, Chicago, Illinois

LISTENING **CD 3:13**

The Carousel Waltz by Richard Rodgers and Oscar Hammerstein

Featured as the overture in the musical *Carousel,* this waltz can be heard in parks all over the world wherever carousel rides are still enjoyed by "children" of all ages.

Describe the tone colors and meter of "The Carousel Waltz" after you have listened to it. What kind of scene can you imagine in the musical as you listen to this?

A Peruvian Classic

Andean instruments that are centuries old are still used in Andean folk music today.

Concerts played in parks throughout the United States often include **folk music**. Sometimes called the "first popular music," folk music is usually characterized by simple lyrics about everyday life and a simple instrumental accompaniment. "El cóndor pasa" is a folk song from the Andean region of Peru. The folk music of Peru has its origins in pre-Incan civilization. While this song dates back only to the eighteenth century, it also helps us imagine what music may have sounded like more than 5,000 years ago in South America. Since many versions of this song have been recorded over the years by different artists, "El cóndor pasa" has enjoyed considerable popularity in the United States. Simon and Garfunkel's recording from the 1960s is among the most popular versions.

LOG ON

music.mmhschool.com
Learn more about traditional South American music.

LISTENING **CD 3:14**

El cóndor pasa Andean Folk Song

Joël Francisco Perri is known as the "master of the Indian flute." He plays three different kinds of Indian flutes: the kena, or shepherd's flute; the zapoñas, or pan flute; and the rondador, a pan flute from Ecuador.

Read the lyrics below from the Simon and Garfunkel rendition as you listen to this instrumental recording. Discuss the possible meaning of the lyrics.

I'd rather be a sparrow than a snail. Yes I would. If I could, I surely would.
I'd rather be a hammer than a nail. Yes I would. If I could, I surely would.
Away, I'd rather sail away like a swan that's here and gone.
A man gets tied up to the ground. He gives the world its saddest sound.
I'd rather be a forest than a street. Yes I would. If I could, I surely would.
I'd rather feel the earth beneath my feet. Yes I would. If I could, I surely would.

It's About the Life and the Music . . .

If someone asked you how to describe **rap music**, what would you say? Is it more than just spoken words with an optional melody line?

Rap is a genre of rhythm-and-blues music that includes a rhythmic vocal line spoken or sung over an instrumental accompaniment. It often uses a call-and-response format common in traditional African American music. Musical interest is often achieved by the timing of lyrics over complex rhythmic patterns. Rap lyrics are most often about relationships, inner-city life, and political issues.

LISTENING CD 3:15

Park Rap 1 by Chris Judah-Lauder

This recording features Boomwhackers® playing a rhythmic accompaniment. A more typical accompaniment would include a bass guitar, drums, keyboard, other unpitched percussion, and vocal sound effects.

Play the rhythmic accompaniments on Boomwhackers® or on any pitched or unpitched percussion instruments. Practice each line separately. Then play the three parts together.

Perform the following lyrics on top of the recorded accompaniment "Park Rap 1," looking for places in the text to add unpitched percussion or short vocal sound effects.

Park Rap 1

Music and Lyrics by Chris Judah-Lauder

Refrain

In the park, man, in the park
In the park, man, in the park.

Verse 1

A hangin', a runnin', a walkin' all around.
The park is cool with its many a sounds.
The birds, the wind, the bikers on the street.
Makin' their sounds (pause) so sweet.

Verse 2

Teens are talkin'. Kids hard at play.
Grandma and grandpa enjoying their day.
Then there's the critters that run all free.
Some walk around and others climb a tree.

Verse 3

Concert time with the big jazz band.
Guitar and bass, and keyboard land,
Listen to the vibes as they fill the air.
Tap those toes and give a care.

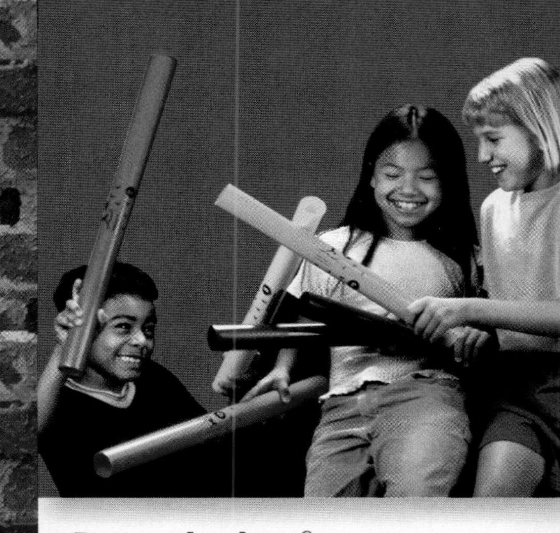

Boomwhackers® Percussion Tubes
Boomwhackers are brightly colored tubes of varying lengths that can be used to play melodies, rhythms, or chords. They are played by simply tapping the tubes on the floor, a table or chair, or on other tubes. They can be used to play up to three octaves of notes. A cap can be fastened to the end of a tube to lower the pitch one octave.

See *Spotlight on MIDI* for an activity about creating your own rap.

Music Journal

What lyrics can I create about the sights and sounds of "music in the parks" to perform with the accompaniment for "Park Rap 1"?

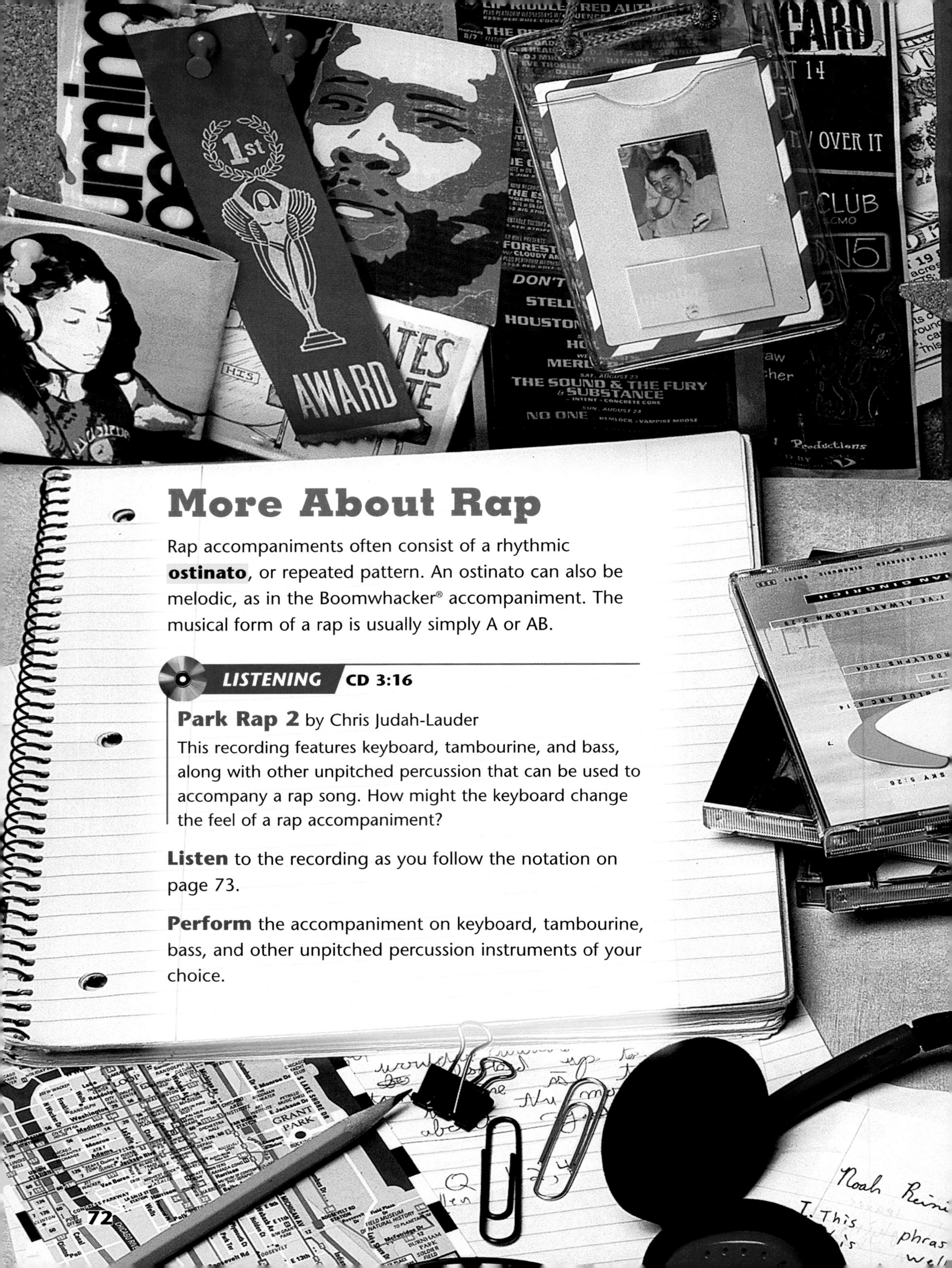

More About Rap

Rap accompaniments often consist of a rhythmic **ostinato**, or repeated pattern. An ostinato can also be melodic, as in the Boomwhacker® accompaniment. The musical form of a rap is usually simply A or AB.

LISTENING **CD 3:16**

Park Rap 2 by Chris Judah-Lauder

This recording features keyboard, tambourine, and bass, along with other unpitched percussion that can be used to accompany a rap song. How might the keyboard change the feel of a rap accompaniment?

Listen to the recording as you follow the notation on page 73.

Perform the accompaniment on keyboard, tambourine, bass, and other unpitched percussion instruments of your choice.

Computer-generated sounds from synthesizers have been used since the late 1970s and early 1980s to create the rhythm backgrounds used by many rap and other popular artists. Various sounds are combined, or synthesized, electronically to produce a layered sound in music.

music.mmhschool.com
Read more about developments in digital sound.

Perform the lyrics from page 71 with the recording for "Park Rap 2," looking for places in the text to add unpitched percussion or short vocal sound effects.

Music Journal

What musical criteria can I use to describe the similarities and differences between the two rap accompaniments?

LESSON 4

Parades and Processions

Parades are yet another example of how communities come together to celebrate events like holidays and sports victories. The music at parades is as varied as the reasons for having them in the first place. Some parade music, such as in the electrical parades at Disneyland, is performed completely on analog synthesizers, while other parade music is performed by live marching bands. Parade "acts" include performers like Broadway singers in New York's Thanksgiving Day Parade and Irish step dancers in Chicago's St. Patrick's Day Parade. Jugglers and clowns walk alongside civil leaders and politicians. Truly, parades bring people together in a unique way! Parades are a very special kind of ceremonial procession!

Powwow dancer (left); powwow dancer processional, or Grand Entry (right)

 **LISTENING** CD 3:17

Processional Medley (montage)

This medley of processional music includes "Olympic Fanfare," "Honor the Earth Powwow—Grand Entry," "Agahu Suite from *Dance Suites from West Africa,*" and "Just a Closer Walk with Thee."

Listen to "Processional Medley" and notice the different moods that various processionals can convey.

Identify which excerpt you think you are hearing, based on the titles provided.

Create movements for each excerpt that reflect the various moods. Include body percussion as well as "steps."

The American team (above) entering Olympic Stadium during the opening ceremonies of the 2000 Olympics, Sydney, Australia

Analog synthesizers have been used in Disneyland's electrical parades since their beginning in 1972. The technology that made these parades possible began as early as the 1950s when experiments with rearranging recorded sounds began. Max Mathews wrote an article in 1963 entitled "The Digital Computer as a Musical Instrument." And in 1964 three synthesizers were invented in different places at about the same time. The most famous was by Robert Moog of Trumansburg, New York.

Careers

Music Journal

How can I describe at least three distinct kinds of processional music in terms of style, tempo, dynamics, mood, and tone color?

Marching Band Music

Marching bands perform primarily in parades and at football games. They are often joined by drum majors and baton twirlers who add to the crowd's enthusiasm! But like so many other styles of music, marching band music can be best appreciated when you're actually a part of it!

LISTENING **CD 3:18**

National Emblem by E. E. Bagley

Composer E. E. Bagley never took music lessons in his entire life! He learned music by simply playing along with others who did study music. A trombonist and cornetist, as well as a cartoonist, Bagley is remembered mostly for composing this march.

Identify the A and B sections as you listen to the recording.

Clap the following rhythm patterns.

Perform the following rhythmic accompaniment to "National Emblem" on finger cymbals, ride cymbals, drum sticks, bass drum, or other percussion instruments.

Playalong

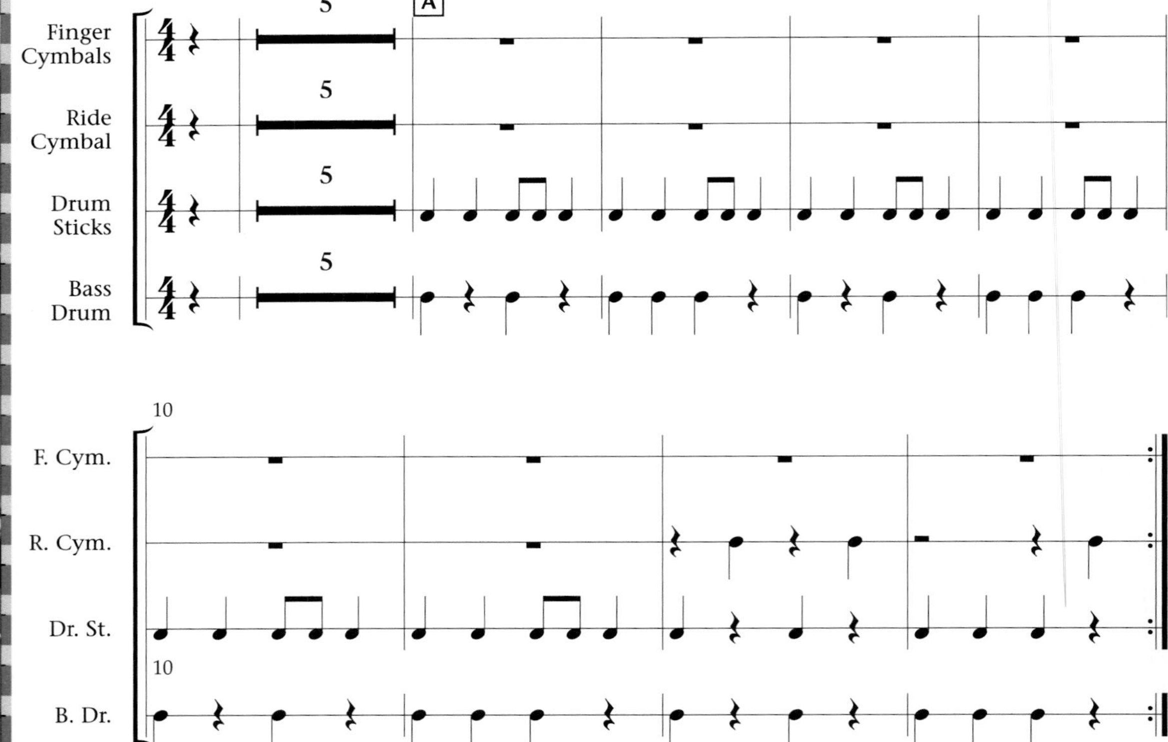

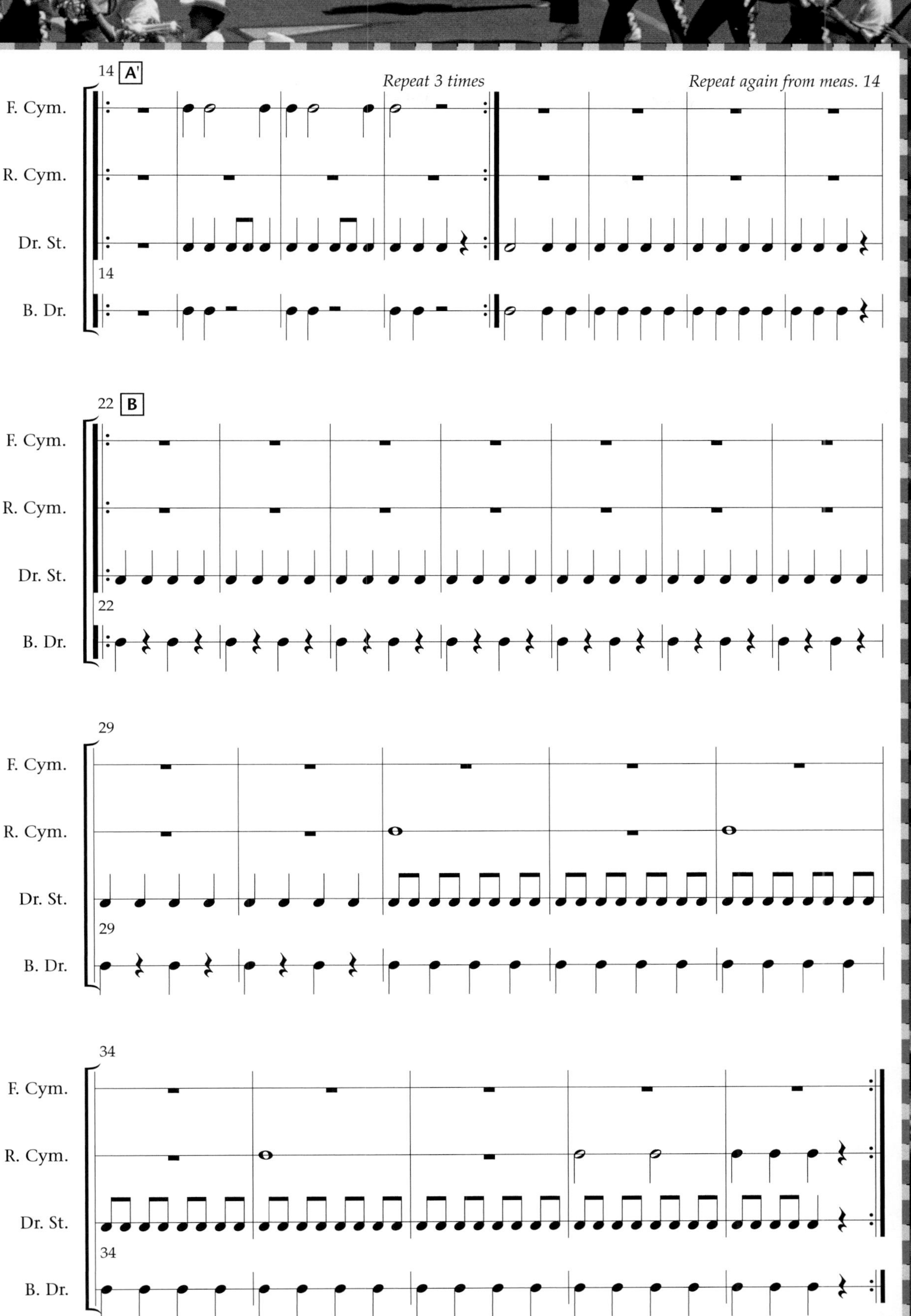
14 A'
Repeat 3 times
Repeat again from meas. 14
F. Cym.
R. Cym.
Dr. St.
14
B. Dr.
22 B
F. Cym.
R. Cym.
Dr. St.
22
B. Dr.
29
F. Cym.
R. Cym.
Dr. St.
29
B. Dr.
34
F. Cym.
R. Cym.
Dr. St.
34
B. Dr.

Meet the Musician

ON NATIONAL RADIO!

Name: Jarrod Lentz
Age: 17
Instrument: Voice
Hometown: Palmyra, PA

Even before he was born, music was a part of baritone Jarrod Lentz's life. "My mother played classical music to me through headphones when I was still in the womb," he explains. "Apparently the piece I responded to most, by kicking and so forth, was the Dvorak *New World Symphony*. Now when I listen to that piece I have a corny attachment like it's something I've known forever!"

Jarrod is being trained as a classical singer; but his ultimate dream is to make a name for himself in the world of musical theater. He recently had the summer of his life at Interlochen Arts Camp, where he performed in the musicals *Pirates of Penzance* and *How to Succeed in Business Without Really Trying*.

Prior to going to arts camp, Jarrod spent a few summers performing in a unique environment. He worked as a costumed character at Hershey Park, entertaining the amusement park crowd. Jarrod dressed up as several characters, including a Hershey Bar, a Hershey's Peanut Butter Cup, a chocolate syrup bottle, and a Rollo. As a musician, Jarrod's favorite character to play was, of course, a Hershey's Symphony Bar.

RECORDED INTERVIEW

Listen to Jarrod's performance of "Bright is the Ring of Words" **(CD 3:19)** and "The Vagabond" **(CD 3:20)** by Ralph Vaughan Williams and his interview **(CD 3:21)** on the national radio program From the Top.

Looking Back

You have explored the many ways that your community experiences and enjoys music—with celebrations of cultural heritage, with formal and informal ceremonies, in its parks and on its streets, and in its parades and processionals. Which of the examples in this unit most closely reflect celebrations and ceremonies in your own community? What new events or music might you want to promote in your community?

Music Journal

What could I do to help plan music for events in my own community that would appeal to many people and would encourage people who are reluctant to participate to get more involved?

Unit 4

On the Broadway Stage

MUSIC in Our CITIES

You cannot talk about a city's cultural life without talking about its music. Since the mid-nineteenth century, musical theater has enjoyed great popularity in America's largest cities. The works of composers and lyricists such as George Gershwin, Jerome Kern, Cole Porter, Leonard Bernstein, Frank Loesser, Rogers and Hammerstein, and Loewe and Lerner are known and loved by generations of music lovers.

By the early 1970s, British and French creative teams were making major contributions to what began as a uniquely American art form. London native Andrew Lloyd Webber's creations include *Cats, Evita,* and *The Phantom of the Opera.* Elton John, also of Great Britain, teamed up with lyricist Tim Rice for such shows as *The Lion King* and *Aida.*

THE LION

BROADWAY

Les Misérables

1920s–1940s

Lady Be Good! (1924), *Show Boat* (1927), *Face the Music* (1932), *Anything Goes* (1934), *Porgy and Bess* (1935), *Carousel* (1945), *Brigadoon* (1947), *Finian's Rainbow* (1947), *Kiss Me, Kate* (1948), *On the Town* (1949), *South Pacific* (1949)

In the 1980s, Frenchmen Claude-Michel Schönberg and Alain Boublil teamed up to create *Les Misérables* and *Miss Saigon.*

The late twentieth century also saw the production of many rock musicals including *Tommy, Jesus Christ Superstar, Jekyll and Hyde,* and *Rent.*

Copyright laws ensure that composers and writers enjoy the fruits of their own labor and can profit from their work. Many Broadway musicals are adaptations of novels or plays that are in the public domain. This means they can be freely reproduced, recorded, or adapted. For works created after 1978, a person's ideas are protected 70 years beyond his or her death. As long as copyright protection is still in effect, however, anyone who wishes to reproduce or adapt a work must get permission.

LOG ON

music.mmhschool.com
Learn more about copyright protection of creative works.

"UNLIKE ANYTHING BROADWAY HAS EVER SEEN!"

ING

1950s–1970s

Guys and Dolls (1950), *Wonderful Town* (1953), *My Fair Lady* (1956), *The Sound of Music* (1959), *Camelot* (1960), *Bye Bye Birdie* (1960), *How to Succeed in Business Without Really Trying* (1961), *West Side Story* (1961), *Cabaret* (1966), *Evita* (1976), *Annie* (1977)

1980s–2000s

Cats (1982), *Les Misérables* (1987), *The Phantom of the Opera* (1988), *Miss Saigon* (1991), *Rent* (1996), *Chicago* (1996), *The Lion King* (1997), *Aida* (1998), *42nd Street* (1980, 2001), *Hairspray* (2002), *Nine* (1982, 2003)

Les Misérables

Like many other Broadway musicals, *Les Misérables* is an adaptation of an existing work. It is based on Victor Hugo's novel of the same title. The main character is Jean Valjean, who has spent nineteen years in prison for stealing a loaf of bread. His adopted daughter, Cosette, sings about her hopes and dreams for a better life in "Castle on a Cloud."

The light instrumentation for the recording is appropriate for supporting the young soloist's voice. Strings, harp, guitar, alto flute, English horn, and orchestral bells are used in the accompaniment.

Listen to the repeated and contrasting sections in each verse and determine which of the following sequences represents the form of the song.

AAAA or ABA or AABA

When music contains a repetition after one contrast, it is described as having **ternary form**.

Describe the musical contrasts between the different sections.

Castle on a Cloud

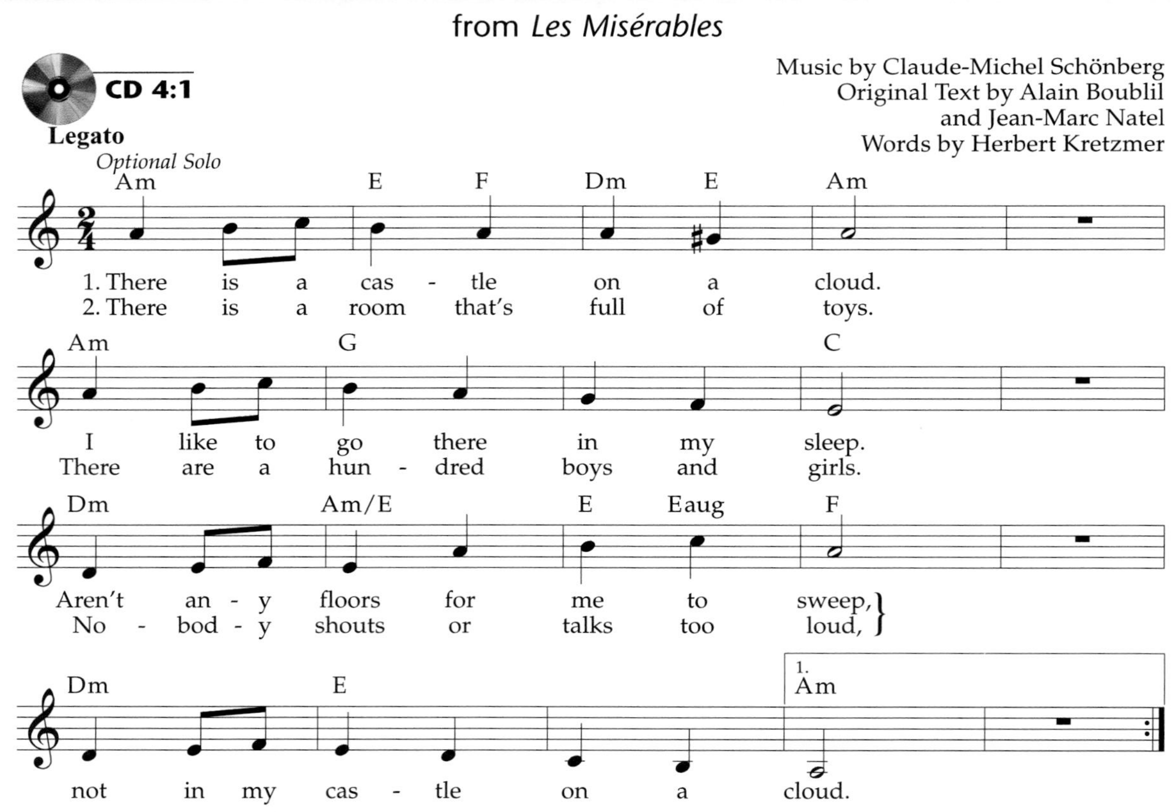
from Les Misérables
Music by Claude-Michel Schönberg
Original Text by Alain Boublil
and Jean-Marc Natel
Words by Herbert Kretzmer
CD 4:1
Legato
Optional Solo
Am E F Dm E Am
1. There is a cas - tle on a cloud.
2. There is a room that's full of toys.
Am G C
I like to go there in my sleep.
There are a hun - dred boys and girls.
Dm Am/E E Eaug F
Aren't an - y floors for me to sweep,
No - bod - y shouts or talks too loud,
Dm E 1. Am
not in my cas - tle on a cloud.

Play the following melodic accompaniment for "Castle on a Cloud" on keyboard, bells, or recorder.

Recorder Part
A
Fine
B
D.C. al Fine
4

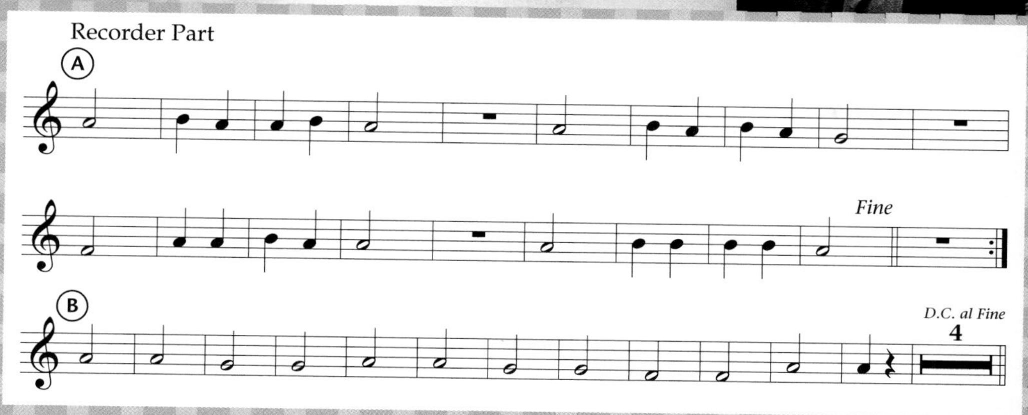

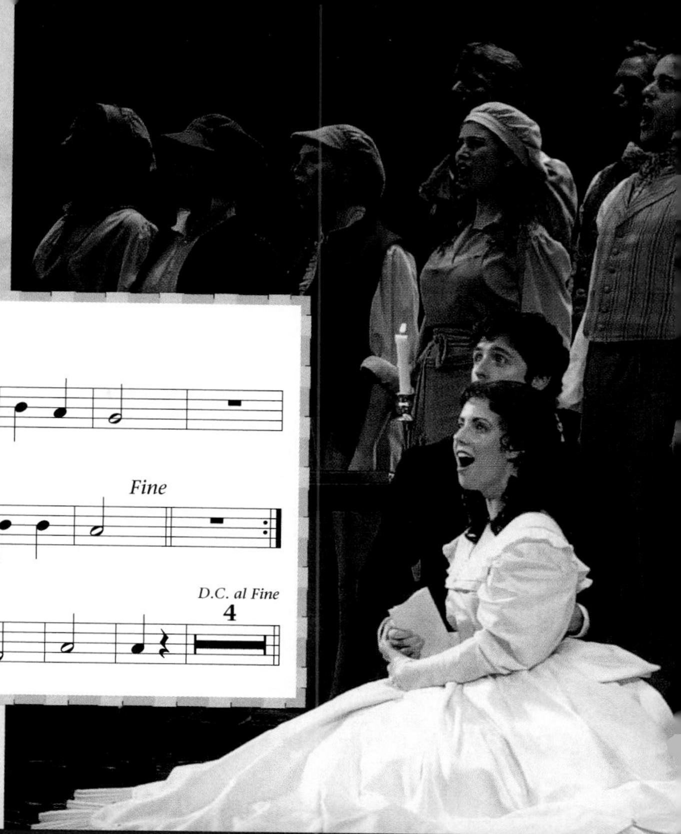

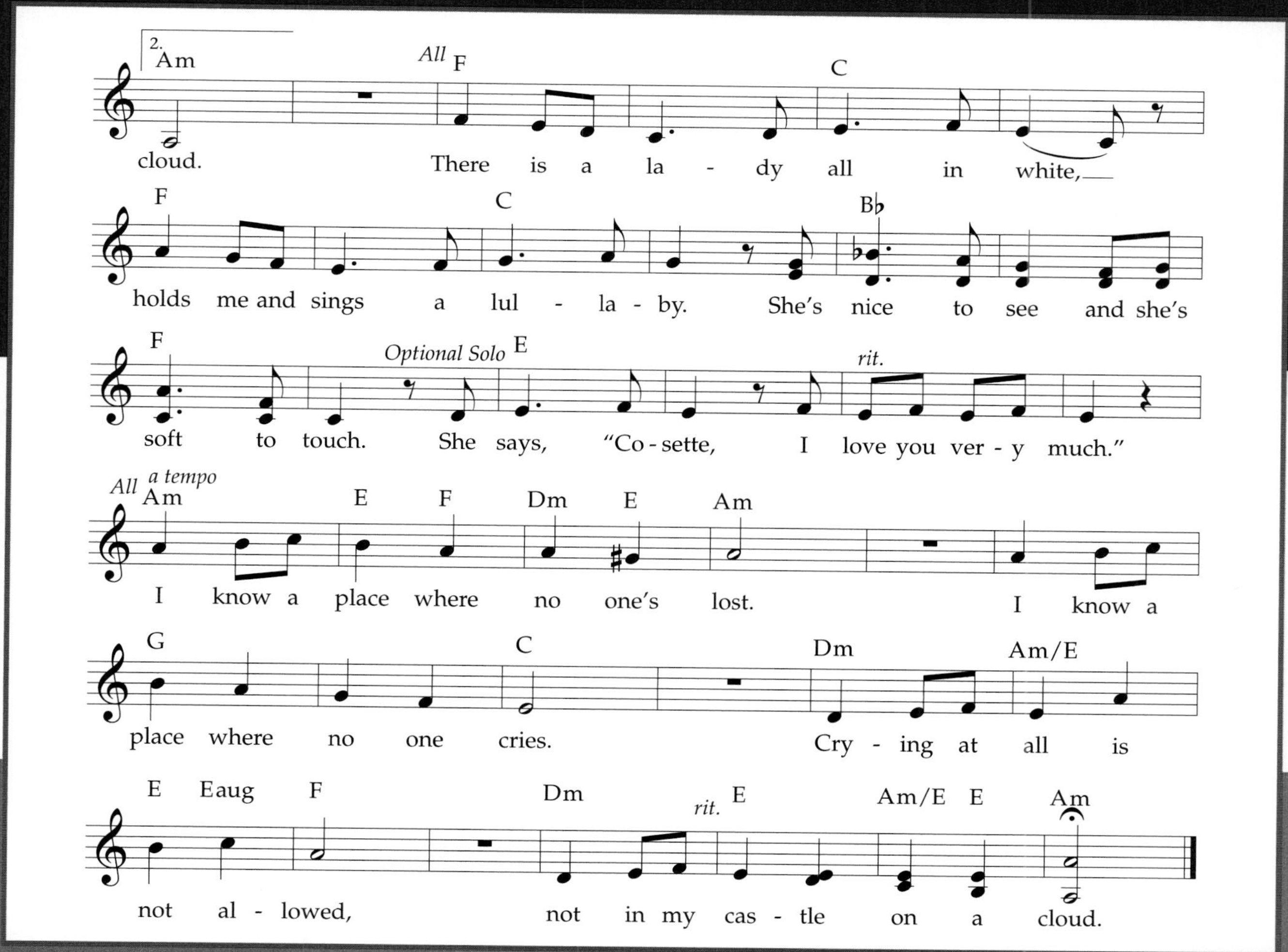

2.
Am All F C
cloud. There is a la - dy all in white,
F C B♭
holds me and sings a lul - la - by. She's nice to see and she's
F Optional Solo E rit.
soft to touch. She says, "Co - sette, I love you ver - y much."
All a tempo Am E F Dm E Am
I know a place where no one's lost. I know a
G C Dm Am/E
place where no one cries. Cry - ing at all is
E Eaug F Dm rit. E Am/E E Am
not al - lowed, not in my cas - tle on a cloud.

The Lion King

The Lion King tells the story of Simba, a young lion cub eager to become a proud ruler like his father, Mufasa. When Simba's jealous Uncle Scar plots to take the throne, Simba is exiled from the kingdom that is rightly his. While in exile, Simba meets Rafiki—a wise, mystic baboon who helps Simba reclaim his true destiny as king. "Circle of Life" celebrates Simba's return to the throne.

LISTENING CD 4:5

Circle of Life (choral arrangement) by Elton John and Tim Rice

In this SATB arrangement of "Circle of Life," the voices are accompanied by strong rhythm and percussion instruments that have the same driving force that you would expect to hear in a Broadway production.

Describe the form of the song, taking clues from the lyrics.

Describe the musical mood of the repeated and contrasting sections.

Meet the Musicians

Careers

The King's Singers ensemble was formed in 1968. Three of the original six members were students at King's College in Cambridge, England. Their repertoire includes everything from medieval madrigals to popular songs arranged especially for their six-part singing. Since their repertoire spans five centuries, they are said to take their audiences on a virtual tour of music history at their concerts. A total of eighteen men have been members over the years.

LISTENING CD 4:6

Circle of Life (The King's Singers) by Elton John and Tim Rice

The King's Singers are an all-male singing ensemble whose hallmark is their close six-part harmonies. Although they often sing a cappella (without accompaniment), they are accompanied on this recording by the Metropole Orchestra of the Netherlands.

Compare the King's Singers' performance of "Circle of Life" with the choral arrangement you just heard. Use musical terms to describe the differences.

The "Circle of Life" is completed in this final scene from *The Lion King*.

CIRCLE OF LIFE

FROM *THE LION KING*
BY ELTON JOHN AND TIM RICE

FROM THE DAY WE ARRIVE ON THE PLANET AND, BLINKING, STEP INTO THE SUN,
THERE'S MORE TO BE SEEN THAN CAN EVER BE SEEN, MORE TO DO THAN CAN EVER BE DONE.
SOME SAY, "EAT, OR BE EATEN." SOME SAY, "LIVE AND LET LIVE!"
BUT ALL ARE AGREED AS THEY JOIN THE STAMPEDE, YOU SHOULD NEVER TAKE MORE THAN YOU GIVE ...

REFRAIN
IN THE CIRCLE OF LIFE. IT'S THE WHEEL OF FORTUNE.
IT'S THE LEAP OF FAITH. IT'S THE BAND OF HOPE ...
'TIL WE FIND OUR PLACE ON THE PATH UNWINDING
IN THE CIRCLE, THE CIRCLE OF LIFE.

SOME OF US FALL BY THE WAYSIDE, AND SOME OF US SOAR TO THE STARS.
AND SOME OF US SAIL THROUGH OUR TROUBLES, AND SOME HAVE TO LIVE WITH THE SCARS.
THERE'S FAR TOO MUCH TO TAKE IN HERE, MORE TO FIND THAN CAN EVER BE FOUND.
BUT THE SUN ROLLING HIGH IN THE SAPPHIRE SKY KEEPS GREAT AND SMALL ON THE ENDLESS ROUND ...
(REFRAIN)

Rent

The award-winning 1996 musical *Rent* is based on Giacomo Puccini's opera *La Bohème,* which was first performed in 1896. A hit musical in its own time, *La Bohème* is an opera about loyal friendship among starving bohemian artists. It is set in Paris during the 1830s. In creating this rock musical version of *La Bohème,* composer Jonathan Larson sets the story in the East Village of New York City at the end of the twentieth century. *Rent* examines modern issues such as racism, poverty, homelessness, and debilitating illness.

A bohemian lifestyle refers to the unconventional lifestyle of writers, artists, and musicians struggling to make a living at their crafts. Devoting themselves completely to their creative work, they sometimes choose to live on meager incomes and in crowded living quarters.

LISTENING CD 4:7

Seasons of Love from *Rent*

(choral arrangement) by Jonathan Larson

"Seasons of Love" opens Act II of *Rent*. In this song, the cast members reflect on the riot that closed Act I. It asks the question: How do you measure a year in the life of a woman or a man?

Listen to "Seasons of Love" and notice its two main sections: verse and refrain. The two-part form illustrated in "Seasons of Love" is called AB, or binary form.

Seasons of Love by Jonathan Larson

from *Rent*

Five hundred twenty-five thousand six hundred minutes (three times)
How do you measure, measure a year?
In daylights, in sunsets, in midnights, in cups of coffee;
In inches, in miles, in laughter, in strife?
In five hundred twenty-five thousand six hundred minutes?
How do you measure a year in the life?
How about love? (three times)
Measure in love.
Seasons of love. (two times)

In truths that she learned or in times that he cried,
In bridges he burned or the way that she died.
It's time now - to sing out though the story never ends.
Let's celebrate, remember a year in the life of friends.
Remember the love. (three times)
Measure in love.
Seasons of love. (three times)

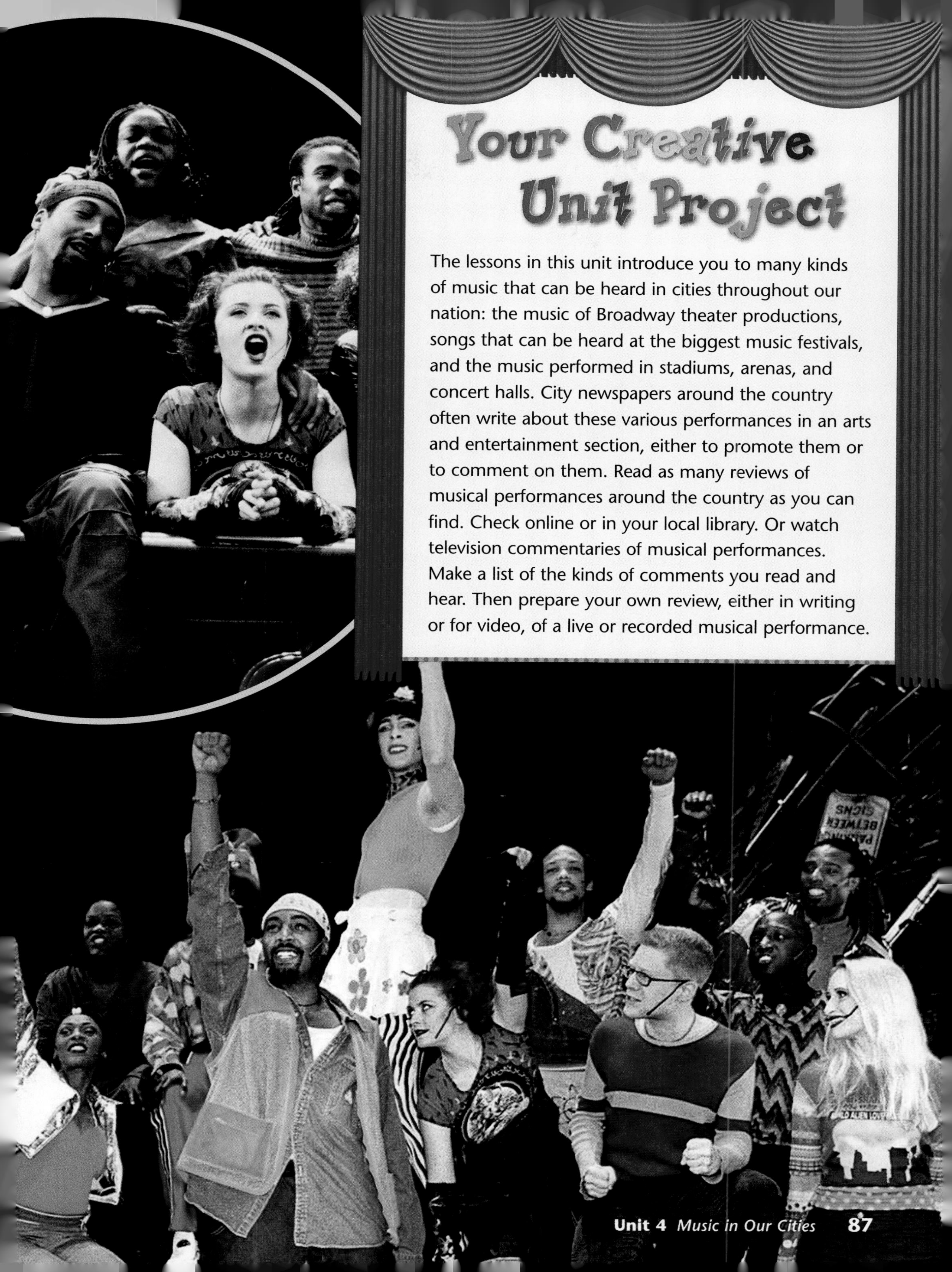

Your Creative Unit Project

The lessons in this unit introduce you to many kinds of music that can be heard in cities throughout our nation: the music of Broadway theater productions, songs that can be heard at the biggest music festivals, and the music performed in stadiums, arenas, and concert halls. City newspapers around the country often write about these various performances in an arts and entertainment section, either to promote them or to comment on them. Read as many reviews of musical performances around the country as you can find. Check online or in your local library. Or watch television commentaries of musical performances. Make a list of the kinds of comments you read and hear. Then prepare your own review, either in writing or for video, of a live or recorded musical performance.

Major Music Festivals

LESSON 2

Just as local communities enjoy music as they celebrate the heritage of their people, many of our nation's cities enjoy music festivals on an even grander scale. With its large and diverse populations, a city often draws people together from its many smaller communities and neighborhoods for big events. Some of these events, such as Musikfest in Bethlehem, Pennsylvania, specifically celebrate music itself! Others, such as Mardi Gras or Oktoberfest, help us celebrate a particular holiday or season.

Buckwheat Zydeco

The annual Mardi Gras festivities in New Orleans, Louisiana, are among the most popular in the country. *Mardi Gras* is French for "Fat Tuesday." The carnival season begins in early to mid January and lasts until February. In some religious traditions, Fat Tuesday is the last day before a season of prayer and fasting. Music often comes to mind when people talk about the city of New Orleans or about Mardi Gras.

Read the notation for "Mardi Gras Mambo" as you listen to the recording. Notice where the improvised solos occur.

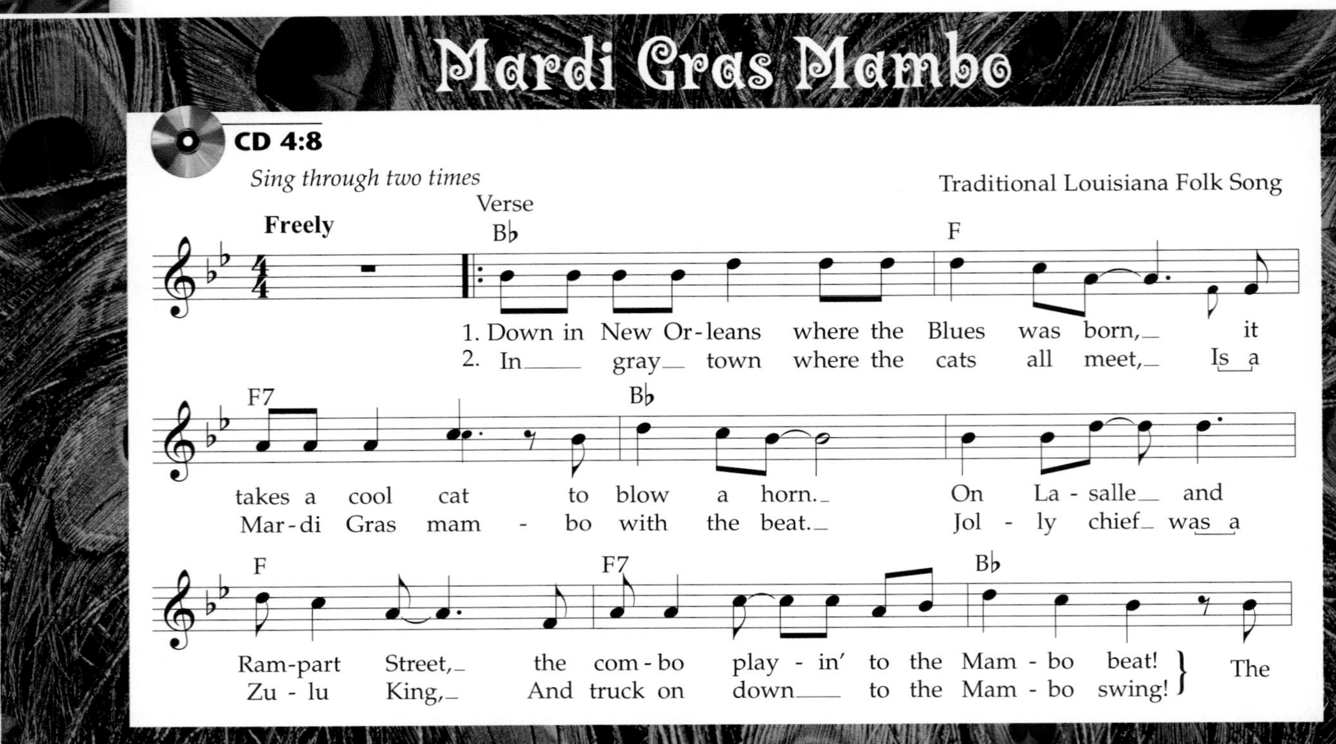
Mardi Gras Mambo
CD 4:8
Sing through two times
Traditional Louisiana Folk Song
Freely
Verse
B♭
F
1. Down in New Or-leans where the Blues was born,_ it
2. In_ gray_ town where the cats all meet,_ Is a
F7
B♭
takes a cool cat to blow a horn._ On La - salle_ and
Mar-di Gras mam - bo with the beat._ Jol - ly chief_ was a
F
F7
B♭
Ram-part Street,_ the com-bo play - in' to the Mam - bo beat!
Zu - lu King,_ And truck on down_ to the Mam - bo swing!
The

A Mardi Gras favorite, this song is in a style called **zydeco**. Zydeco blends blues, jazz, French, African, and Caribbean music. "Mardi Gras Mambo" often features improvised solos on trombone, trumpet, and saxophone. This recording features Stanley "Buckwheat" Dural's accordion playing.

Mardi Gras celebration in New Orleans, Louisiana

The rubboard, an unusual homemade instrument, is played in the recording of "Mardi Gras Mambo." Hung over the shoulder, the rubboard is a piece of metal with ridges. A rhythmic, scratchy sound is produced by rubbing spoons over the metal.

Sing "Mardi Gras Mambo."

Create and perform movements to accompany your singing.

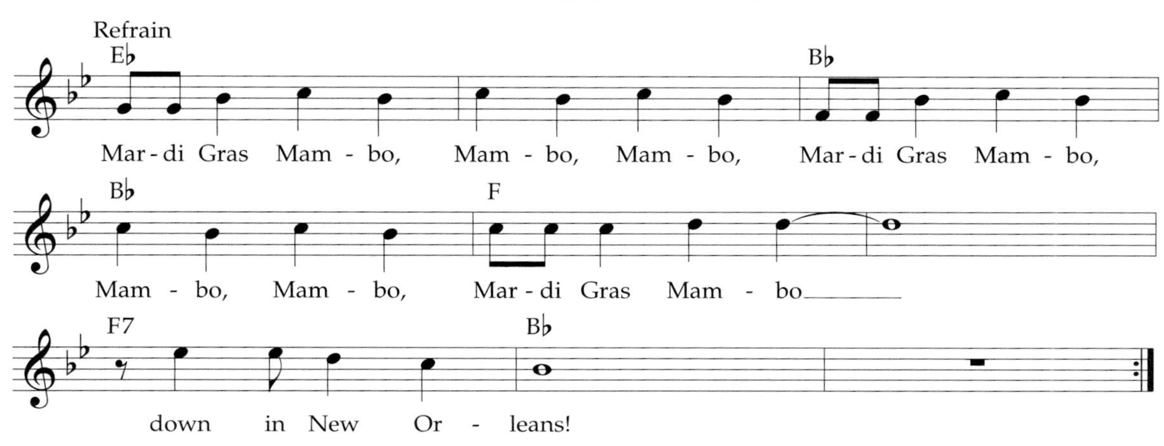

Repetition in Festival Music

At large city festivals, the music gives people of all ages and musical abilities opportunities to participate. The music that people most readily catch on to uses repetition. You have already learned about the rondo form in which there are repeated and contrasting sections. This can occur in both vocal and instrumental music. So whether you are singing or dancing, the music quickly becomes familiar. This makes it easy to join in the fun.

Cinco de Mayo dancers

Mariachi band members performing

LISTENING **CD 4:9**

Los mariachis Mexican folk song

The instruments played in "Los mariachis" were originally used only during Catholic Masses. Mexicans of Spanish descent began using them to make popular music in the mid-nineteenth century. The word *mariachi* describes the street musicians in a mariachi band as well as the music they perform.

Music Journal

What kinds of dance movements do the musical characteristics of the different sections of "Los mariachis" suggest to me?

Read the listening map below and pat the steady beat each time you hear the A section of "Los mariachis."

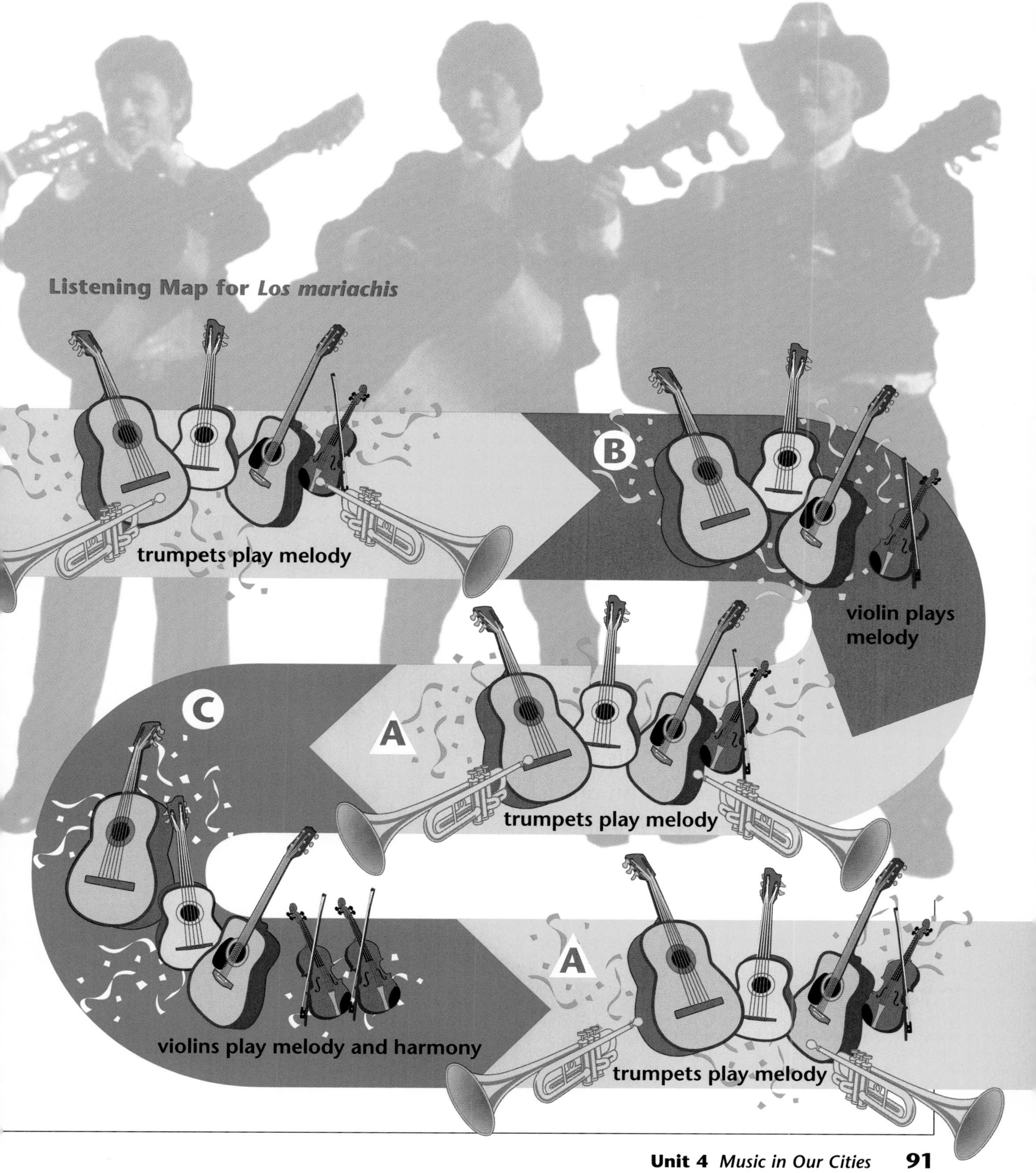

Listening Map for *Los mariachis*

trumpets play melody

B

violin plays melody

A

trumpets play melody

C

violins play melody and harmony

A

trumpets play melody

Music That Motivates

It is not often that you can read about a song so powerful that it inspired a national project that made its way into the hearts of people throughout the country. The song "Don't Laugh at Me" did just that. Soon after the song was performed at the Kerrville Folk Festival in Kerrville, Texas, in 1996, it became the centerpiece of a project called Operation Respect.

In 2000, folk singer Peter Yarrow founded Operation Respect to help children of all ages learn to respect and live in peace with one another in what he calls ridicule-free zones. In classrooms and camps across the nation, the program teaches people how to resolve conflicts in a safe environment.

Read the notation for "Don't Laugh at Me" as you listen to the recording. Be sure to follow the abbreviations *D.C., D.S. al Coda, coda* and *fine. D.C. (Da capo)* means to go back to the beginning, or the top, and start again. *D.S. al Coda (Dal segno al Coda)* means to go back to the sign 𝄋 and continue until you come to *To Coda.* Then skip to the term *Coda* to finish (at the *fine*).

Sing the song with the recording or with guitar accompaniment.

The Kerrville Folk Festival drew about 3,000 people back in 1972 when it first began. By the 1990s, more than 25,000 people were attending. It is America's largest and longest-running festival that features the work of original songwriters.

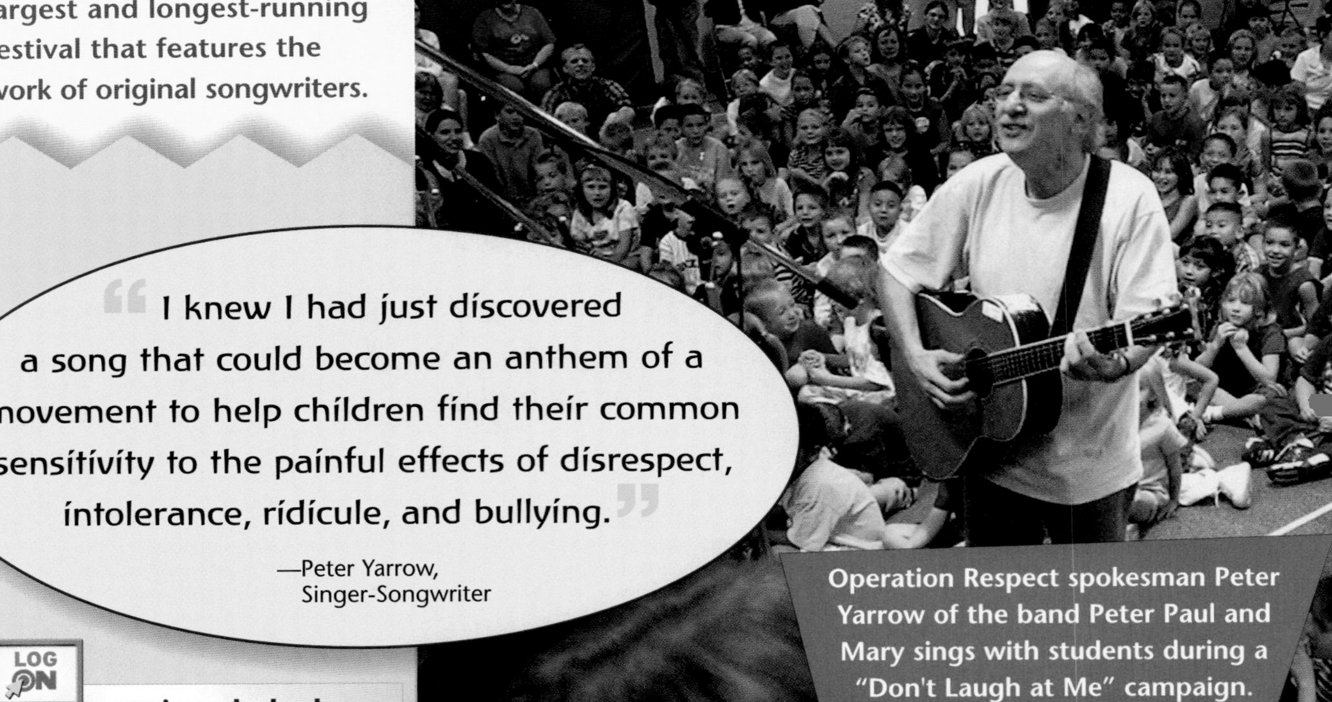

Operation Respect spokesman Peter Yarrow of the band Peter Paul and Mary sings with students during a "Don't Laugh at Me" campaign.

> "I knew I had just discovered a song that could become an anthem of a movement to help children find their common sensitivity to the painful effects of disrespect, intolerance, ridicule, and bullying."
>
> —Peter Yarrow, Singer-Songwriter

LOG ON

music.mmhschool.com
Learn more about Operation Respect and the Kerrville Folk Festival.

Don't Laugh at Me

CD 4:10
Words and Music by
Steve Seskin and Allen Shamblin
Freely
Eb
1. I'm a lit - tle boy with glass - es, the one they call a geek; a lit-tle
(2.) kid on ev - 'ry play-ground the one that's cho - sen last; I'm a
3. I'm the beg - gar on the cor - ner, you've passed me on the street, and I
Cm
girl who nev - er smiles 'cause I've got brac - es on my teeth and
sin - gle teen - age moth - er try-in' to o - ver - come my past. You don't
wouldn't be out here beg - gin' if I had e - nough to eat, and
Ab Eb/G Fm7 Bb
I know how it feels to cry my - self to sleep.
have to be my friend, but is it too much to ask?
don't think I don't no - tice that our eyes nev - er meet.
1.
2. I'm the
2., 3. Refrain
Eb
Don't laugh at me. Don't call me names.
Cm Ab Bb Eb
Don't get your plea - sure from my pain. In God's eyes, we're all the same.
Cm Ab Bb Eb
(3rd time) To Coda
Some-day we'll all have per-fect wings. Don't laugh at me.
1. Cm Ab Bb
(to Vs. 3) D.C.
2. Bridge
Cm Ab Eb/G
I'm fat, I'm thin, I'm short,
Fm7 Bb Ab Eb/G
rit.
Fm7 Bb
D.S. al Coda
I'm tall, I'm deaf, I'm blind. Hey, aren't we all?
Coda
Cm Ab Bb Ebmaj7
Don't laugh at me.

In Arenas and Stadiums

LESSON 3

From the Acropolis in Athens, Greece to California's Hollywood Bowl, and from New York City's Madison Square Garden to Louisiana's Superdome, arenas and stadiums around the globe serve as popular venues for large concerts and festivals. Many of these arenas also host sports events and conferences of many kinds. They draw the world's most popular performers. Their seating capacity is larger than concert halls and theaters. And the **acoustics** can be astounding! Acoustics are the characteristics of a space that determine the quality and control of sound waves within that space.

Many kinds of music can be heard in the world's largest arenas, from classical to new age and from rock and roll to country. This lesson highlights the variety of music you might hear in an arena or stadium.

LISTENING CD 4:11

Arianna by Claudio Monteverdi and Paul Schwartz

"Arianna" is the only surviving piece from a 1608 Monteverdi opera of the same title. Composer-producer Paul Schwartz uses the original melody and lyrics from Monteverdi, but then transforms the piece with a sound and style that appeal to an audience far beyond opera fans. "Arianna" is from the album *Aria 2: New Horizon* which includes other "recomposed" pieces. The album was No. 3 for the year 2000 on Billboard's Classical Chart.

Aerial view of an ancient theater near the Acropolis; ca. 1970-1997 Athens, Greece

Listen to "Arianna." The Italian lyrics, in typical operatic fashion, tell of the lament of Arianna for a lover who has died.

Play the harmonic accompaniment to "Arianna."

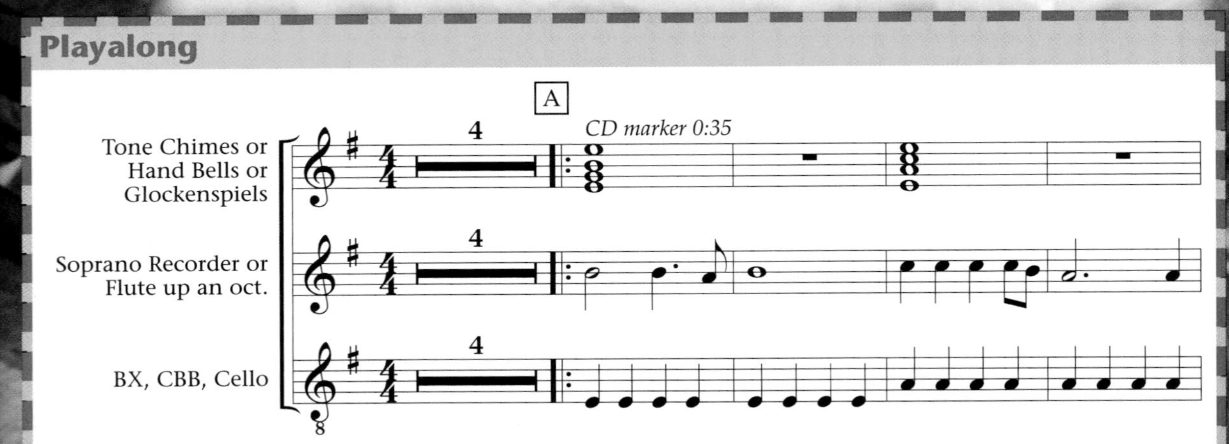

Hollywood Bowl in southern California is one of the largest natural ampitheaters in the world. It opened in 1922. Lloyd Wright, son of famous architect Frank Lloyd Wright, designed two of the shells.

In 1936, the all-time attendance record of 26,410 was set.

music.mmhschool.com
Learn more about famous arenas.

Mary Chapin Carpenter

Like many recording artists of the late twentieth and early twenty-first centuries, Mary Chapin Carpenter has enjoyed popularity with a wide variety of audiences. What was remarkable about her, though, was her perseverance as a female artist in times when the country music scene was largely dominated by male artists. And, unlike herself, many of her female contemporaries did not write their own songs.

Always true to herself and her own life experiences, Carpenter has written songs that convey strong emotions about a range of situations from the everyday to the political that many people easily relate to. Her strong, clear singing voice contributes to powerful performances that are often said to be very moving.

LISTENING **CD 4:12**

Down at the Twist and Shout

by Mary Chapin Carpenter

The venue for this live recording from January 1997 is the Super Dome in New Orleans, Louisiana, where singer and songwriter Mary Chapin Carpenter is joined by BeauSoleil at Super Bowl XXXI. BeauSoleil has been called America's best Cajun group and even the best Cajun band in the world. From Lafayette, Louisiana, this Grammy-winning group adds elements of zydeco, New Orleans jazz, Tex-Mex, country, and blues to their local Cajun musical tradition.

Read through the lyrics before you listen to the recording.

Describe the musical style or styles that you might expect to hear with these lyrics.

Meet the Musician

Mary Chapin Carpenter was born and raised in New Jersey. After spending time on the folk scene in Washington, D.C., she is now based primarily in Virginia. The winner of five Grammys and two Country Music Association awards for Female Vocalist of the Year, Carpenter has been recording since the late 1980s.

In 1994, her Grammy nomination for Record of the Year marked the first time a country hit received such a nomination without crossing over to the "pop" music charts. The song was "He Thinks He'll Keep Her." While many of her songs are considered characteristically "folk" music, they also include more than just hints of pop, blues, and country. Her lyrics and music have inspired artist Donna Mintz, whose work appears on one of Carpenter's albums.

Down at the Twist and Shout

Music and Lyrics by Mary Chapin Carpenter

Refrain
Saturday night and the moon is out,
I wanna head on over to the Twist and Shout,
Find a two-step partner and a cajun beat.
When it lifts me up I'm gonna find my feet.
Out in the middle of a big dance floor,
When I hear that fiddle wanna beg for more.
Wanna dance to a band from a-Lou'sian' tonight.

Verse
And I-a never have a-wandered down to New Orleans;
I never have drifted down a bayou stream.
But I heard that music on the radio,
And I swore some day I was gonna go
Down-a Highway 10, past-a Lafayette,
Then to Baton Rouge, and I won't forget
To send you a card with my regret
'Cause I'm never gonna come back home.
(repeat refrain)

(interlude with jam on guitar and piano)

Verse
They got a alligator stew and a crawfish pie,
A golf storm blowin' into town tonight.
Livin' on the delta, it's quite a show.
They got hurricane parties every time it blows.
Well here up north it's a cold, cold rain
And there ain't no cure for my blues today
Except when the paper says: BeauSoleil is a-coming into town. Baby, let's go down!
(repeat refrain)

(interlude with French vocals and then jam on accordion)

Verse
So bring your mama, bring your papa, bring your sister, too!
They got-a lots of music, lots of room.
And when they play you a waltz from 1910,
You're gonna feel a little bit young again
But you learn to dance with your rock and roll.
You learn to swing-a with a do-se-do
But you learn to love at the fais-do-do
When you hear a little jolie blon'.
(repeat refrain)

(tag with jam on guitar and violin)

Listen to "Down at the Twist and Shout" and discuss the variety of

That Old Time Rock and Roll

Grammy Award recipients not only include some of the world's newest stars, but also performers who have been around for more than a few decades. Let's take a look at the top ten touring artists and groups from the summer of 2002. Three acts debuted back in the 1960s. Five were first popular in the 1970s. Creed and The Dave Matthews Band were the only newcomers on this top ten list.

LISTENING **CD 4:13**

Old Time Rock and Roll by George Jackson and Thomas E. Jones III

The 1979 recording by Bob Seger and The Silver Bullet Band is considered a twentieth-century rock classic. This recording of this anthem to rock and roll is by the Flying Burrito Brothers.

Listen to the recording.

Improvise a rhythmic or melodic accompaniment on the instrument of your choice.

Describe the musical styles mentioned in the lyrics and your familiarity with each of them.

Bob Seger and The Silver Bullet Band

Old Time Rock and Roll

original lyrics by George Jackson
and Thomas E. Jones III

Just take those old records off the shelf.
I'll sit and listen to 'em by myself.
Today's music ain't got the same soul.
I like that old time rock and roll.

Don't try and take me to a disco.
You'll never even get me out on the floor.
In ten minutes I'll be late for the door.
I like that old time rock and roll.

Refrain

Still like that old time rock and roll.
That kind of music just soothes my soul.
I reminisce about the days of old
With that old time rock and roll.

Won't go and hear 'em play a tango.
I'd rather hear some blues or funky old soul.
There's only one sure way to get me to go.
Start playin' old time rock and roll.

Call me a relic, call me what you will.
Say I'm old-fashioned. Say I'm over the hill.
Today's music ain't got the same soul
Like that old time rock and roll.

Music Journal

What examples do I know of each of the musical styles mentioned in the lyrics to "Old Time Rock and Roll"? What would I want to say in my own song lyrics about my favorite style of music?

Bob Seger

LESSON 4

In the Concert Halls

If you have ever enjoyed live music performances, then you probably know how much of a difference acoustics can make. While outdoor arenas can have outstanding acoustics, either naturally or because of amplification, concert halls are designed and decorated specifically with great acoustics in mind. Whether a hall seats 2,000 people or 200, architects design them so that the sound can be clearly heard wherever a person might sit.

Concert-hall acoustics enable the listener to hear all the parts of an ensemble, even in music that uses complex layering strategies. One such ensemble is the **gamelan**, which is made up of gongs, metallophones, rhythmic drums, flutes, and stringed instruments. In a gamelan ensemble, which is the traditional instrumental ensemble of Indonesia, each instrument has a distinctive quality. As individual performers repeat rhythmic patterns, individual sounds combine with others to create ever-changing layers of sound. The concert hall is an ideal place to listen to the music of a gamelan ensemble.

Carnegie Hall, New York City

Meyerson Hall, Dallas, TX

LA Concert Hall, Los Angeles, CA

Sydney Opera House, Sydney, Australia

Gamelan musicians perform during a temple festival, Bali, Indonesia

LISTENING CD 4:14

Gêndhing KÊMBANG MARA (excerpt) Balinese gamelan music

This excerpt is performed by a gamelan ensemble in Bali, Indonesia. It is in a style used to accompany dance, drama, and puppet theater.

Listen to "Gêndhing KÊMBANG MARA," focusing on the sounds of individual instruments and the ensemble.

Members of gamelan ensembles may perform music based on reading and performing the same rhythm pattern. However, instead of performing all the notes, performers alternate with other ensemble members to share notes of the rhythm pattern. This creates an interesting melodic quality.

Clap the following gamelan rhythm.

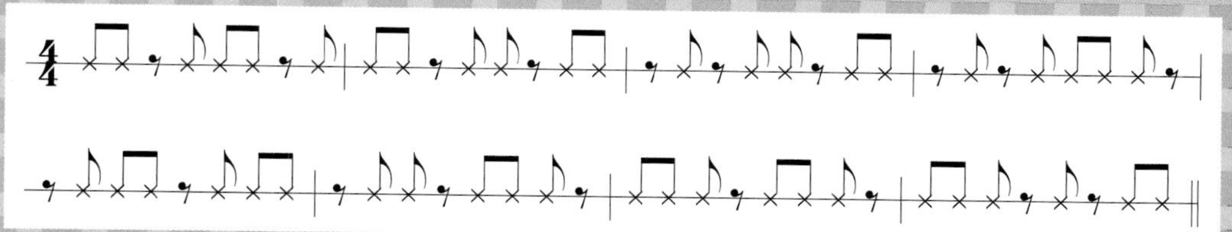

Perform the rhythm pattern in gamelan style with a partner using unpitched percussion instruments. Each person claps or pats every *other* note.

Gamelan ensembles also use melodic patterns when they perform. Some patterns are four notes.

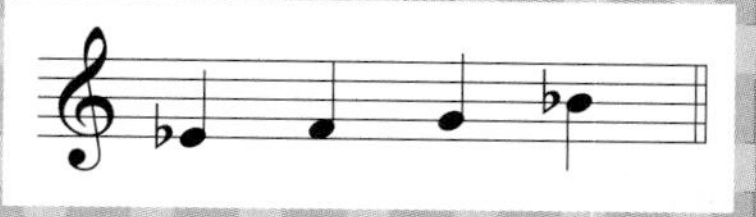

Notate a melodic pattern using the four-pitch scale and the rhythm pattern above.

Perform your melodic pattern with the rhythm pattern on pitched instruments such as bells, xylophone, or keyboard. Do so in gamelan style with a partner, alternating notes.

A Concert Hall Favorite

A popular composition performed by a symphonic orchestra in a concert hall is "Seventeen Come Sunday." Written by the English composer Ralph Vaughan Williams, the piece is one movement, or selection, from a group of individual musical selections making up the *English Folk Song Suite*. A **suite** is a collection of individual pieces combined to create a longer musical work.

Different places have different expectations for experiencing music. When an audience listens to "Seventeen Come Sunday," each person is expected to observe social customs or **concert etiquette** appropriate for attending a concert-hall performance. Speaking, using cellular phones, or rustling paper all distract from the audience's ability to enjoy and listen attentively to the music being performed.

LISTENING **CD 4:15**

Seventeen Come Sunday

by Ralph Vaughan Williams

"Seventeen Come Sunday" features a folk song melody as the main musical idea, or theme, of the piece. A folk song is a song that emerges from a culture or a group of people, usually of unknown authorship. The theme is repeated several times with contrasting larger musical sections being heard at other times.

Listen and identify how many times you hear the theme. Touch each note of the theme as you listen.

Analyze the listening map for "Seventeen Come Sunday." Find the order of the sections, repeat signs, first and second endings, and *Da Capo* and *D.S.* indications.

Listen to "Seventeen Come Sunday" and follow the listening map. Touch each note and measure as you hear it played.

Listening Map for *Seventeen Come Sunday*

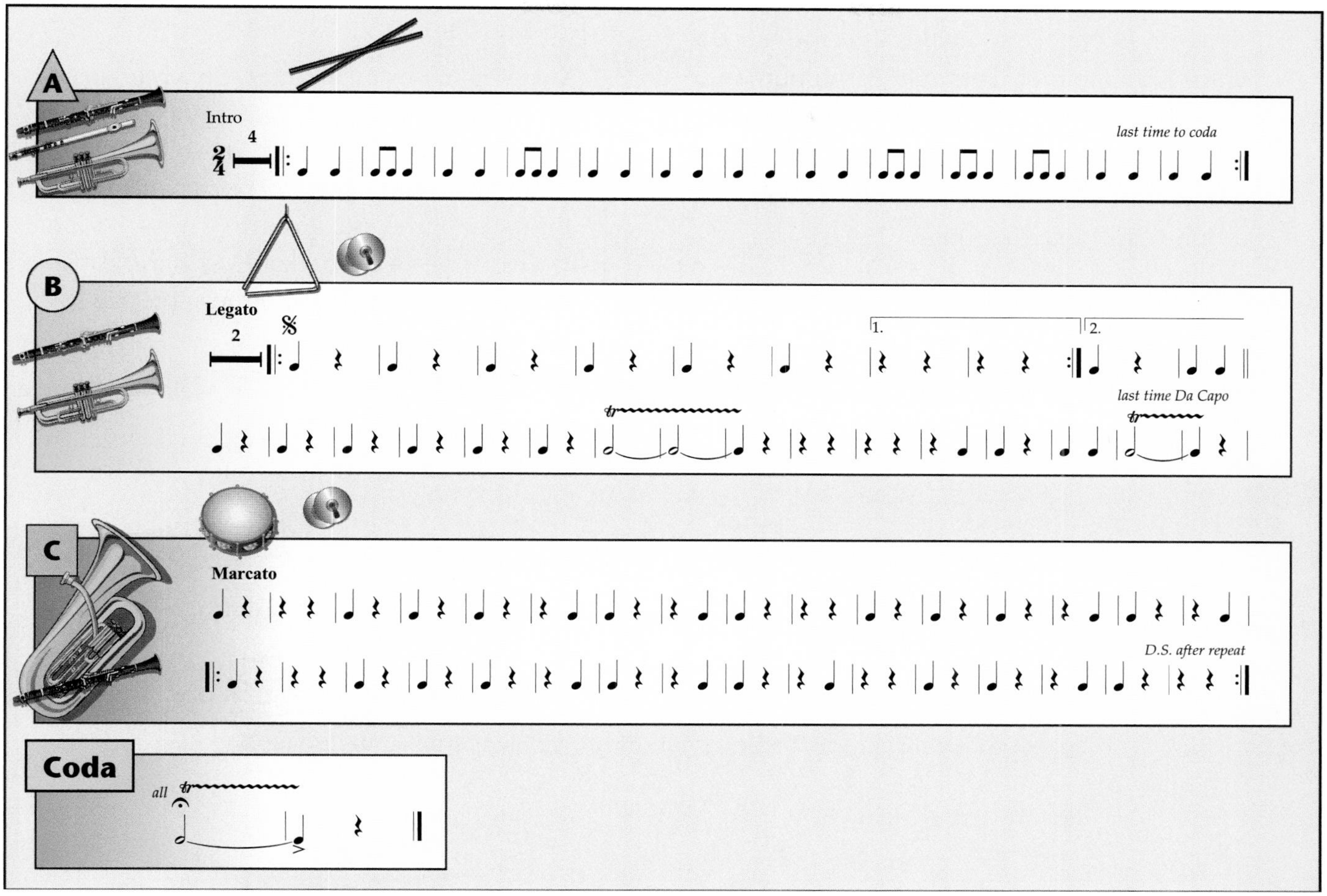

A

Intro

4

last time to coda

B

Legato

2

1.

2.

last time Da Capo

C

Marcato

D.S. after repeat

Coda

all

Ralph Vaughan Williams (1872–1958) was born in Gloucestershire, England. His grandmother had encouraged him to play violin and piano. Later on, as a teacher, he encouraged many other young musicians. He loved the folk music of his homeland and often used this music in his compositons. Vaughan Williams composed operas, symphonies, and choral works, as well as dance and ballet music.

Music Journal

How would I describe proper concert etiquette in three different settings, including a concert hall?

A Taste of the Non-Traditional

Jing Ling Tam is a choral music educator in Arlington, Texas. She is especially interested in exploring and teaching people about the many different expressive qualities that the human voice is capable of. Sometimes the human voice is used to create sounds that are non-traditional or unusual. Imitating the wind, a car, or a ringing phone is using the voice in a non-traditional manner.

Sing the excerpt below after you have listened to the selection.

LISTENING CD 4:16

Magnificent Horses arranged by Jing Ling Tam

"Magnificent Horses, a Fantasy on a Mongolian Folk Tune" was arranged by Jing Ling Tam. She created a musical structure in which the folk tune is sung over a supporting accompaniment of other voices. She uses voices in a non-traditional manner to create the background accompaniment sounds of horses. The folk melody enters as the horses conclude their galloping.

Magnificent Horses

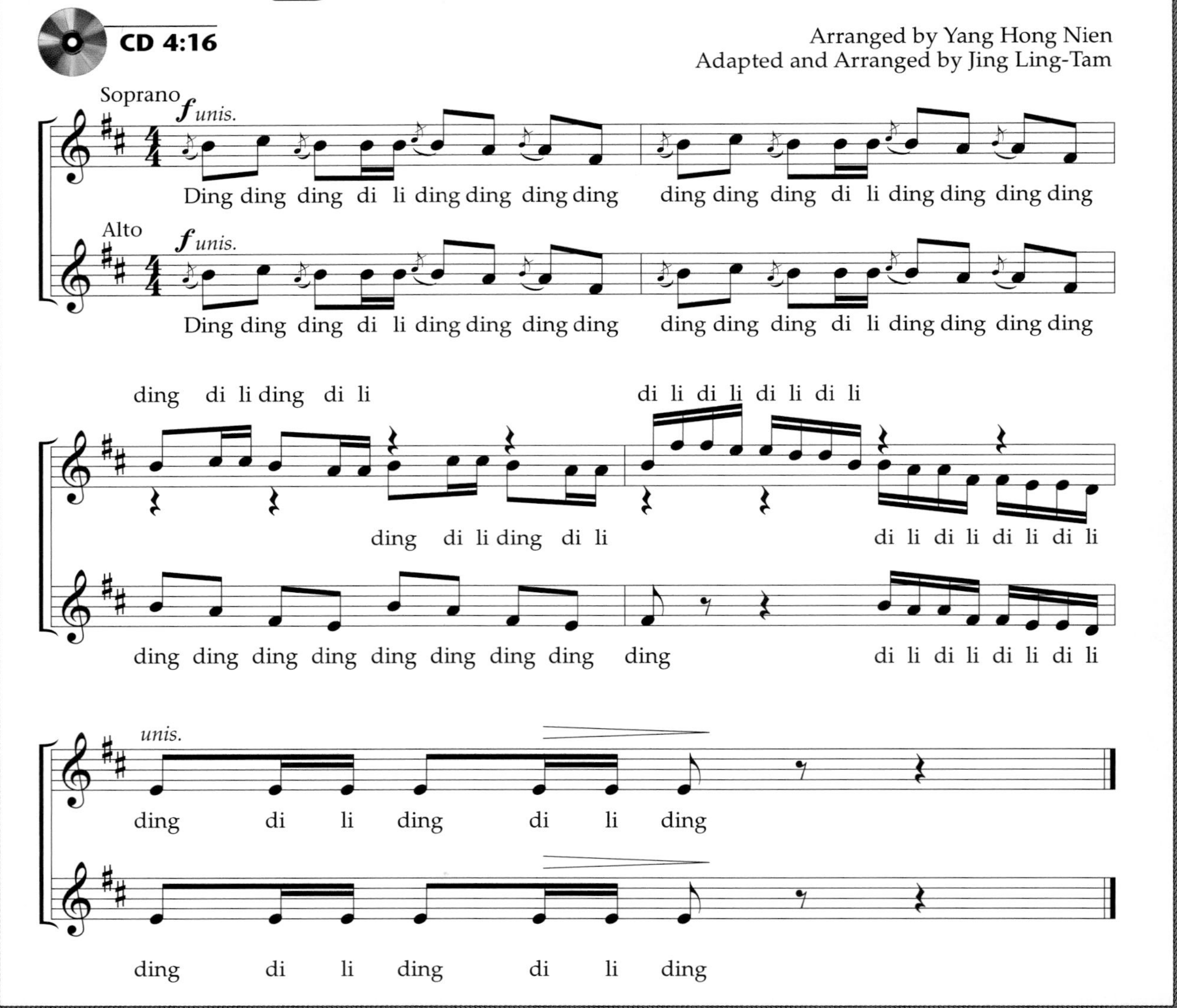

CD 4:16

Arranged by Yang Hong Nien
Adapted and Arranged by Jing Ling-Tam

Soprano *f unis.*
Ding ding ding di li ding ding ding ding ding ding ding di li ding ding ding ding

Alto *f unis.*
Ding ding ding di li ding ding ding ding ding ding ding di li ding ding ding ding

ding di li ding di li di li di li di li di li
ding di li ding di li di li di li di li di li

ding ding ding ding ding ding ding ding ding di li di li di li di li

unis.
ding di li ding di li ding

ding di li ding di li ding

Looking Back

As you prepare to write your review of a musical performance, recall the variety of performance venues featured in this unit. How did the places where people performed affect the *success* of their performances? What performances did you find most motivating? Most significant, either musically or socially? How closely do the selections in this unit represent your own experience or knowledge of music in our nation's cities?

Unit 5

Our Musical Legacy

Lesson 1 Baroque Highlights

Who are some of your favorite songwriters, composers, and performing artists of all time? Does your list stretch beyond the last year? The last decade? Might it even span across centuries? If your list is on the short side, then listen closely to this rather "lively" conversation. Even if you are already familiar with the works of some of these composers, you just might learn something new!

George Frideric Handel (1685–1759)

Franz Joseph Haydn (1732–1809)

Johann Sebastian Bach (1685–1750)

Wolfgang Amadeus Mozart (1756–1791)

1600 Baroque 1750

1750 CLASSICAL 1800

RECORDED INTERVIEW **CD 4:17**

Composers Forum

This "radio interview" gives you a personal glimpse into the lives and minds of some great composers of centuries gone by. Listen to Johann Sebastian Bach, Wolfgang Amadeus Mozart, Fanny Mendelssohn Hensel, and Igor Stravinsky respond to questions about themselves and the music of the times in which they lived and worked.

Each of the composers "interviewed" is from one of the four major historical periods of music in the Western world since about 1600. German composer and organist Johann Sebastian Bach was a genius of the Baroque era. Wolfgang Amadeus Mozart was a child prodigy of the Classical period. Fanny Mendelssohn Hensel composed vocal and piano music during the Romantic era. And Russian-born Igor Stravinsky was one of the most multi-talented and inventive composers of the twentieth century. Can you name any other composers from any of these periods?

Listen to "Composers Forum."

Compare the responses of the four composers to the interview questions.

LOG ON

music.mmhschool.com
Learn about radio programs that feature composers and songwriters of the past and present.

Ludwig van Beethoven
(1770–1827)

Fanny Mendelssohn Hensel
(1805–1847)

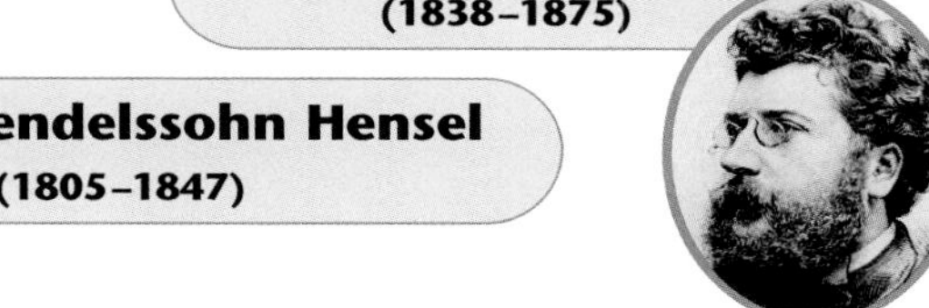

Georges Bizet
(1838–1875)

Igor Stravinsky
(1882–1971)

1800 Romantic 1900 1900

Johann Sebastian Bach

Johann Sebastian Bach (1685–1750)

One very important musical instrument during the **Baroque period** (1600–1750) was the **pipe organ**. The sound of a pipe organ is produced by wind moving through pipes. With its ability to create and produce many different sounds, it was perhaps the greatest musical-technological marvel of the seventeenth century. Listeners were amazed as organists showed off the capabilities of the pipe organ by performing and improvising on their own and others' compositions.

1600 Baroque 1750

LISTENING **CD 4:18**

Toccata and Fugue in D Minor

by Johann Sebastian Bach

A **toccata**, usually a keyboard piece, gives a performer an opportunity to display his or her manual dexterity and coordination. Some critics have questioned whether or not Bach actually composed this piece, calling it "atypical" of Bach's compositions. However, other critics point out that one thing that was typical of Bach was his frequent departure from custom.

Listen to "Toccata and Fugue in D Minor." As you listen, identify the order in which you hear either a fast-moving musical line or sustained chords.

Pipe organ at the Abbey of Ottobeuren, Germany

Listening Map for *Toccata and Fugue in D Minor*

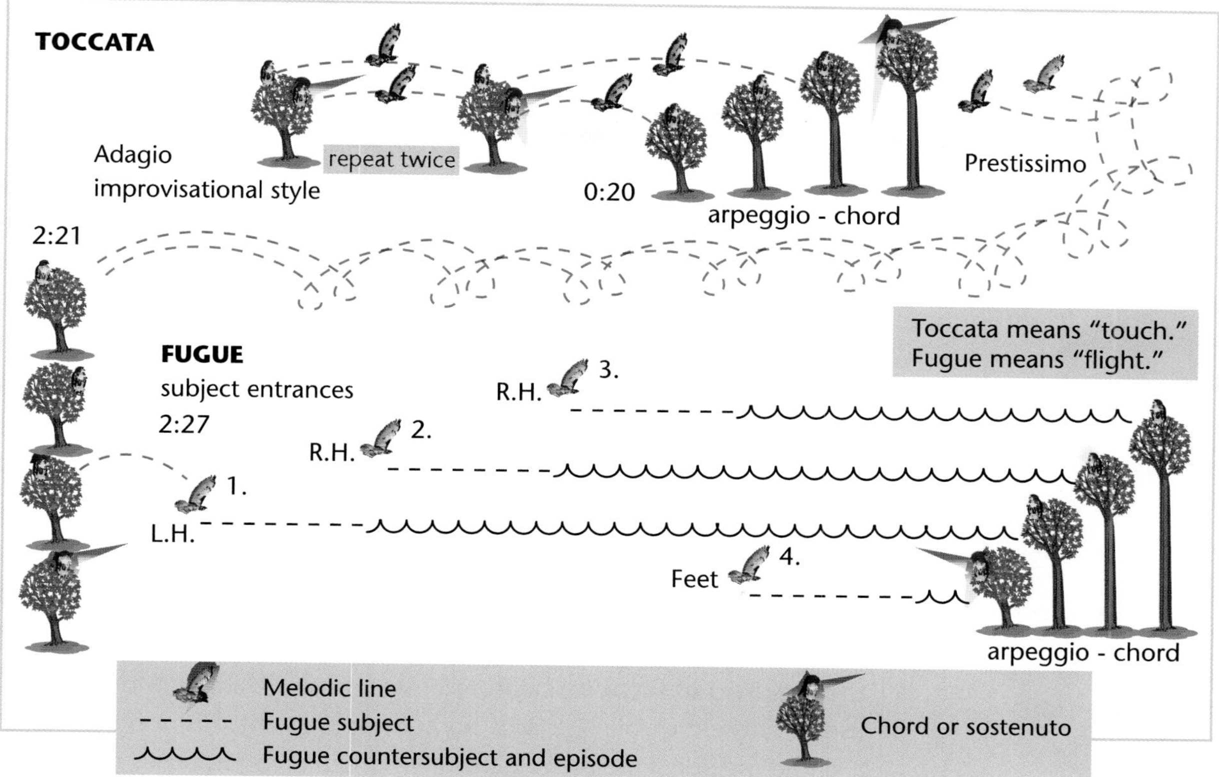

The Baroque period stretched from about 1600 to 1750, ending with the death of the great composer and organist Johann Sebastian Bach (1685–1750). Baroque musical concepts began in Italy and were quickly exported to the courts of important European monarchs in France and Austria.

Making a living in the arts during the Baroque period was often difficult. Many courts, however, employed composers and musicians as a means for glorifying their own monarchs and monarchies. Much of the music of the Baroque period was written at the command of a king or another noble. Performance "opportunities" were more often than not "command" performances.

Bach's vocation was to compose and perform music for the church. As a church composer and musician, Bach was responsible for creating music for all church services and festivals. In addition to composing, he also played the organ and directed the choirs. One reason Bach composed as much music as he did was that this was how he earned his living. He worked for numerous churches throughout his career. Through recordings his musical legacy is more alive today than when he was living.

Music Journal

What are some of the similarities and differences in how composers earned their living in the major historical periods discussed in this unit?

George Frideric Handel

The late Baroque period featured many composers whose music is part of a rich legacy that many music lovers still enjoy today. Along with Bach, George Frideric Handel (1685–1759) is one of the most widely known composers whose music is still being performed throughout the world. Like Bach, Handel was born in Germany.

After studying law, Handel moved to Italy to study music. Eventually he moved to London, where he began composing large extended compositions for chorus and orchestra called **oratorios**. Handel's 1741 oratorio *Messiah* contains the famous "Hallelujah Chorus." This is the most frequently performed choral work of all time.

George Frideric Handel (1685–1759)

1600 Baroque 1750

LISTENING **CD 4:19**

Hallelujah Chorus from *Messiah*

by George Frideric Handel

This chorus illustrates Handel's skill in changing musical texture, using **monophony**, **homophony**, and **polyphony** to highlight the meaning of the words and to create musical variety. Monophony uses a single melodic line with no accompaniment. Homophony uses a single melodic line above harmony parts. Polyphony uses two or more independent melodic lines sounding together.

Listen to the "Hallelujah Chorus" from *Messiah*. Notice the musical differences when the chorus is singing in unison without accompaniment (monophony), singing different parts at the same time with the same words (homophony), and singing at different times with the same words (polyphony).

1. Introduction
2. Theme A
Hal - le - lu - jah, Hal - le - lu - jah, Hal - le -
lu - jah, Hal - le - lu - jah, Hal - le - lu - jah,

LOG ON

music.mmhschool.com
Read about some of the many opportunities to perform Handel's *Messiah* today.

3. Theme B

for the Lord God Om-nip - o - tent reign - eth. Hal - le-
lu - jah, Hal-le - lu - jah, Hal-le - lu - jah, Hal-le - lu - jah.

4. Theme B repeated higher

for the Lord God Om-nip - o - tent reign - eth. Hal - le-
lu - jah, Hal-le - lu - jah, Hal-le - lu - jah, Hal-le - lu - jah!

5. Theme C

The king-dom of this world is be - come

6. Theme D

And He shall reign for ev - er and ev - er

7. "King of Kings and Lord of Lords" is heard in long note values; "forever and ever" is added in shorter note values. Gradually, this moves higher and higher.

8. Theme D repeated

And He shall reign for ev - er and ev - er,

9. "King of Kings and Lord of Lords" is heard in long note values; "forever and ever" is added in shorter note values.

10. The coda ends with four "hallelujahs" followed by a dramatic pause and a final "hallelujah" in very long note values.

Vivaldi and Purcell

The musical legacy from the Baroque period is wide and diverse. In addition to writing music for organ and voice, composers were also writing for instrumental ensembles. By the late 1600s, instrumental compositions often consisted of three or four longer musical sections unified by the repetition of a musical section called a **ritornello**. This resulted in music exhibiting loud and soft dynamics created by using a small group of soloists called the **concertino** contrasted with the full orchestral ensemble called the **tutti**. **Concerto** is a term used to describe music contrasting an orchestra with solo instruments.

Antonio Vivaldi

LISTENING **CD 5:1**

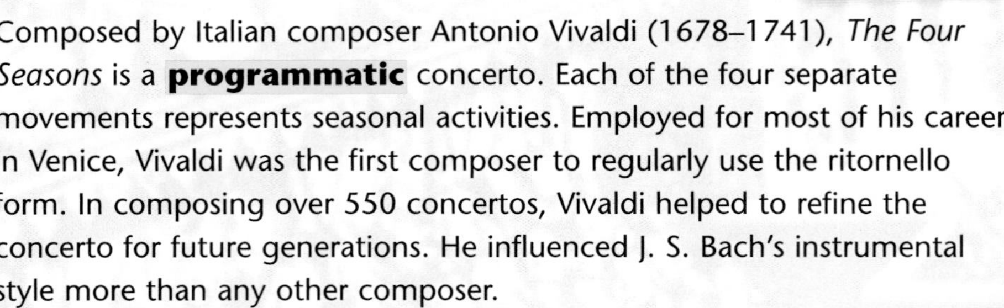

Spring (Allegro) from *The Four Seasons* (excerpt)

by Antonio Vivaldi

Composed by Italian composer Antonio Vivaldi (1678–1741), *The Four Seasons* is a **programmatic** concerto. Each of the four separate movements represents seasonal activities. Employed for most of his career in Venice, Vivaldi was the first composer to regularly use the ritornello form. In composing over 550 concertos, Vivaldi helped to refine the concerto for future generations. He influenced J. S. Bach's instrumental style more than any other composer.

Listen to "Spring" from *The Four Seasons*. Notice how the music has variety through the dynamic changes resulting from the alternating use of tutti and concertino sections.

LISTENING CD 5:2

Entrada from *The Indian Queen*

by Henry Purcell

Henry Purcell

One of Purcell's most important legacies is the music he composed for the theater. This legacy consists of songs, dances, and instrumental music for plays and "semi-operas" like *The Indian Queen* (1695). In Purcell's time, these opened with a festive march-like section called an **entrada**. His sense of drama and musical invention, especially his sensitivity to words in choral music, had great influence on his contemporaries and future generations of composers.

Listen to "Entrada" from *The Indian Queen*. Notice the march-like, noble, and dignified quality of the music, the four distinct sections, and the use of the trumpet as the solo instrument accompanied by a string orchestra.

Your Creative Unit Project

Choose two composers from two different periods to compare. Explore the sources and inspiration for the composers' works. Find out what you can about who influenced each composer personally and musically. Also explore what composers and performers their own works may have influenced in turn.

As an alternative project, use the selections you will perform and listen to throughout this unit to create your own "mix" of favorite music from the various periods of music history. Use other selections as well. Be sure to include at least two compositions from each period. You can also include earlier pieces from the Ancient, Medieval, and Renaissance periods and later pieces from the twenty-first century.

Music Journal

How might I describe the influence of Vivaldi and Purcell on Bach?

LESSON 2

Classical Traditions

During the Classical period (1750–1830), composers broke from the elaborate, ornamental style of the Baroque era. Classical composers emphasized simplicity, logic, and order. Still largely dependent on the patronage of royal sponsors, they also began to write music for a broader audience that included the musically unsophisticated. Composers, often performing their own compositions, began to give concerts that were governed by neither religious nor political patronage. The concerts were supported entirely by ticket sales to the public. Both the opera and the symphony quickly achieved popularity. For the first time, the most highly skilled performers of the time were in the public eye (and ear).

The musical style of the Classical period is exemplified in the music of three composers whose names you might recognize: Wolfgang Amadeus Mozart, Franz Joseph Haydn, and Ludwig van Beethoven.

Detail of Arch of Trajan
Benevento, Italy

View of the Temple of Neptune with the Basilica of Paestum beyond; ca. 460 B.C. Paestum, Italy

Wolfgang Amadeus Mozart (1756–1791)

Ludwig van Beethoven (1770–1827)

Franz Joseph Haydn (1732–1809)

1750 CLASSICAL 1830

Franz Joseph Haydn

Haydn is often called "the father of the symphony" because he developed many of the features of the symphony, string quartet, and piano trio. Haydn's musical career began during his childhood when he was a professional choir singer in Vienna, Austria. As an adult, he remained in Austria and became the official musician for Prince Esterházy. The prince and his family championed Haydn's compositions and helped him become one of the best-known composers in all of Europe. Haydn wrote more than 100 symphonies and many works for string quartets and other instrument ensembles. Haydn was one of the first composers to write using the rondo form. In classical simplicity, he created variety by simply introducing new themes in between repetitions of the principal theme in a work.

Franz Joseph Haydn
(1732–1809)

LISTENING **CD 5:3**

Rondo all'Ongarese by Franz Joseph Haydn

Also known as "Gypsy Rondo," this is the final movement of Haydn's Piano Trio No. 39 in G. Gypsies are nomadic people believed to have come originally from India or Egypt. Their dance music was familiar in the many European countries they lived in. "Rondo all'Ongarese" can be translated, "rondo in a Hungarian style." When composing, Haydn sometimes drew upon folk melodies of his native Austria and surrounding regions.

1750 CLASSICAL 1830

LOG ON

music.mmhschool.com
Learn more about Haydn and other classical composers.

Listen to "Rondo all'Ongarese" to identify the repetitions of the principal theme, or A section.

Determine which of the following describes the form of this piece.

A A A   A B A   A B A C A

Dachstein Mountains and the Hallstatter Sea, Hallstatt, Austria

Wolfgang Amadeus Mozart

Mozart was a child prodigy who began to play the piano at age three and was writing large pieces for orchestra by age nine. The 1984 movie *Amadeus*, while somewhat fictionalized, showcased Mozart's genius and is based on his life.

Wolfgang Amadeus Mozart at the piano

1750 CLASSICAL 1830

LISTENING CD 5:4

Rondo "alla turca" from Piano Sonata in A major by Wolfgang Amadeus Mozart

One of Mozart's best-known compositions for piano is "Rondo 'alla turca,'" also known as a movement from the Piano Sonata in A Major K. 331. *Alla turca* means "in Turkish style." During Mozart's time, the Turks were invading Mozart's country of Austria. And "all things Turkish" were of interest to Austrians. Turkey was considered an exotic place of adventure. Mozart wanted to give his audiences a sense of the sounds of Turkey.

Folk musician troupe at the Topkapi Palace, Istanbul, Turkey

Read this rhythm pattern by saying *march* for each quarter note and *everybody* for each group of four sixteenth notes.

Play this same pattern on drumsticks every time you hear it in "Rondo 'alla turca.'" How many times do you hear this pattern?

Like other composers from the Classical period, Mozart repeated musical ideas to unify and order a composition. Mozart, however, gave the rondo form far greater variety than his predecessors. Mozart created new musical ideas (Sections B, C, D, and E) to contrast with the unity provided by the reoccurring A section. The form of "Rondo 'alla turca'" can be described as: A B A C D E D C A B A C Coda (ending)

See ***Spotlight on MIDI*** for an activity with Mozart's Rondo "alla turca."

Play both of the rhythmic patterns to accompany the A and C sections as you listen to "Rondo 'alla turca.'"

Listening Map for *Rondo "alla turca" from Piano Sonata in A Major*

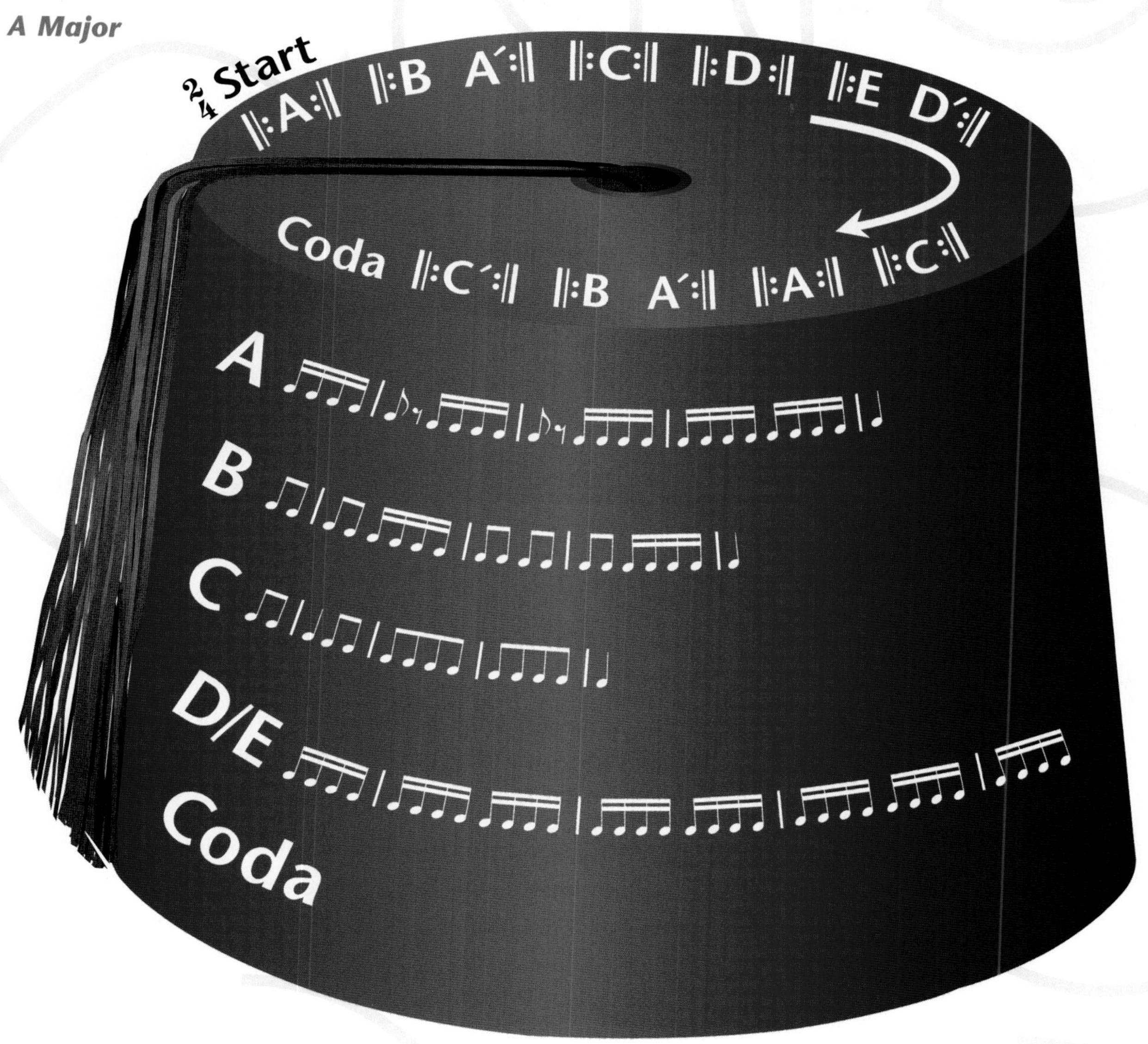

Listen for the repetition of the A theme as you follow the listening map for "Rondo 'alla turca.'"

Compare the approach to rondo form in "Rondo all'Ongarese" and "Rondo 'alla turca.'"

Ludwig van Beethoven

Like Haydn and Mozart, Beethoven came from the German-Austrian traditions that dominated the Classical period. Born in Bonn, Germany, he began musical study with his father at the age of four. Later in his life he studied piano with Franz Joseph Haydn. However, unlike Haydn, who was a court composer, Beethoven was a freelance composer, barely making a living wage.

In the middle period of Beethoven's career, when he did some of his most creative writing, he began to lose his hearing. During the final years of his life, Beethoven became totally deaf. One story tells how at the end of one performance of his Ninth Symphony, at which Beethoven was sitting in the front row of the audience, someone had to tug at Beethoven's sleeve to encourage him to turn around and bow to the standing ovation from the audience that he could not hear.

LISTENING **CD 5:5**

1750 CLASSICAL 1830

Symphony No. 7, Second Movement

by Ludwig van Beethoven

Beethoven wrote the Seventh Symphony about the time he began to lose his hearing. With ten variations on a common theme, Beethoven features the strings and the woodwinds in this movement.

Perform this rhythm pattern from the Second Movement by patting the quarter note on your knees and clapping the eighth notes. This basic rhythm pattern serves as a building block to create unity throughout the piece.

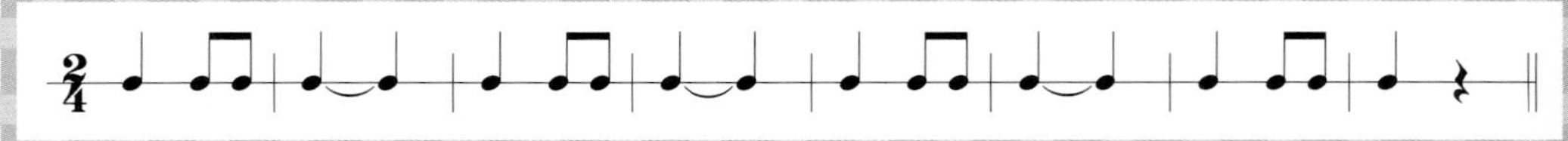

Listen to the Second Movement and move the tennis balls as indicated. This will help you feel the expressiveness of the slow tempo while learning to keep the beat. First, practice saying the pattern to prepare for moving the tennis balls.

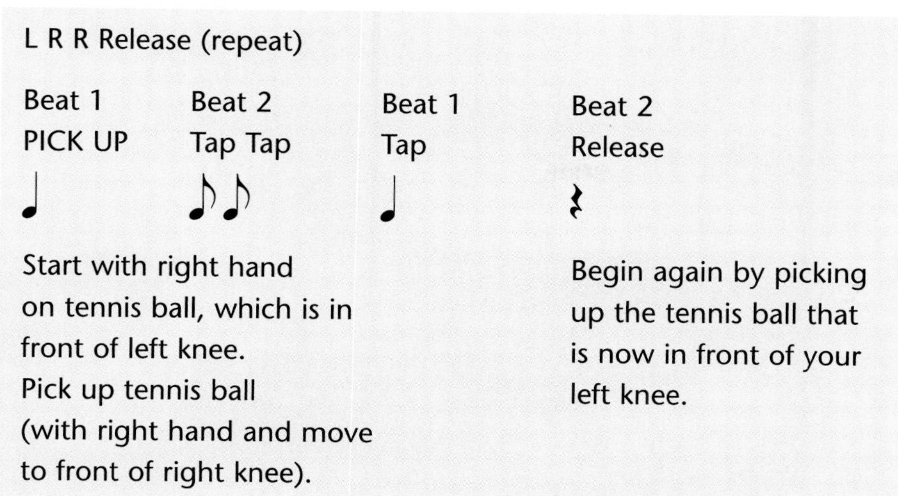

L R R Release (repeat)
Beat 1
PICK UP
Beat 2
Tap Tap
Beat 1
Tap
Beat 2
Release
Start with right hand on tennis ball, which is in front of left knee.
Pick up tennis ball (with right hand and move to front of right knee).
Begin again by picking up the tennis ball that is now in front of your left knee.

Listening Map for *Symphony No. 7, Second Movement*

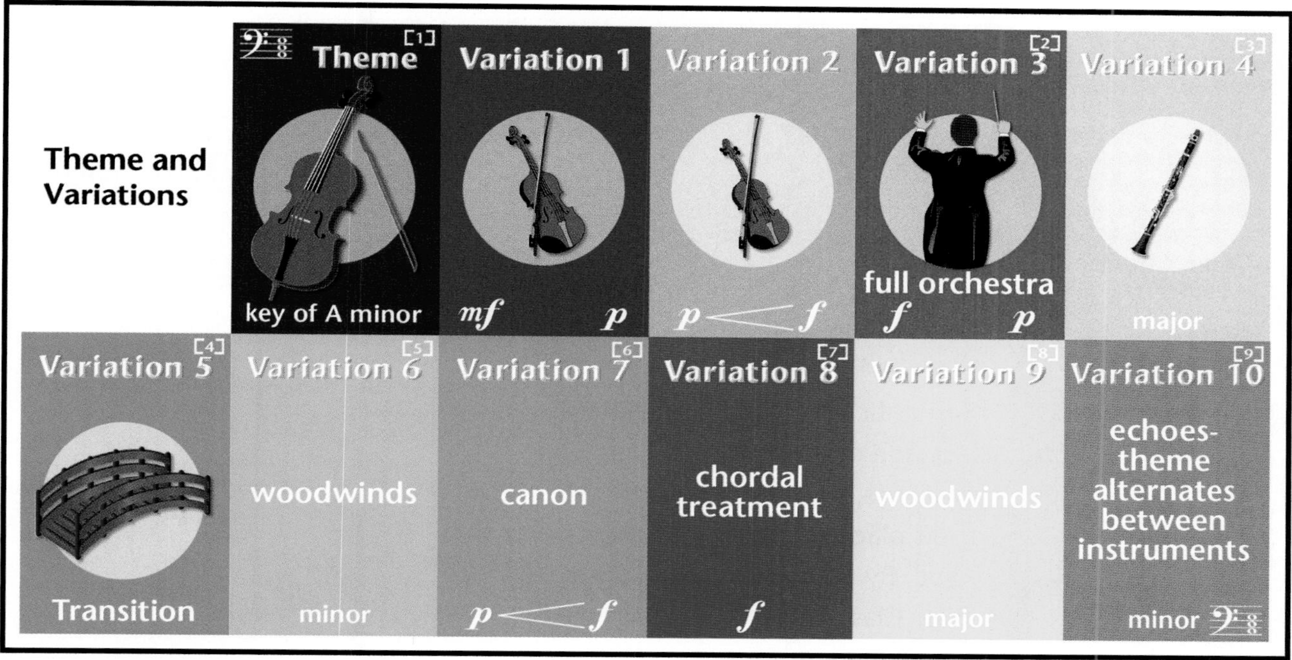

Listen to the first portion of the Second Movement of Beethoven's Seventh Symphony and determine the order of the A, B, C, and D sections. Use the change of instruments and dynamic levels to help you make your decisions.

How did Beethoven create variety in the section of Movement 2?

The Romantic Era

LESSON 3

Romantic composers used the language of music to paint pictures, tell stories, and take audiences to far-off places depicted as colorful and exotic. By contrast, composers in the earlier Classical period had created music based on formal principles of clarity, order, and balance.

Watercolor sketch for a production of *Salomé*, an opera by German composer Richard Strauss (1864–1949)

Opera flourished in the late eighteenth and early nineteenth centuries. While some people today may find it difficult to understand and appreciate opera, opera music was actually crafted in a way that was meant to help audiences grasp things quickly. Although opera music is usually sung in a non-English European language, certain phrases and musical techniques functioned as musical signposts so that audiences could immediately recognize the villain, the heroine, and moments of high drama. What contemporary uses of music can you think of in which the music serves to intensify emotions in dramatic scenes or images?

Orchestral compositions were a favorite for many Romantic composers. These composers, helped by skilled conductors, drew out the tone colors of each instrument and section to create rich and vibrant musical textures. Some of the music they wrote was so demanding that instruments such as horns required improvements in their manufacturing in order to perform the compositions.

Romanticism's appeal to the emotions was characteristic of the other fine arts of the time as well, such as Romantic poetry and art. The ideals of Romanticism sometimes took the form of a natural, free-flowing style in art and architecture. In contrast, there was more symmetry and balance in the art and architecture of the Classical period.

Art Gallery

Luncheon of the Boating Party by Pierre-August Renoir, **Oil on canvas, 1881**

Meet the Musician

Georges Bizet (1838–1875) went to the Paris Conservatory at the age of nine. He was an outstanding student, winning numerous prizes for his piano and organ performances as well as his compositions. His big break came in 1857 when he won the *Prix de Rome* which gave him money to study and compose in Rome for four years. He wrote the music for *L'Arlésienne* after his return to Paris. The opera *Carmen*, Bizet's masterpiece, came in 1875. Set in Seville, Spain, *Carmen* featured daring and exotic subject matter characteristic of the opera stage—love and fatal jealousy. Deemed too "steamy" for conservative Paris audiences, the opera closed after only 37 performances. Ironically, *Carmen* is now probably the most-performed opera in the entire world.

1800 Romantic 1900

Georges Bizet

Georges Bizet was a French composer from the Romantic period best known for his opera *Carmen*. However, his other works remain favorites with audiences because of his beautiful melodies, exciting rhythms, and powerful orchestrations. One of his most popular works is a series of 27 short pieces that he wrote as **incidental music** for a play called *The Woman of Arles*. Arles is a city in the south of France. *L'Arlésienne* is the French title of the play. Incidental music is the music that played underneath the action onstage. The first performance of *The Woman of Arles* that included incidental music was not received well. Audiences had not yet grown to appreciate the use of music as background for drama. Bizet later organized the 27 pieces into a set called *Suites*.

Agnes Baltsa as Carmen in Bizet's opera with José Carreras

Fedora Barbieri as Carmen in Bizet's opera *Carmen*

LISTENING **CD 5:6**

Carillon from *L'Arlésienne, Suite No. 1*

by Georges Bizet

A carillon is one of the world's largest musical instruments! It is a set of large tuned bells, usually hung in an outside tower. The bells can be heard for miles around. The carillon is played from a keyboard made of broomstick-like keys called batons. Unlike the piano keyboard, the batons are played with fists rather than fingers. The largest bell in a carillon can weigh as much as five tons.

Listen to "Carillon" and describe how Bizet imitates the sound of bells by using the instruments of the orchestra.

Listen again and describe how Bizet uses loud and soft contrasts to organize "Carillon." How does the dynamic range he uses contribute to the emotional qualities of the piece?

Play this melody during the A section of "Carillon." It repeats 56 times.

Perform this rhythm pattern during the B section. It repeats 89 times.

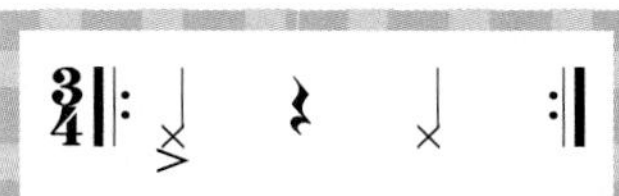

Play this melody during the return of A. It repeats 39 times.

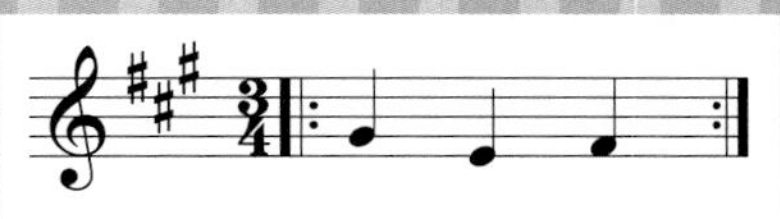

Unity and Variety

Bizet uses a structural musical device called **ostinato**, which is a repeated musical figure. The use of ostinato creates a powerful sense of unity that gives the composer creative freedom to craft the other parts. Why do you think Bizet used only 39 repetitions of the ostinato during the return of A?

See ***Spotlight on MIDI*** for an activity with another selection from Bizet's *L'Arlésienne.*

Fanny Mendelssohn Hensel

During the Romantic period, composers were often influenced by the work of fine artists such as poets. The German poet Heinrich Heine (1797–1856) wrote the text for "Schwanenlied" (Swan's Song). Fanny Mendelssohn Hensel, sister of famous composer and pianist Felix Mendelssohn, used this text to compose her famous **art song** of the same title. An art song is music written for solo voice and instrumental accompaniment, usually keyboard.

LISTENING **CD 5:7**

Schwanenlied by Fanny Mendelssohn Hensel and Heinrich Heine

Sung in the original German, this performance demonstrates how in setting a text to music, an art song composer aims to enhance the emotional power of the text.

Listen to "Schwanenlied" and read the English translation of the German text. The text is set in **strophic form**. Heine's poem contains two verses that have the same number of lines, the same rhyme scheme, and the same meter. Both verses are set to the same music. This is a form often found in folk and popular music.

Schwanenlied

(Swan's Song)

Verse 1

A star falls down from its sparkling heights.
That is the star of love that I see falling.
So many white leaves fall from the apple tree.
The teasing breezes come and playfully use them
for their games.

Verse 2

The swan sings in the ponds and glides back and forth,
And ever so softly singing he dips into the sweet
watery grave.
It is so still and dark, leaves and blossoms have
disappeared.
The star's brilliance is gone. The swan's song has
died away.

Listen again to "Schwanenlied" and determine which of the musical characteristics below best describes the text and the music. What words might you use to describe the general mood of the text?

slow/fast major/minor mostly loud/mostly soft

music.mmhschool.com
Learn more about the use of poetic meter in folk and popular music.

Fanny Mendelssohn Hensel (1805–1847) was the oldest of four children in a very musically talented family. Like her brother Felix, she was both a composer and pianist. Although many people are more familiar with the works of her brother Felix, Fanny was considered an important musical advisor to her brother, who often talked to her about his musical ideas before writing them down.

Fanny's earliest works were actually published under Felix's name. Queen Victoria's favorite Mendelssohn song, "Italien," was actually composed by Fanny. During Fanny's lifetime, only five collections of her songs and a piano trio were published.

1800 Romantic 1900

The Last Hundred Years

LESSON 4

In the twentieth century, pride in one's heritage and country became very important. Composers of opera music wrote in their native languages and used folklore as the basis of their stories. Many American composers were immigrants from Europe, and their music often reflected the musical traditions of their native lands. Popular songs were sometimes adapted for more stylish and innovative settings. In America, jazz and spirituals became an important source for composers such as George Gershwin. In Brazil and other places, composers like Heitor Villa-Lobos notated and wrote arrangements of folk tunes not previously written down.

George Gershwin

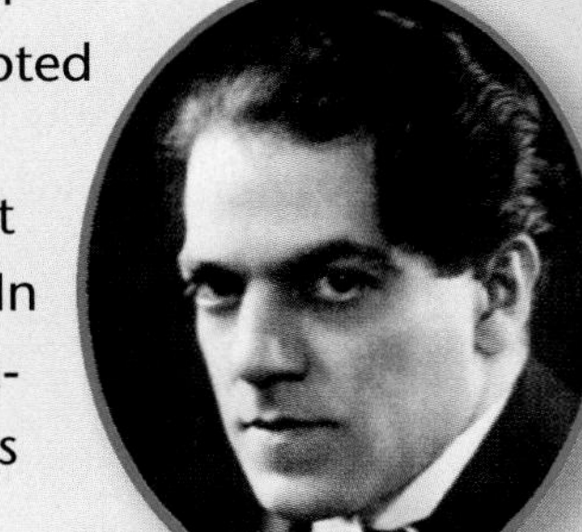
Heitor Villa-Lobos

LISTENING **CD 5:8**

Galop (excerpt) from *Suite No. 2 for Small Orchestra*

by Igor Stravinsky

In 1942, Igor Stravinsky was commissioned by Russian-born American ballet choreographer George Balanchine to write a short "circus polka" for elephants! Prior to this, Stravinsky had written mostly for the theater.

Listen to "Galop." Notice the changing meters, syncopations, ostinatos, sudden changes of key, and lively rhythms.

Igor Stravinsky

Not all twentieth-century composers used folk and popular themes. Some experimented with harmonic devices like **dissonance** and **atonality**. Dissonance is the sounding of a combination of pitches that creates harmonic tension and sounds incomplete. Atonality is characterized by the absence of a tonal center and places equal emphasis on all 12 tones of the chromatic scale. Arnold Schönberg introduced the twelve-tone approach to music, which was a dramatic move from the eight-tone scale in which a tonal center is so important.

Arnold Schönberg

Meet the Musician

ON NATIONAL RADIO!

Name: Sebastian Chang
Age: 12
Instrument: Composition, Piano
Hometown: Trabuco Canyon, CA

Sebastian Chang wants to be the next Leonard Bernstein, and he's well on his way. Sebastian already conducts, composes, plays piano, and teaches. Bernstein's music, especially "West Side Story," is high on his favorites list. "It's a classic," Sebastian says. "I would love to see it performed onstage."

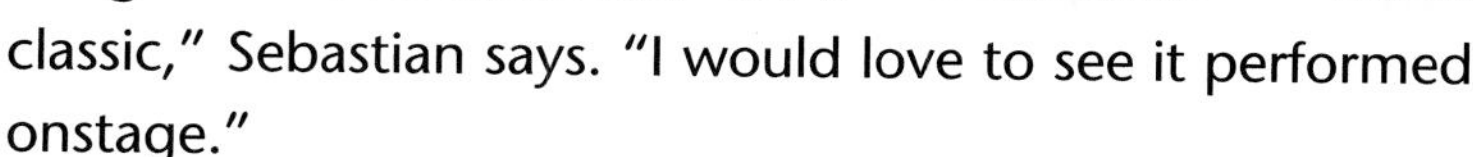

Sebastian is already a veteran composer. "I've been writing my own music since the age of five, but I started playing piano at four," he says. Sebastian actually started composing because the classical pieces he was then studying—works by Mozart and Beethoven—just weren't interesting enough to him!

"I began to wonder, 'Is this all there is to music?' So my teacher started giving me lessons on improvisation," he says. Sebastian enjoys listening to many different types of music and exploring different styles by writing his own pieces in those styles. "It helps to expand my understanding of concepts relating to different sounds," he explains.

In addition to being an outstanding composer, Sebastian is also a talented gymnast. He recently won first place in the state championships on the rings. Just like music, gymnastics provide him with another opportunity to express himself. "It's all a matter of technique," he says. "The better your technique, the easier it is."

RECORDED INTERVIEW

Listen to Sebastian's performance on piano of his own composition "Moonlight Masquerade for Violin and Piano" **(CD 5:9)** and his interview **(CD 5:10)** on the national radio program From the Top. Fifteen-year-old violinist Stephan Jackiw joins Sebastian on this recording.

The 1889 Universal Exposition in Paris was a major influence on French composers. One of the first multicultural, worldwide music events, musicians gathered from around the world to share their music. French composers experienced the music and dance of such faraway places as Bali in southern Indonesia. Claude Debussy was one such composer who discovered a lot of "new" material to "imitate" in his own music.

The new field of **musicology** also exposed young composers to a vast tradition of music they had never known. For the first time, many of these composers were exposed to the styles of previous generations. Many composers experimented with unconventional rhythms and harmonies but used baroque or classical forms to organize their music.

Díane Warren

Diane Warren (b. 1956) is one of the most prolific female composers of popular music in the twentieth century. She has written and co-written hit songs for performing artists such as Ziggy Marley, Michael Bolton, Chicago, Cher, Patti LaBelle, Barbra Streisand, Gloria Estefan, Bette Midler, Celine Dion, Starship, Joe Cocker, Selena, Faith Hill, Tim McGraw, The Jacksons, Brian McKnight, Natalie Cole, Reba McEntire, Whitney Houston, Aerosmith, and Meat Loaf. She has a knack for taking everyday situations and turning them into songs. In 1998, the American Society for Composers and Performers named her Songwriter of the Year for the fourth time. Warren is known best for her love songs.

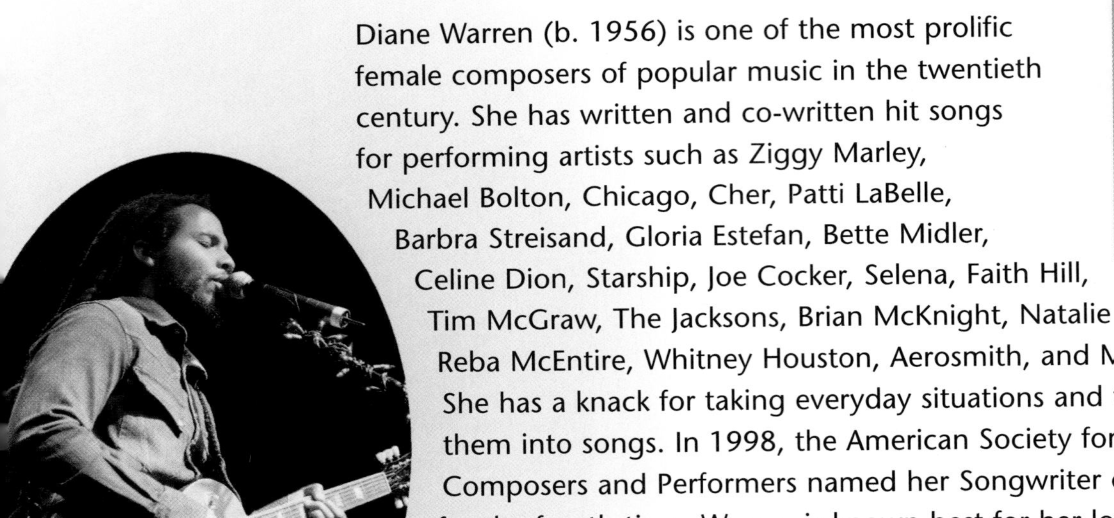

Diane Warren

Ziggy Marley

Give a Little Love

CD 5:11

Words and Music by
Al Hammond and Diane Warren

Refrain 1
D A7 D
We got to give a lit-tle love, have_ a lit-tle hope, make_ this world a lit-tle bet-
A7 D 2 A7 D 3
- ter. Oh-oh whoah, Oh - oh whoah.
Verse D A7 D
1. Liv-ing in this cra-zy world,_ so caught up in the con-fu - sion.
2. Got the wars_ on our minds,_ got the trou-bles on our shoul - ders.
D A7 D
Noth - ing is mak-ing_ sense_ for me_ and_ you.___
Some-times it seems_ so much_ what we_ go_ through._

May-be we can find a way, there's got to be a so-lu - tion,
May-be if we take the time, time to un-der-stand each oth - er,
How to make a bright - er day, What do we do?
We can learn to make it right. What do we do?
Refrain 2
We got to give a lit-tle love, have a lit-tle hope, make this world a lit-tle bet - ter.
Try a lit-tle more, hard - er than be-fore, let's do what we can do to-geth - er. Oh
whoah-oh, We can ev-en make it bet - ter, yeah. Oh whoah, la, la, la,
On-ly if we try.
to Bridge
(last time repeat Refrain 2 ad lib)
We got to
Bridge
If ev-'ry-bod-y took some-bod-y by the hand, May-be
ev-'ry-one could learn to love and un-der-stand.
Oh whoah, We can real-ly make it bet - ter, yeah.
2nd time to Refrain 2
Oh whoah, la, la, la, On-ly if we try. (We got to)

Steve Reich

Careers

Steve Reich (b. 1936), a composer influenced by African drumming and the Balinese gamelan, developed **mimimalism** into a fine art. Featuring repetitive melodic, rhythmic, and harmonic ideas, minimalism was a popular style in the late twentieth century. The subtle changes in these repetitive musical ideas are sometimes compared to the way colors change when a kaleidoscope is gently turned.

LISTENING **CD 5:14**

Clapping Music by Steve Reich

"Clapping Music" (1972) is a purely rhythmic piece composed for two pairs of hands. No other instruments are used. There are 13 sections of 12 beats. The first performer claps the same 12 rhythmic patterns throughout. The second performer starts the rhythmic pattern in unison with the first performer, then shifts the downbeat over one beat at the beginning of each new section. Eventually the two performers will be playing in unison at the end. This technique is called **phasing**.

Listen to the recording and notice where the second performer shifts ahead one beat.

Experimental music was fueled in part by new technology in the late twentieth century. Natural sounds could be electronically altered or imitated. "Synthesized" music is created with computers and other electronics instead of instruments. Electronic and digital devices made it possible for people who did not read music at all to create and form original compositions.

LOG ON

music.mmhschool.com
Read about composers who have been influenced by Steve Reich's experimental music.

Steve Reich

Music Journal

What questions would I ask if given the opportunity to interview four composers or songwriters of my own time?

Looking Back

Now that you've experienced a whirlwind of a journey across more than three centuries of music, what music did you most enjoy learning about? What new information was most interesting to you? Have you ever heard or performed any music by the composers you've read about?

Discuss which selections from each period of music history were most interesting to you. Be sure to share your reasons for your opinions. Is there anything that all the composers shared in common? What made each composer unique?

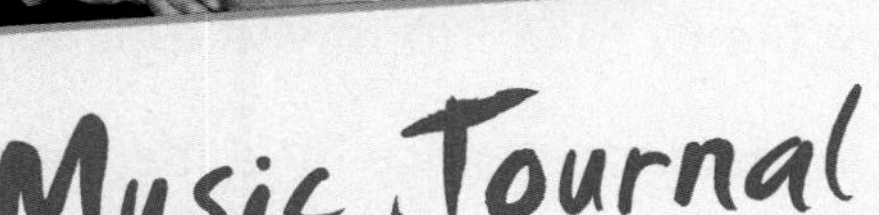

Music Journal

Who are some of my favorite composers and songwriters of all time? How much thought have I given to them as opposed to the people who perform their works? How can this increase my appreciation of the music?

Unit 6

The Many MOODS of Music

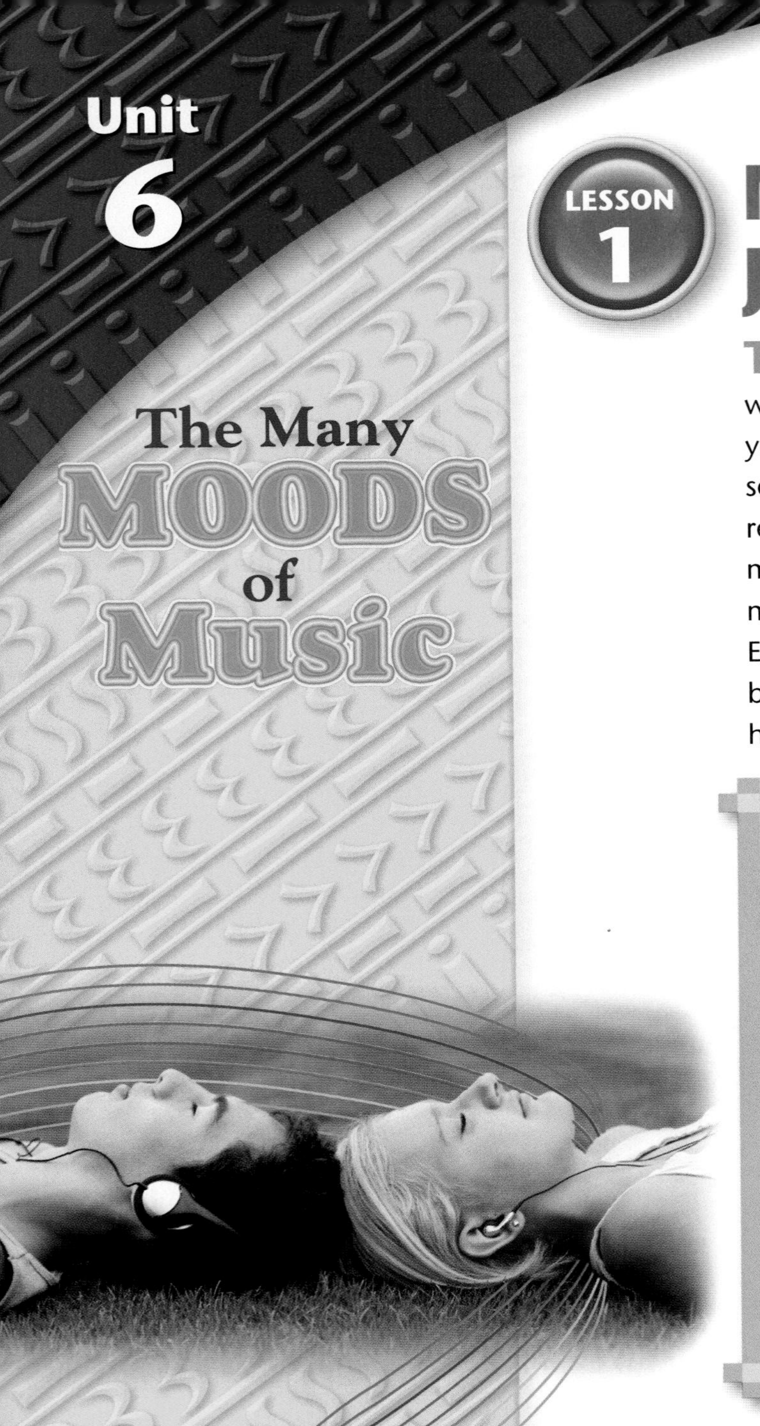

LESSON 1 Music Expresses Joy

Think about the many places you have been where music was playing in the background. Have you noticed the different kinds of music in these settings? Background music in a mall or a restaurant is probably different from what you might hear in a doctor's office. In what settings might you hear music that is soothing? Energizing? What purpose do you think background music can serve in the settings you have identified?

What kinds of music would you choose or expect to hear in each of the following situations? Explain your choices.

1. working with classmates at a school car wash
2. a family barbecue in your backyard
3. on a CD which is a gift for a sick friend
4. a family road trip to visit a national park
5. a memorial service for a friend who has died

Music plays a powerful role in our lives. It can help you express feelings that are difficult to put into words. Music can help shape your feelings as well. Playing or listening to an upbeat song can almost instantly pick you up when you're feeling a little down. When you're a bit stressed out, playing or listening to quiet music can calm you.

LISTENING **CD 5:15**

Mood Music (montage)

In this recording, you will hear excerpts from "Come On-A My House," "Only Time," "Lead Man Holler," and "Peace in this House." Each song expresses a distinct mood. You will also hear the complete version of each song in Unit 6.

Listen to "Mood Music" and write down a word or two to describe the mood each excerpt suggests. Discuss how changes in tempo, choice of instruments, and other expressive elements influence the effect that the music has on you.

Music Journal

What specific songs have I listened to or performed which have made me feel happy, sad, or peaceful? What musical characteristics helped evoke these feelings?

Happy Face

In a world that can be frightening at times, a positive attitude goes a long way. Many songs have been written specifically to encourage people to smile, laugh, or just to look at the brighter side of life. How many songs can you think of that aim to bring joy to the people who listen to and perform them?

The mood of a song is determined as much by its lyrics as by the music itself. The lyrics and music of a song often go hand in hand in a very powerful way. Think again about the songs you heard in "Mood Music." What role did the lyrics play in your decisions about the mood of each excerpt? What role did the music play?

LISTENING **CD 5:16**

Happy Face by Beyoncé Knowles, Rob Fusari, Calvin Gaines, Gill Lee, and Falonté Moore

The song "Happy Face," made popular by Destiny's Child, demonstrates how well lyrics and music can work together to convey a mood of happiness and optimism.

Listen to "Happy Face" and discuss how well the music supports the positive message of the lyrics.

Sharing good times with your friends and family is guaranteed to put a smile on your face!

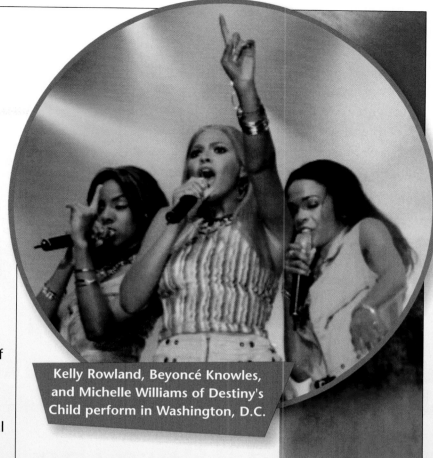

Kelly Rowland, Beyoncé Knowles, and Michelle Williams of Destiny's Child perform in Washington, D.C.

The message of the lyrics for "Happy Face" is simple. The music is more complex. This complexity is created by a **texture** that weaves together various pitches, rhythms, and tone colors. Texture is the way in which melody and harmony are combined to create layers of sound. One way to create musical interest is to use **accidentals**. An accidental is a sharp ♯, flat ♭, or natural sign ♮ that raises or lowers a note in a measure. It introduces a pitch that is not normally part of the **scale** for that key. A scale is an ordered series of pitches.

"Happy Face" also uses an unusual chord progression: E-A-C-G. Since the song is written in E major, the scale is built on the pitch series, E-F♯-G♯-A-B-C♯-D♯-E. The song also uses the pitches C and G, which are not part of the E major scale. They are from the scale for E minor: E-F♯-G-A-B-C-D-E. "Happy Face" also uses the chords C and G. Chords taken from a different but related scale are called **borrowed chords**.

Clap the following rhythm patterns.

Play these same patterns on percussion instruments with the recording of "Happy Face."

Singing with Pride

"God Bless the U.S.A." is another example of how music and lyrics work well together to create a certain kind of feeling. As you listen to and sing this song, think about the feeling of pride it expresses. Discuss how the melodic sequence, the major key, and the rhythmic patterns help support this feeling. Discuss expressive elements, such as changes in dynamics, that you can use in your performance.

God Bless the U.S.A.

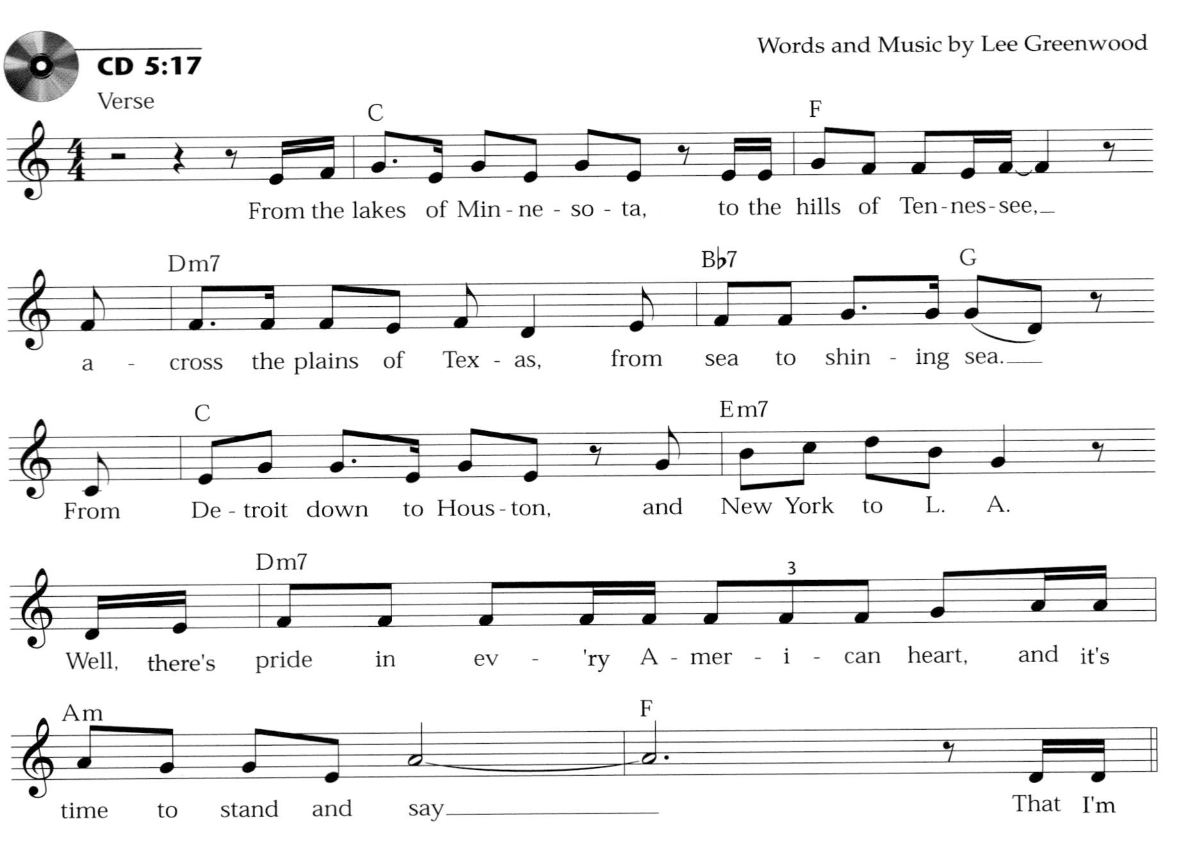
Words and Music by Lee Greenwood
CD 5:17
Verse
C
F
From the lakes of Min - ne - so - ta, to the hills of Ten-nes-see,
Dm7
B♭7
G
a - cross the plains of Tex - as, from sea to shin - ing sea.
C
Em7
From De - troit down to Hous - ton, and New York to L. A.
Dm7
3
Well, there's pride in ev - 'ry A - mer - i - can heart, and it's
Am
F
time to stand and say That I'm

Refrain
G F C
proud to be an A-mer-i-can where at least I know I'm free.
G F C
And I won't for-get the men who died, who gave that right to me.
F G Am C F Em7
And I'd glad-ly stand up, next to you and de-fend her still to-day.
Dm7 C F Dm7/G C
'Cause there ain't no doubt I love this land. God bless the U. S. A.

Lee Greenwood, Rally for America, May 2003, Huntington, West Virginia

Rhythm Does the Trick

Syncopation is one musical element that often supports a joyful feeling in a song. Musical **anticipation** is another element that can do this. Anticipation is when an upbeat, or weak beat, is tied to the downbeat, or the accented first beat in a measure. This rhythmic device can drive a song forward and contribute to a joyful quality. "Happy Face" makes use of this device, as does "Come On-A My House."

LISTENING **CD 5:20**

Come On-A My House by William Saroyan and Ross Bagdasarian

"Come On-A My House" is a 1951 classic. Rosemary Clooney's recording spent twenty weeks on the Billboard chart, including eight weeks at No. 1.

Listen to the recording of Rosemary Clooney singing "Come On-A My House" as you follow the lyrics on page 139. Discuss your initial reaction to the song. Use two or three adjectives to describe the feelings it conveys.

Identify where anticipation occurs as you listen.

Singer Rosemary Clooney performing onstage

Come On-A My House

by William Saroyan and Ross Bagdasarian

Come on-a my house, my house. I'm gonna give you candy.
Come on-a my house, my house I'm gonna give-a you
Apple a plum and apricot-a too eh.
Come on-a my house, my house-a come on,
Come on-a my house, my house-a come on.
Come on-a my house, my house. I'm gonna give-a you
Figs and dates and grapes and cakes eh.
Come on-a my house, my house-a come on,
Come on-a my house, my house-a come on.
Come on-a my house, my house. I'm gonna give you candy.
I'm gonna give you everything.

(instrumental interlude)

Come on-a my house, my house. I'm gonna give you Christmas tree.
Come on-a my house, my house I'm gonna give-a you
Marriage ring and a pomegranate too ah.
Come on-a my house, my house-a come on,
Come on-a my house, my house-a come on.
Come on-a my house, my house I'm gonna give-a you
Peach and pear and I love your hair ah.
Come on-a my house, my house-a come on,
Come on-a my house, my house-a come on.
Come on-a my house, my house. I'm gonna give you Easta egg.
I'm gonna give you everything.

Meet the Musician

Rosemary Clooney (1928–2002) Rosemary Clooney was from Maysville, Kentucky. Deserted by her parents while she was in her teens, she took her first singing job in 1945 to buy food for herself and her younger sister, Betty. At age twenty-three, Clooney had her first smash hit with "Come On-A My House." For the next fifty years, she was known to her millions of fans as simply "Rosie." Having enjoyed much success as a singer and TV actress, Clooney was best known and loved for her singing, dancing, and acting role in the classic movie *White Christmas* (1954), which also starred the legendary Bing Crosby.

Your Creative Unit Project

As you work through the lessons of Unit 6, keep a journal of ideas for creating your own mood montage. Identify at least five different moods or feelings you want to convey through your musical selections. Write a narration to connect the selections which identifies the feelings evoked by each selection and describes how musical elements were used to express that mood or feeling. Present your montage to the class.

Music Expresses Sorrow

Sadness is a feeling that is often hard to express. But when you find a way to express sadness, you will usually find that you are not alone. People who have experienced similar hurts, losses, and sadness often find comfort in sharing their experiences with one another.

LISTENING CD 6:1

Tears in Heaven (choral arrangement) by Eric Clapton and Will Jennings

Popular songs are sometimes based on the painful experiences of the people who wrote them. For example, Eric Clapton's 1992 song "Tears in Heaven" is his expression of the grief and sadness he felt when his four-year-old son died in an accident.

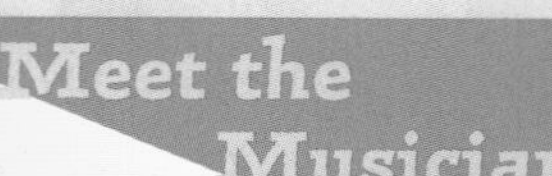

Eric Clapton (b. 1945) A triple inductee into the Rock and Roll Hall of Fame, Clapton has entertained fans for more than four decades with his blues-influenced guitar playing. His talent blazed in the sixties and seventies as a pop singer and guitarist with John Mayall's Bluesbreakers, Cream, Blind Faith, and Derek and the Dominoes. In the eighties, his career as a solo artist enjoyed equal success. After a period of artistic uncertainty and personal disaster, Clapton returned to triumphant form in 1993, attracting a new generation of fans with the relaxed virtuosity of his album *MTV Unplugged*, which featured "Tears in Heaven." Clapton's preference for playing traditional blues over a commerical pop style was most evident in his solo career.

Listen to "Tears in Heaven." How do the vocal inflections and guitar licks help contribute to the strong emotion this song can convey?

Play the melodic accompaniment below to the refrain of "Tears in Heaven" on recorder, bells, or keyboard.

Sing the refrain with expression.

Perform the vocal line and melodic accompaniment together.

Tears in Heaven

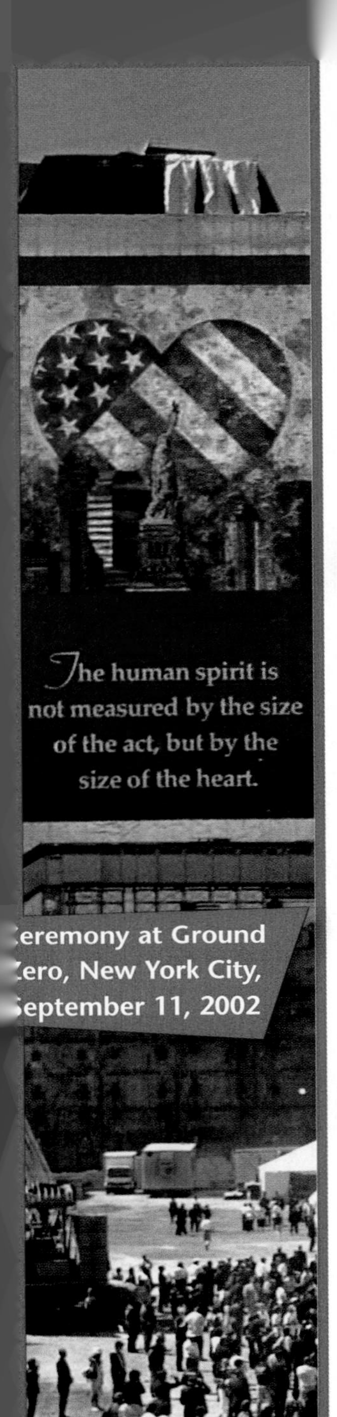

The human spirit is not measured by the size of the act, but by the size of the heart.

Ceremony at Ground Zero, New York City, September 11, 2002

Music Helps Us Grieve

While music can help you express sad feelings, it can also help you grieve. Grief is the process of dealing with a loss. Music can play an important part in this process. It can be a source of comfort and a way to honor the memory of a loved one.

On March 11, 2002, the loved ones of people who died as a result of the tragic events of September 11, 2001, gathered at Ground Zero in New York City. As the names of these victims were read, many musicians played softly in the background.

LISTENING **CD 6:2**

Only Time by Enya, Nicky Ryan, and Roma Ryan

After September 11, 2001, many news broadcasts featured the song "Only Time." The song's simple melody and slow tempo comforted many people. The lyrics ask several questions and suggest that "only time" might offer some answers.

Identify additional musical elements that people might find soothing as you listen to "Only Time."

Play the following harmonic progression on keyboard, bells, or handbells to accompany the first section of the song before the key change.

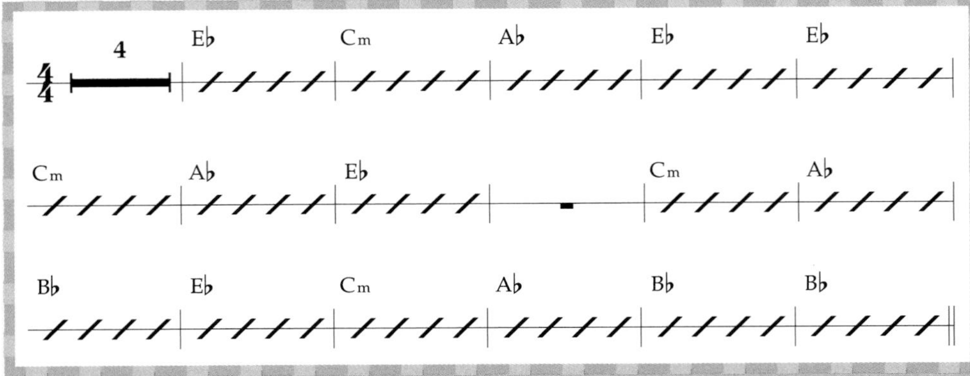

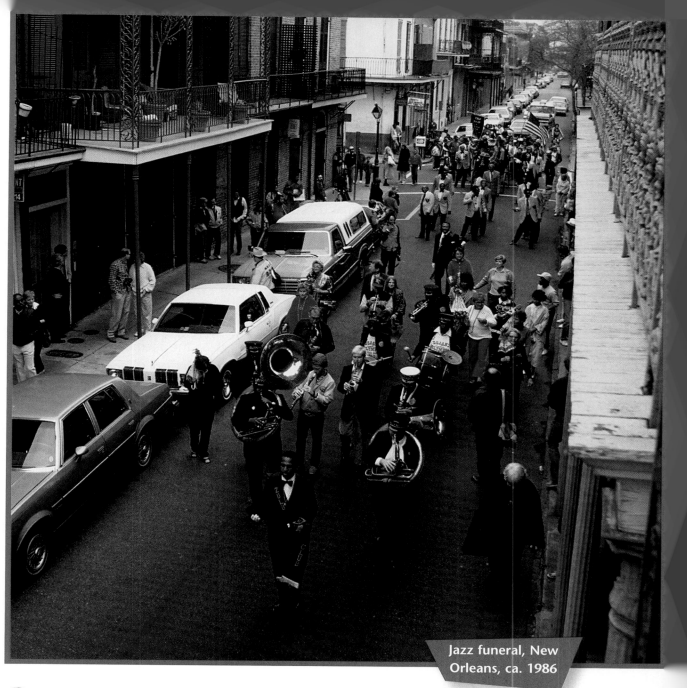

Jazz funeral, New Orleans, ca. 1986

 **LISTENING** **CD 6:3**

New Orleans Jazz Funeral (excerpts)

Recorded in 1991, these authentic excerpts are performed by the Magnificent Seventh's Brass Band. The introductory narration is followed by excerpts from "In the Sweet By and By" and "Just a Closer Walk with Thee." These dirges are typically played on the way to the funeral. The concluding excerpt is from "Didn't He Ramble," which is part of the joyous sendoff after the funeral is completed.

Listen to "New Orleans Jazz Funeral."

Compare the processional dirges and the sendoff music. Discuss the differences and what thoughts, feelings, and beliefs you think are being conveyed in each.

LOG ON

music.mmhschool.com Read the history and myths associated with the origins of "Taps."

Read the history of the City of Washington Pipe Band.

Bugler playing "Taps" at an American cemetery in Makati, Philippines, Memorial Day, 2002

Timeless Traditions

When people die in the line of duty, military and police forces, and firefighters honor the deceased in formal ceremonies. "Taps" is traditionally played at the conclusion of most military funerals. The official bugle call since 1862, "Taps" can be found in military manuals dating back to 1835. It was probably an adaptation of another call that originally signaled troops to prepare for their bedtime roll call.

LISTENING CD 6:4

Taps Traditional

Just after three o'clock on the afternoon of November 24, 1963, bugler Sgt. Keith Clark stepped forward to play "Taps" at the funeral of President John F. Kennedy. Comprised of just twenty-four notes, "Taps" is one of the most universally heart-wrenching melodies ever heard. In 1963, our nation was in mourning, and for the Kennedy family it was a moment of private grief. That day at Arlington National Cemetery, Sgt. Clark missed a note. Somehow, his poignant error seemed right.

Listen to "Taps" and describe the feelings it evokes.

Notate the melody on staff paper.

LISTENING CD 6:5

Amazing Grace (violin and bagpipe version) by John Newton

This violin and bagpipe rendition of "Amazing Grace" is performed by the City of Washington Pipe Band. "Amazing Grace" is one of the most recognizable **hymns** ever written. A hymn is a four-part song of praise used in religious services. A familiar hymn, people listening to an instrumental performance often recall the lyrics as well. The lyrics speak of hope and the strength to endure life's most difficult challenges.

Listen to "Amazing Grace" and discuss what musical characteristics may have made it so popular for so long.

The bagpipe has a long and multiethnic history among musical instruments. Variations of the instrument can be traced to countries around the world, including parts of the Middle East and Eastern Europe. Early bagpipes were made primarily from the remains of animals. The skin was used to form the bag, while the pipes were made from the bones. Perhaps owing to the loudness of the bagpipes, they were sometimes used in battle to inspire soldiers and to remind them of their previous victories.

In addition to Enya's "Only Time," "Amazing Grace" was another song frequently played in the days following September 11, 2001. It was often performed on bagpipes as a tribute to those who perished that day—especially at the funerals of police officers, firefighters, and emergency services workers.

RECORDED INTERVIEW **CD 6:6**

Richard Scott Blair

Scottish bagpiper Richard Scott Blair played "Amazing Grace" at the funeral of President John F. Kennedy in 1963. He also played at the memorial service for Laurel Clark, who perished in the 2003 Space Shuttle Columbia disaster.

Listen to Dr. Blair talk about some of his most memorable experiences playing the Scottish bagpipes.

See ***Spotlight on MIDI*** to further explore musical moods.

Music Journal

Which song in this lesson do I think provides the best comfort for grief? Why?

LESSON 3

Music in the Workplace

Sung in rhythm with particular kinds of work, **work songs** are often characterized by strong rhythms that help workers move together as they work. These songs help pass the time when the work gets tedious. Sometimes they are simply sung at the end of a work day as a way to celebrate.

A schoolroom in New York, New York, ca. 1886

Coal miners in Pennsylvania

American farm workers, ca. 1940

Planting corn in Shenandoah Valley, Virginia, 1941

LISTENING CD 6:7

African Postal Workers

This music features postal workers from the University of Ghana sorting and stamping letters. One worker keeps the beat by clicking scissors. A second worker whistles the melody. Two other workers sit across from each other at a table, stamping their ink pads and letters in an elaborate rhythm.

Listen to "African Postal Workers."

Improvise your own rhythmic accompaniment as you listen to the recording again.

Postal workers in Chicago, Illinois, 1927

Factory assembly line, ca. 1930

Transcontinental Railroad completed in British Columbia, Canada, November 1885

Music Journal

What rhythm patterns can I imagine and notate that might represent the actions of workers shown in the photographs on pages 146 and 147?

A Caríbbean Work Song

Work songs present a story addressing the type and nature of work that people do. Sometimes work songs are light and humorous. Other times they are very serious. "Lead Man Holler" is a work song about the heavy physical work of some laborers on Caribbean islands.

The instruments used in this recording of "Lead Man Holler" include a cow bell, conga drum, maracas, and shakers. They are just a few of the traditional instruments used in performing Caribbean music.

Sing "Lead Man Holler" along with the recording.

Identify the musical form.

Play the following rhythms during the verses.

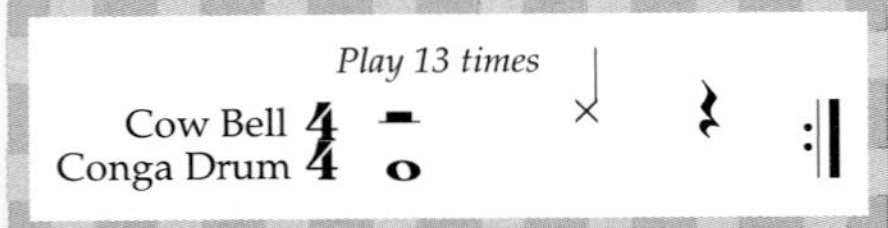

Play 13 times
Cow Bell
Conga Drum

Play the following rhythms during the refrain.

Play 5 times
Play 4 times
Maracas/
Shakers

Play the following rhythms during the coda.

Maracas/
Shakers

MAP

UNITED STATES

CARIBBEAN

Lead Man Holler
CD 6:8
Words and Music by Irving Burgie
Verse 1 B♭5
You hear me call - in' at the crack of dawn,
B♭5 F5/B♭ B♭ E♭ F
Jump up broth - er, come an' face the morn.
B♭5 F5/B♭ B♭5
For - get your ach - in' from the day be - fore,

B♭5 F5/B♭ B♭5
'cause to - day we goin' to do that an' more.
Refrain
B♭5 B♭
Lead man hol-ler Wo. All men fol-low,
B♭ F5 B♭ B♭5 F5
down you go for a work - an' dol - lar, yes he hol - ler
2nd time to Coda
B♭ F5 B♭5
Wo. All men fol-low, down you go for a work-in' dol-lar.
B♭5
Verse 2
I'd like to tell you 'bout yes-ter - day.
B♭ E♭/B♭ B♭5 E♭ F
You worked right well, I am proud to say.
B♭ E♭/B♭ B♭5
I want ev - 'ry man to try his will,
B♭ E♭/B♭ B♭5
an' make yes - ter - day look like you were
B♭5
D.S. al Coda
stand - in' still.
Coda
B♭ F5 B♭5
Down you go for a work - in' dol - lar.
B♭ F5 B♭5
Down you go for a work - in' dol - lar.

Meet the Musician

Tennessee Ernie Ford (1919–1991) was born in Bristol, Tennessee. As a child, he sang and played trombone. As an adult, he first worked as a radio DJ. His recording career started in 1948, and his big break came in 1955 with his booming baritone performance on "Sixteen Tons." Singing everything from rock and roll to gospel music, Ford recorded over one hundred albums. Along with "Sixteen Tons," Ford also had Top Ten hits with "The Ballad of Davy Crockett" (1955) and "Hicktown" (1965). In 1990, Ford was inducted into the Country Music Hall of Fame.

An American Work Song

Many familiar work songs are folk songs created by unknown workers. In 1946, composer and performer Merle Travis wrote the song "Sixteen Tons" about the work of his father, a Kentucky coal miner. This is an example of a *composed* work song. The lyrics of the refrain include one of his father's favorite sayings: "I can't afford to die. I owe my soul to the company store." The lyrics also include excerpts from a letter his brother wrote: "It's like working in the coal mines. You load sixteen tons and what do you get? Another day older and deeper in debt."

LISTENING **CD 6:11**

Sixteen Tons (Tennessee Ernie Ford) by Merle Travis

When Tennessee Ernie Ford performed this song on TV and for an audience of 30,000 people at the 1955 Indiana State Fair, it was an instant success. Recording the song later that year, Ford snapped his fingers to kick off the tempo. This "mistake" was left on the recording. In eleven days, 400,000 records were sold; in twenty-four days more than 1,000,000 had sold. By the 60th day of release, more than 2,000,000 copies had been sold, making it the most successful single recording ever sold up to that point in time.

Listen to this version of "Sixteen Tons."

Sing the version of "Sixteen Tons" on page 151.

Create new verses for "Sixteen Tons" and share them with the class.

SIXTEEN TONS

LESSON 4

Music and the Quest for Peace

Music has the power to inspire peace on many levels. It can soothe an individual, or it can bring the entire world together. "Peace in this House" expresses a vision of peace that is full of hope.

Peace in this House

Words and Music by Mac Huff

Verse

Dm *mp - mf* 15 Bbmaj7 Dm

1. Peo - ple, O my peo - ple, all com - mu - ni - ty.
2. Bro - ther, O my bro - ther fam - i - ly of man.

Bbmaj7 Gm7 Dm

Peo - ple, O my peo - ple, seek - ing un - i - ty.
Bro - ther, O my bro - ther come and take my hand.

Gm Bb C

To - geth - er we are strong. To - geth - er joined in
To - geth - er we can see. To - geth - er we'll be

1. Asus A7 2. Asus A7 Dm

song. free. Let there be peace.

Refrain

Dm *mp* F Gm7/F F Gm7/F

Let there be peace in this house, let there be hope in our

C/E C Dm

hearts, let there be joy, let there be life, let there be love.

C F Dm G/B

Let there be peace in our voice so that our dreams may nev - er

Bb C Dm

cease in a house that's built on love, let there be peace.

Anti-war demonstration in New York City during the Vietnam War, April 1968

A Song with a Vision

John Mellencamp's "Peaceful World" combines traditional blues and country with the more contemporary sounds of rap and rhythm and blues.

India.Arie and John Mellencamp

LISTENING CD 6:18

Peaceful World

by John Mellencamp

In the original recording, John Mellencamp performs the rap parts while India.Arie sings the more melodic sections of the song. Both pop artists use vocal improvisation in which they make up the melodies on the spot. How well do you think the artists on this recording imitate the original artists?

Listen to "Peaceful World."

Identify the rap and sung parts and discuss which sections seem to be improvised.

Perform the refrain in spoken rhythm. Then sing the refrain.

Refrain
E B C♯m B
Come on, ba - by, take a ride with me, I'm up from In-di-an-a down to Ten-nes-see.
E B A B
Ev - 'ry - thing is cool as can be in a peace - ful world.

Improvise new verses about peace in a rap style.

Music Journal

What two songs with "conflicting" styles can I combine to create a song like "Peaceful World" that symbolizes unity and peace between two different groups?

Art Gallery

Song of Peace

British artist Briton Riviere (1840–1920) demonstrated artistic talent from a very early age. When he was only seven, Riviere created a remarkable drawing of a wolf's head while visiting the Zoological Gardens. As seen in *Song of Peace,* Riviere frequently expressed sympathy between people and animals. This piece may also have been inspired by the biblical concept of peace symbolized by a lion and a lamb (unlikely comrades) lying down together.

Meet the Musician

ON NATIONAL RADIO!

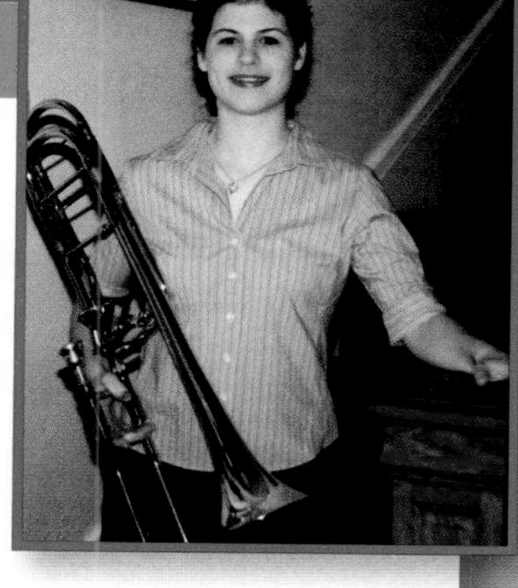

Name: Amanda Stewart
Age: 17
Instrument: Trombone
Hometown: Oakland, MD

When Amanda Stewart first took up the trombone she was about three inches shorter than the instrument. "I wanted to play 'horn,' as I called it, since I was four years old, but my parents felt I was too young," she explains. When Amanda was six, she was finally allowed to get a trombone, but her short arms made it impossible to push the slide out far enough to reach all the notes.

Not content to be so limited, Amanda devised clever ways around the problem. Once, during a performance when she had to play a low C, she tied a string around her finger and reeled back the slide after hitting the note. Another time she bounced the slide off the floor to get it back.

Amanda's practice room is as unique as she is. Her family owns a funeral parlor, and Amanda likes to practice in the casket room. Since the funeral parlor is part of her family's home, Amanda likes to scare her friends by playing hide and seek in the casket room whenever they visit. When she's not playing trombone or scaring her friends, Amanda enjoys Tae Kwon Do and participating in her church youth group.

RECORDED INTERVIEW

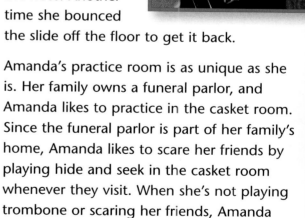

Listen to Amanda's performance of the Concertino for Trombone, Third Movement (Allegro Giocoso) by Lars-Erik Larsson **(CD 6:19)** and her interview **(CD 7:1)** on the national radio program From the Top.

A Historic Occasion

One of the most important celebrations of peace took place in 1989 with the tearing down of the Berlin Wall. The destruction of the wall was a symbol of liberty, reunification, and peace for the German people and for the world.

To celebrate this newfound peace, musicians from all over the world came to Berlin for two Christmas concerts in 1989. American conductor and composer Leonard Bernstein conducted an international orchestra and chorus in a performance of Ludwig van Beethoven's "Symphony No. 9." Bernstein's place at the podium was significant given his Jewish heritage and the profoundly difficult relationship between Germany and the world's Jews following the Holocaust of World War II.

LISTENING CD 7:2

Symphony No. 9, Fourth Movement (excerpt) by Ludwig van Beethoven

This movement is more commonly known as the "Ode to Joy." For the 1989 Berlin performances, Bernstein changed the German word for joy *(freude)* to the word for freedom *(freiheit)*. At that performance people from East and West Germany as well as the four countries to whom the post-World War II partitions of Berlin had been assigned (the United States, France, Great Britain, and the Soviet Union) joined together for the historical event.

Listen to this movement and move your hands to show the upward and downward movement, or shape, of the melody. The shape of the melody is called the **melodic contour**.

Perform the phrases of the main theme on recorder or keyboard. Discuss which phrases sound similar and which sound different.

Looking Back

Music gives us the power to express and experience many emotions in a way that words alone cannot. It can increase our joys, soothe us in sad times, inspire us to work together, and give us hope for peace. What music from this unit or from your own experience has most effectively expressed your own thoughts and feelings?

Music Journal

In what ways has music inspired me to work harder at something? How has music helped to change my attitude or feelings about something or someone? How can I use the music that I love to inspire or help someone else?

Unit 7

Expressing with Music

LESSON 1 Movement Sends a Message

RECORDED INTERVIEW CD 7:3

John Jacobson

Nobody can introduce you to the world of movement in music better than a **choreographer**. A choreographer creates, plans, and arranges body movements, steps, and patterns for dancers. The music itself is often the starting point. Listen to John Jacobson talk about what inspires his work as a choreographer. Jacobson says that a very important part of his work is building self-confidence in the students with whom he works.

Careers
John Jacobson
We Go Together
CD 7:4
from the musical Grease
Words and Music by Jim Jacobs and Warren Casey
B♭ Gm Cm
mp
1. We go to - geth - er, like ra - ma la - ma la - ma ka
2. We're one of a kind like dip da dip da dip
F B♭
ding - a da ding - a dong, Re - mem - bered for
doo wop - a doo - bee doo, our names are
Gm Cm
ev - er as shoo - bop - sha - wad - da wad - da
signed boog - e - dy boog - e - dy boog - e - dy boog - e - dy
F B♭
mf
yip - pi - ty boom de - boom Chang chang
shoo - by doo wop she - bop Chang chang
Gm Cm F
cresc.
chang - it - ty chang shoo-bop, that's the way it should
chang - it - y chang shoo-bop, we'll al - ways be like

Sing and improvise movement to "We Go Together."

be. Wha oooh, yeah! one.
Wa - wa - wa - waah. When we go
out at night, and stars are shin - ing bright
up in the skies a - bove. Or at the
high school dance where you can find ro - mance,
may - be it might be love.
Vocal ad lib.
26
We're for each oth - er like - a
wop ba - ba lu - mop and wop bam boom. Just like my
broth - er is sha - na - na - na - na - na - na - na, yip - pi - ty - dip - de doom
Chang chang chang - it - ty chang shoo - bop,
We'll al - ways be to - geth - er.
cresc.

Movement Brings the Music to Life!

"Twist and Shout" is a song that just isn't the same without the dance steps that the lyrics sing about! The dance craze that started in 1960 with Chubby Checker's release of the song "The Twist" lives on in songs like "Twist and Shout."

Review the dance steps to the Twist on page 11.

CD 7:7

Words and Music by
Bert Russell and Phil Medley

B♭7 E♭ A♭ B♭7
Well, shake it up ba - by, now. (Shake it up ba - by.) Twist and

E♭ A♭ B♭7 E♭ A♭
shout. (Twist and shout.) Come on, come on, come on, ba - by now. (Come on ba -

B♭7 E♭ A♭ B♭7
- by,) Come on and work it on out. (work it on out.) Well, work it on out,

E♭ A♭ B♭7 E♭ A♭
now. (Work it on out.) You know you look so good. (Look so good.)

B♭7 E♭ A♭ B♭7
You know you got me go - in' now, (Got me go - in') just like I knew you would.

E♭ A♭ 1. B♭7 2. B♭7
(Like I knew you would.) Well, shake it up ba -

Meet the Musician

ON NATIONAL RADIO!

Name: Sean Hurlburt
Age: 18
Instrument: Saxophone
Hometown: Palo Alto, CA

Saxophonist Sean Hurlburt, from Palo Alto, CA, originally chose to play music because it was the least of three evils. He remembers having three choices when he was in middle school: band, home economics, or dance. Not wanting to be teased by his peers, he says, "I decided to go with band."

Although he felt that way in middle school, these days 18-year-old Sean is totally into both music *and* dance. "I started out awhile back with hip-hop classes, and then I branched out into other kinds of dance like tap, jazz, and even ballet," he says. "I think the one thing that connects music and dance is the rhythm."

Sean realized just how much he appreciated playing saxophone after a close call when he accidentally dropped his and thought it might be broken beyond repair. "It crashed to the ground with a thud," he recalls. "When I realized none of the keys were working I almost cried." Sean's mom came to the rescue, rushing the banged-up sax to the instrument trauma center. It took weeks to restore, and Sean learned how much he missed playing it. Since then, the first thing Sean does when he wakes up every morning is rush to play his saxophone. "It's like that morning cup of coffee to me," he says. "Invigorating!"

RECORDED INTERVIEW

Listen to Sean's saxophone performance of Concertino da Camera, First Movement by Jacques Ibert **(CD 7:10)** and his interview **(CD 7:11)** on the national radio program From the Top.

Movement Brings the Message to Life!

Gospel music has long played an important role in worship for African American communities and is a popular style in the world of musical entertainment. Often featuring both solo and ensemble singing, gospel music can be highly ornamented with shouts and **glissandos**, as well as improvised lyrics, melodies, and rhythms. A glissando is the continuous movement from one pitch to the other. An accompanying gospel band might include an organ, percussion, bass, piano, and various solo instruments such as trumpet or saxophone.

I've Got a Robe
CD 7:12
Traditional Spiritual
Arranged by David Parker
Verse
1. I've got a robe, you've got a robe, all of God's chil-dren got a robe. When I get to hea-ven goin' to put on my robe, I'm goin' to walk a-round hea-ven all day!
2. I've got shoes, you've got shoes, all of God's chil-dren got shoes. When I get the hea-ven goin' to put on my shoes, I'm goin' to talk and spread the news!
No Chord
When I get there how hap-py I will be,
When I get there my Sav-ior's face I'll see. Well!
Sing: 2, 3
Hea - ven! all day!
Sing: 1, 2, 3, 6, 7, 10, 11, 12
(Walk) a-round hea-ven all day! Walk a-round hea-ven all day! Walk
Sing: 3, 4, 5, 8, 9
Walk, and tell the sto - ry,

LOG ON

music.mmhschool.com
Learn more about the history of Gospel music.

Improvise movements to "I've Got a Robe" as you sing it through the first time.

Create movements that you can perform together with your class.

Music Journal

Which popular performers do I think have probably been influenced by gospel music? What is it about their performance that leads me to believe this?

More Fun with Movement

Another form of dance movement popular in the United States is line dancing. One reason it is so popular is that you don't always need a partner to participate. You might think that line dancing is only for country music fans, but line dancing is actually performed to many kinds of music. "Zudio" is a street game that uses line dance movements.

CD 7:15

Zudio

Traditional

A Refrain

Here we go, Zu - di - o, Zu - di - o, Zu - di - o, Here we go, Zu - di - o all day_ long.
Mov - in' down the av - e - nue the av - e - nue the av - e - nue, Mov - in' down the av - e - nue all day_ long.
Here_ comes the oth - er one the oth - er one the oth - er one, Here_ comes the oth - er one

1., 2. all day_ long.
3. all day_ long.

B Verse

1. I woke up in the morn - ing and my bo - dy said, Ooh, ah,_ got a pain in your head, Ooh, ah,_ got a pain in your side, Ooh, ah,_ got a pain in your back,
2. I went_ to the doc - tor and_ there I said, Ooh, ah,_ got a pain in my head, Ooh, ah,_ got a pain in my side, Ooh, ah,_ got a pain in my back,
3. I went_ to the doc - tor and the doc - tor said, Ooh, ah,_ fix the pain in your head, Ooh, my,_ fix the pain in your side, Ooh, ah,_ fix the pain in your back,
4. I left_ the_ doc - tor and_ then I said, Ooh, ah,_ no_ pain in my head, Ooh, ah,_ no_ pain in my side, Ooh, ah,_ no_ pain in my back,

C

to the front, to the back, to the side, side, side,_ to the front, to the back, to the side, side, side,_ to the side, side, side._

Sing through "Zudio."

Perform the movements to the game.

A1 Form two lines facing each other, with the head couple at the front of the room. Take four steps forward and four steps back on the steady beat. Clap the steady beat while stepping. On the fourth clap, clap your partner's hand.

A2 One member of the head couple struts "down the avenue" between the two lines.

A3 The other member of the head couple follows, imitating the strut of the first partner. They then face each other at the foot of the line.

B All students create pantomimes illustrating the first two phrases.

C All students take one step to the front (in), one step to the back (out), three steps to the side; repeat. Change direction when moving to the other side.

Sing all three lines of A before singing and pantomiming each new verse of B; sing C after each verse of B.

Your Creative Unit Project

As you listen to various styles of music, there are many ways to respond to it and to help bring the music to life. Movement is just one of those ways. In this unit, you will learn that there are many other ways to be expressive in a musical performance, including the use of vocal techniques and taking liberties with tempos and dynamics. As you read through and participate in the activities of Unit 7, explore your own talents and abilities relating to musical expressiveness. Then choose a musical selection from the lessons or from your own music collection to perform for the class. Work alone or as part of a group to express what you believe the music is trying to communicate to your listeners.

LESSON 2

Instrumental Options

Everyone who has ever composed a piece of music has had to decide what voices and instruments would most effectively communicate the music's meaning and spirit. For people of ancient cultures, as well as for cultures in remote parts of the world today, the choice of instruments was limited to what raw materials were available to make them. Long before modern technology and manufacturing, musical instruments had been made of wood and plant fiber, animal bones and skins, clay and stone, and later, metal.

Aerophones

Bagpipes

Native American flute

Tuba

Idiophones

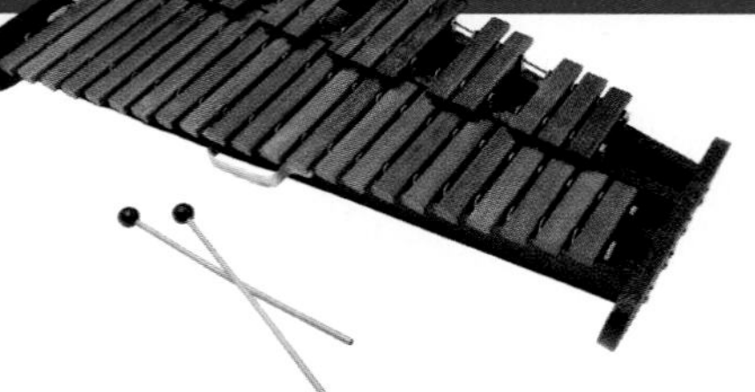

Xylophone

Maracas

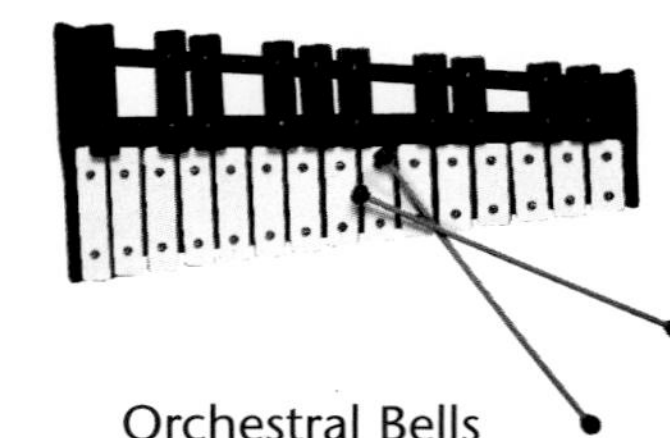

Orchestral Bells

Chordophones

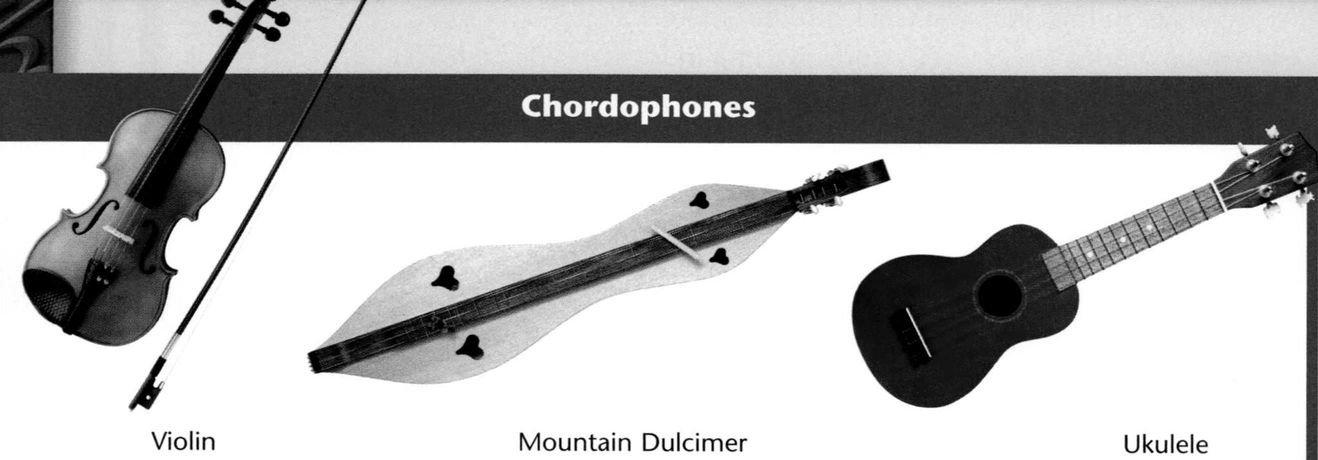

Violin

Mountain Dulcimer

Ukulele

One way to classify musical instruments is based on how their sounds are produced. Most, if not all, instruments of the world fit into one of these categories. **Aerophones** are instruments that produce sound through a vibrating column of air. These include woodwinds and brass as well as pipe organs. **Idiophones** are simple instruments that produce sound by being struck, scraped, or shaken. **Chordophones** are instruments that produce sound when a string or chord is struck, rubbed, or plucked.

Membranophones are instruments that produce sound by striking or rubbing a skin or membrane that is stretched across a resonating air chamber. **Electrophones** are instruments that generate sound from electricity. The tone colors of the various types of instruments add expression and excitement to performances, and they are carefully chosen to express the music that is being performed.

Membranophones

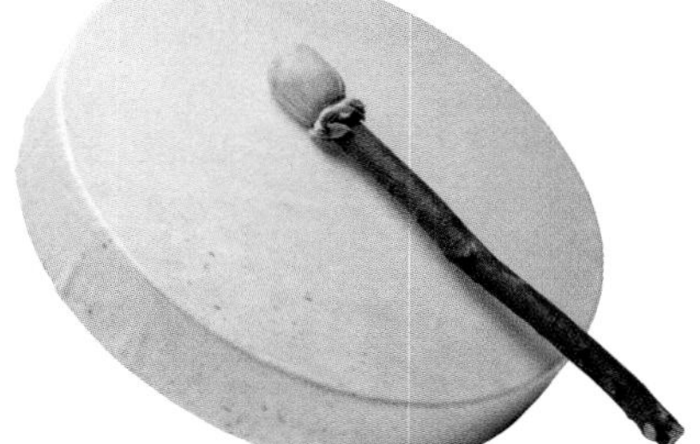

Native American Drum

Snare Drum

Timpani

Electrophones

Electric Guitar

Synthesizer

Music Journal

Based on the descriptions in the text, what other instruments can I include in these classifications according to how their sound is produced? What are my reasons for putting each additional instrument into a particular category?

Experimenting with Instruments

LISTENING CD 7:18

When Johnny Comes Marching Home

by Patrick S. Gilmore

While most songs popular during the Civil War in the United States expressed the fighting spirit of either the North or the South, "When Johnny Comes Marching Home" was sung by people on both sides of the conflict. It became even more popular 30 years later during the Spanish-American War.

Civil War band

Listen to "When Johnny Comes Marching Home."

Identify which group of instruments is used for each of the four verses.

Play "When Johnny Comes Marching Home" on idiophones, aerophones, and membranophones along with the recording. Take turns playing the various instruments to determine which ones you can play most confidently and expressively.

Idiophones

Metals

Woods

Musicians, soldiers, and townspeople from the Civil War era

Meet the Composer

Careers

Composer **Morton Gould** (1913–1996) published his first composition at the age of six. He was the first staff pianist at Radio City Music Hall when it opened in 1932. His compositions include Broadway scores such as *Billion Dollar Baby* (1945) and *Arms and the Girl* (1950). In 1994, he was named Composer of the Year by the Kennedy Center for the Performing Arts, and in 1995 he was awarded the Pulitzer Prize for Music for his composition *Stringmusic*. *Stringmusic* is a suite of five movements.

See **music.mmhschool.com** to learn more about *Stringmusic*.

Variations on a Theme

American composer Morton Gould used many variations on "When Johnny Comes Marching Home" in his 1943 creation "American Salute." Each time the melody is repeated in "American Salute," Gould changes it slightly.

LISTENING **CD 7:19**

American Salute by Morton Gould

Arthur Fiedler conducts this Boston Pops recording of "American Salute." Fiedler, born in Boston in 1894, conducted the Boston Pops for a record 50 years. Under his direction, the Boston Pops was recorded more than any other orchestra in the entire world. "American Salute" is also popular with many drum and bugle corps ensembles.

Listen to "American Salute."

Identify the membranophones and idiophones you hear in this composition.

LOG ON

See **music.mmhschool.com** to learn about a Drum and Bugle Corps performance of "American Salute."

Lyrics Inspire Instrumental Expression

The lyrics for "When Johnny Comes Marching Home" invite various interpretations and possibilities for instrumental accompaniment. Read through the lyrics and describe some additional variations that could help create a meaningful choral arrangement of the song.

1. When Johnny comes marching home again,
   Hurrah! Hurrah!
   We'll give him a hearty welcome then,
   Hurrah! Hurrah!
   The men will cheer, and the boys will shout,
   The ladies they will all come out,
   And we'll all be glad
   When Johnny comes marching home.

2. The old church bell will peal with joy,
   Hurrah! Hurrah!
   To welcome home our darling boy
   Hurrah! Hurrah!
   The village lads and lassies say
   With roses they will strew the way,
   And we'll all feel proud
   When Johnny comes marching home.

3. Get ready for the Jubilee,
   Hurrah! Hurrah!
   We'll give the hero three times three,
   Hurrah! Hurrah!
   The laurel wreath is ready now
   To place upon his loyal brow,
   And we'll all feel proud
   When Johnny comes marching home.

MIDI

See ***Spotlight on MIDI*** to explore musical conversation in a classical piece.

U.S. Marine Drum and Bugle Corps

Exploring Your Own Voice

LESSON 3

Your voice provides countless ways to express yourself. It helps you not only to express your thoughts and personality, but is also an important means of expression when responding to all of life's experiences!

Stop and think about the variety of ways in which you use your speaking voice. Listen to your own unique way of saying simple everyday phrases such as these: "See you later." "Be careful!" "Nice going!" "Watch out!" Listen to how you answer the telephone and if your voice changes depending on who, if you know who, is calling.

Look at the photographs on pages 172 and 173. Use your own voice to speak each part aloud, imitating to the best of your ability the expressiveness you imagine is being used.

"Is that gift for me? Thank you so much!"

"I have a dream that one day this nation will rise up and live out the true meaning of its creed: 'We hold these truths to be self-evident, that all men are created equal.'" From the "I Have a Dream" speech presented by Rev. Dr. Martin Luther King, Jr., August 28, 1963

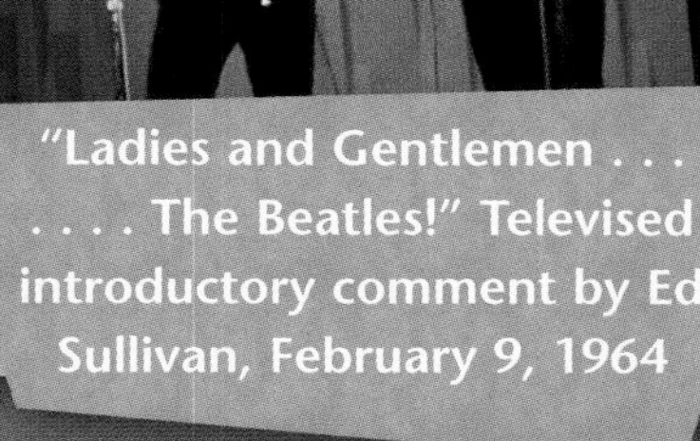

"Ladies and Gentlemen . . .
. . . . The Beatles!" Televised introductory comment by Ed Sullivan, February 9, 1964

Art Gallery

Lincoln gives the Gettysburg Address, Anonymous, color illustration, 19th century
"Four score and seven years ago, our fathers brought forth upon this continent a new nation: conceived in Liberty, and dedicated to the proposition that all men are created equal."
From The Gettysburg Address, given by President Abraham Lincoln on November 19, 1863

"Happy Holidays! Happy New Year!!"

'"Houston, Tranquillity Base here. The Eagle has landed." Statement that mission commander Neil Armstrong sent back to Earth upon landing on the moon July 20, 1969

Music Journal

What example can I describe of a time when I was misunderstood because of the way that I said something? What examples can I describe of how using my voice in different ways to say the same word or phrase changes the meaning of what I'm communicating?

Contrasts in Vocal Music

Both composers and performers of vocal and instrumental music explore different ways to bring the music to life! Some performers can take their listeners beyond a song's literal or obvious meaning.

LISTENING **CD 7:20**

Emergency by Evelyn Maria Harris

Featured on this recording is Sweet Honey in The Rock, a female African American a cappella vocal group founded in 1973. The name comes from a biblical parable that describes a land so rich that when rocks were cracked open, honey flowed from them. Members of the group often compose or arrange the compositions they perform. Evelyn Maria Harris composed the Grammy Award-winning "Emergency" in 1985. In this composition, she uses **voiced sounds** that are not actually sung to help give emphasis, meaning, and musical expression to the lyrics.

Describe the variety of vocal sounds that Harris uses in this composition. How are these sounds descriptive of an emergency situation? Discuss the meaning of the lyrics and how effectively the music brings them to life.

Sweet Honey in The Rock

Emergency

by Evelyn Maria Harris

In 1985, as we flew to Nairobi for the U.N. End of the Decade Conference on Women, a state of emergency was declared in South Africa by the apartheid government. It was hard to believe I was on the same continent. We were in Kenya, a country full of black people, and no one was screaming! None of the newspapers was shouting foul! So I screamed and screamed and . . .

Recording begins here.

Aaaannnnnnn . . .

Workin' in the mines from dawn 'til dusk
Gettin' no money, gettin' nowhere
Diamonds and gold they filter thru my hands
Just like the Krugerrand, the coin of death.

Thousands layin' on the funeral pyre
My sister, my brother, they never afraid
They keep on marching and they keep on singing
With yesterday's coffin on their heads.

Well I'm looking up to heaven for some clear sign
For who to kill now and who to let be
See when you got no freedom and your family is gone
Everybody is your enemy.

So people of the world we got to right this here wrong
We'll wake to the sun and we'll sleep to the breeze
We'll walk hand in hand to the freedom's drum
Cause South Africa she's gotta be free of this emergency.

Chorus 1 and 2
My soul's in a state of emergency . . .

Chorus 3
Apartheid's in a state of emergency . . .

Last Chorus
South Africa's got to be free of this emergency
She gon be so free of this emergency
Gotta be so free, gon be you and me
Emergency—

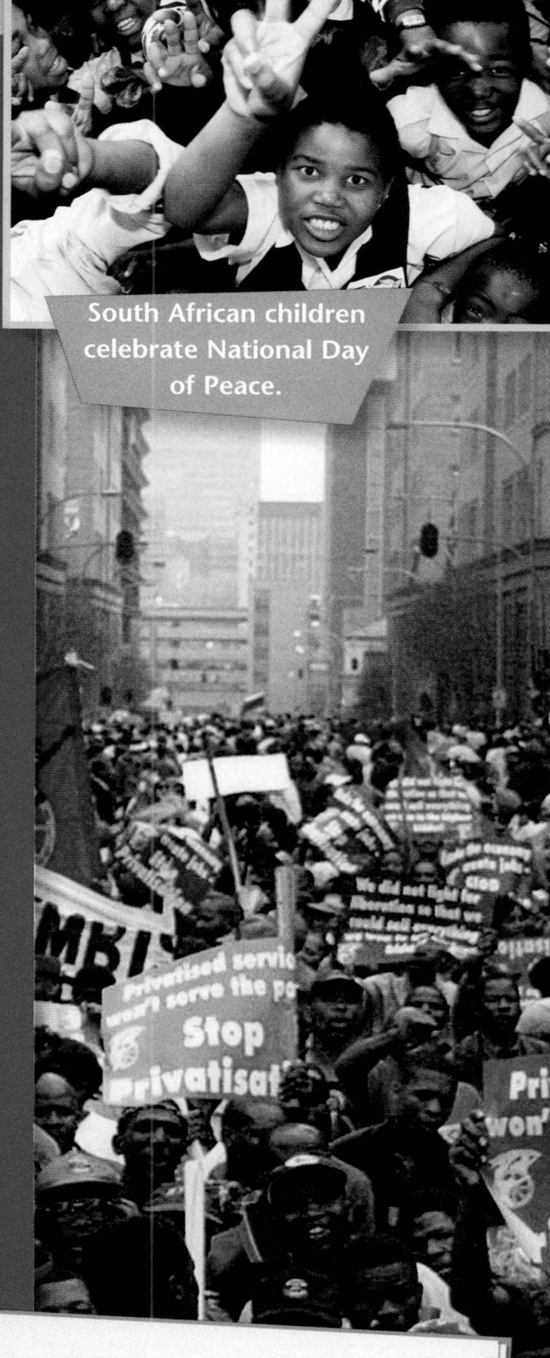

South African children celebrate National Day of Peace.

South African workers march in protest, August 30, 2001.

Music Journal

How could I use my voice in a sound composition that describes or expresses a recent specific experience I had? How would I teach such a composition to my classmates?

Culture Influences the Voice

Using the voice to express emotion and convey meaning can be influenced by cultural differences. Long before Europeans settled in North America, **katadjait** or **"throat songs"** were being sung in Northern Canada. Katadjait are an example of an important style of singing and musical expression resulting from the influences of culture.

LISTENING **CD 8:1**

Song of a Seashore Traditional Inuit

For generations, Inuit women in the village of Povungnituk on the eastern shore of Hudson Bay in the Canadian Arctic have sung and handed down throat songs. Performing in a duet, two women stand close together facing each other. The sounds they produce are created through altering breathing techniques and vocal manipulation. The sounds are meant to imitate the real life environmental landscape of the village. When observing and listening to katadjait, you should expect to hear indoor sounds (babies crying, water boiling, dogs barking) as well as outdoor sounds (wind, water, waves, geese).

Listen to "Song of a Seashore" to identify the outdoor sounds the singers might be trying to imitate.

Listen again to notice how different throat singing is from the singing you are used to hearing.

Describe some of the differences.

LOG ON

music.mmhschool.com
Learn more about throat singing in northern Canada.

Create an environmental landscape composition based on sounds connected with your classroom, school, family, or a special place in your community. Be sure to feature innovative uses of the voice.

Caribou Inuit throat singers dressed in traditional parkas

LISTENING CD 8:2

Papa-oom-mow-mow by A. Frazier, J. E. Harris, C. L. White, and W. Turner, Jr.

"Papa-oom-mow-mow" is one of the most famous rock and roll novelty recordings of all time. Recorded by The Rivingtons and released in the early 1960s, it features voices being used in what were at that time rather unusual ways.

Sing the opening section of "Papa-oom-mow-mow" as you listen to the recording. If the title "Song of a Seashore" helped you identify some of the musical events you might listen for, what do you think will happen musically in a song with the title "Papa-oom-mow-mow?"

Papa-oom-mow-mow
Words and Music by
Alfred Frazier, John Earl Harris,
Carl L. White, and Wilson Turner, Jr.
E♭
Pa pa pa pa pa pa pa oom-ah mow mow_ pa pa oom mow_ mow_ pa pa pa
Repeat ad lib.
oom - ah mow mow mow pa pa oom mow_ mow pa pa pa

For centuries, other instruments have attempted to imitate and copy the expressive qualities of the human voice. Still, of all the musical instruments available to composers, the human voice is the most versatile and expressive. As long as people can speak and sing, they will continue to share the joys of expressing thoughts and ideas through the use of the human voice.

Music Journal

What musical characteristics can I use to compare the performances of "Song of a Seashore" and "Papa-oom-mow-mow?" Which selection do I believe uses the human voice more creatively? Why?

LESSON 4

Dramatic Expression

Opera, a continuously popular form of classical music, has found its way to the Broadway stage on many occasions in recent years. Powerful musical performances are inspired by the dramatic stories on which they are based. As in any great musical theater production, the costumes, scenery, lighting, dancing, and stage spectacles all work together to keep the audience involved and excited while a story is told in song. The theme of love as expressed in opera, as well as non-musical drama, has been the inspiration for many Broadway musicals.

Luciano Pavarotti in *Aïda*, the opera

There are many different treatments of the original opera or drama when the basic story is transferred to the Broadway musical. For example, Leonard Bernstein's *West Side Story* moved Shakespeare's *Romeo and Juliet* to New York City where Romeo and Juliet became Maria and Tony. The musical *Aida* by Elton John and Tim Rice is a rock and roll treatment of the story of Verdi's *Aïda,* set in ancient Egypt. *Miss Saigon* is loosely based on Puccini's *Madama Butterfly* and is set during the Vietnam War.

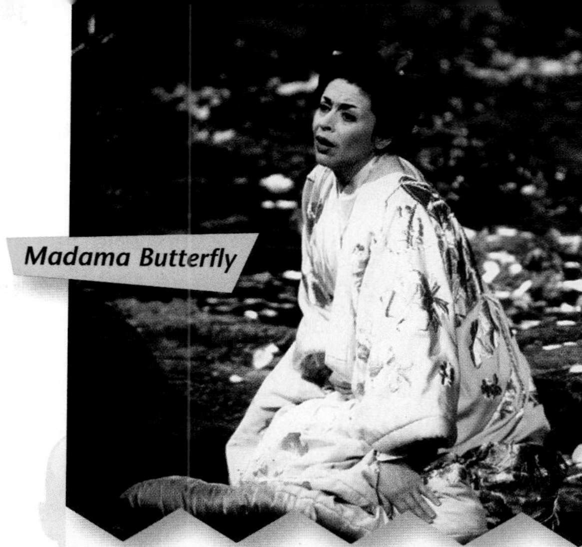
Madama Butterfly

West Side Story started out as "East Side Story." Bernstein planned for a romance between a Jewish boy and an Italian Catholic girl. Many delays and changes resulted in the more modern story of an American-born Polish boy and a Puerto Rican girl who had just come to America.

Romeo and Juliet

Parallel Productions

Puccini's opera *La Bohème* is considered by many to be the greatest love story every told. It's an opera about real people. It's about loyalty in love and friendship. *Rent,* created by the late Jonathan Larson, retells the story in a fresh setting.

It is interesting that *Rent* opened in New York on the 100th anniversary of the opening of *La Bohème. Rent* does more than borrow the story line! It incorporates Puccini's musical themes, plot twists, and even some lyrics from the opera.

Scenes from *La Bohème*

LISTENING **CD 8:3**

Signature Themes (from *La Bohème* and *Rent*)

by G. Puccini and J. Larson

"Signature Themes" includes the introduction to a choral arrangement of selections from the musical *Rent* and an excerpt from Musetta's solo "Quando men vo" from the opera *La Bohème*. These very brief excerpts are probably among the most familiar sounds from these productions.

Listen to "Signature Themes" and describe in musical terms how the excerpts are similar to each other and how they are different from each other.

Describe and discuss the musical differences between the two themes. In your opinion, what makes one more dramatic than the other?

music.mmhschool.com
Read more about Jonathan Larson and other creators of Broadway musicals.

Scene from *Rent*

Mimi and Roger from *Rent*

Rodolfo and Mimi from *La Bohème*

Compare the characters and scenes from *Rent* and *La Bohème* using the brief descriptions below. Discuss how effectively the different settings of the "Signature Themes" (page 180) and the "Death Scene Themes" (page 182) bring the dramatic scenes to life.

Rent

CHARACTERS

Mark—a filmmaker
Roger—a composer
Mimi—Roger's love interest
Collins—a philosopher
Angel Schunard—a musician
Maureen—Mark's former girlfriend
Benny—the landlord

SCENES

Mark and Roger are cold, so they warm themselves by making a fire with Mark's screenplays and Roger's music posters.

Mimi enters Mark's apartment during a power outage seeking a light for her candle. Her song ends with "They call me Mimi."

Roger is attracted to Mimi's "hair in the moonlight."

Angel Schunard is hired to get rid of an annoying dog by drumming non-stop.

After Roger and Mimi's separation, Maureen discovers Mimi "freezing" in a park and brings her to Mark and Roger's apartment.

As Mimi lies dying, she says to Roger, "I should tell you—I love you."

La Bohème

CHARACTERS

Marcello—an artist
Rodolfo—a painter
Mimi—Rodolfo's love interest
Colline—a philosopher
Schaunard—a composer
Musetta—Marcello's former girlfriend
Benoit—the landlord

SCENES

Rodolfo and Marcello warm themselves by burning Rodolfo's five-act drama.

Mimi enters Marcello's apartment looking for a light for her candle. Her aria begins, "They call me Mimi."

Rodolfo sings of Mimi's "sweet visage bathed in a soft lunar dawn."

Schaunard is hired to get rid of an annoying parrot by singing non-stop.

After Rodolfo and Mimi's separation, Musetta meets Mimi, who is "so cold" on the street, and takes her to Marcello and Rodolfo's home.

As Mimi dies, she says "you are my love and all my life."

A Hundred Years Later

The emotion of love in music usually fits into one of three categories:

Lost love   Seeking love   Finding Love

Which one of these phrases best describes the central theme of *La Bohème* and *Rent*?

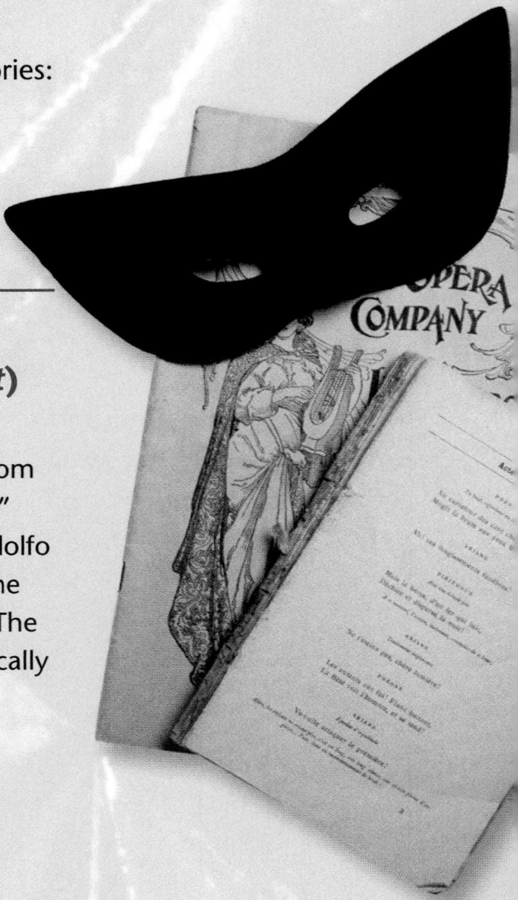

LISTENING **CD 8:4**

Death Scene Themes (from *La Bohème* and *Rent*)

by G. Puccini and J. Larson

"Death Scene Themes" includes part of the song "Without You" from *Rent* and the aria "Che avvien?" from *La Bohème.* In "Without You," Mimi is mourning an impending loss of love. In "Che avvien?" Rodolfo and several others are with Mimi in her final moments of life. At one point, he thinks Mimi is merely resting when in fact she has died. The faces of his friends help him realize the truth, and Rodolfo dramatically throws himself, sobbing, over her lifeless body.

Listen to "Death Scene Themes" and discuss the effectiveness of each of the performances in portraying a death scene.

The death scene from *La Bohème*

Looking Back

Now that you have explored the many ways that music can be used expressively—through movement, instrumentation, singing, and drama—what "talents" of your own have you discovered? Think about some things that you have always wanted to say to somebody but just couldn't find the right words. How effectively could you communicate this through music—either your own or someone else's? What inspiration can you find in an existing work that you might transform for your purposes?

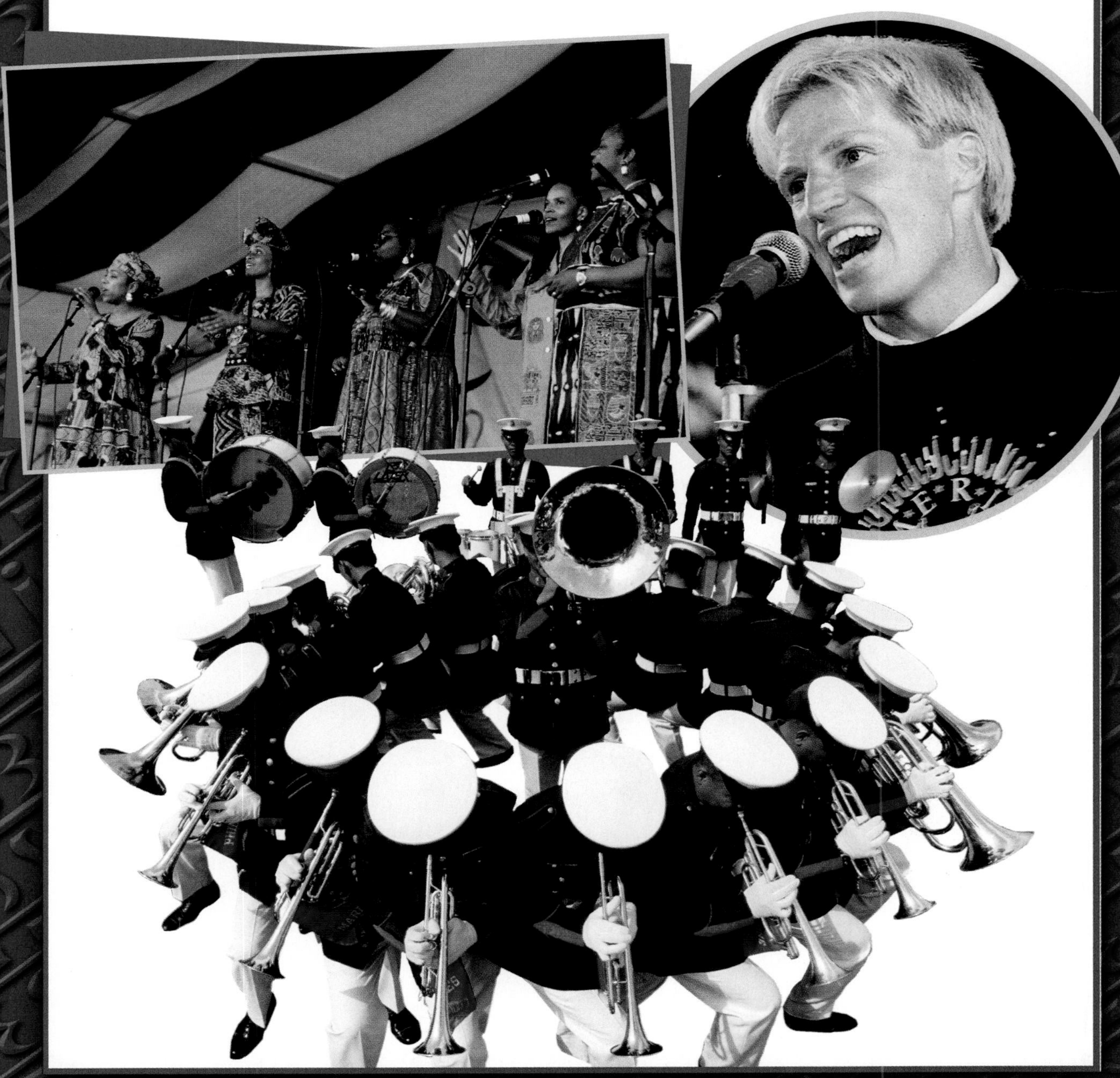

Honoring Your Past

When was the last time you took a close look at a calendar? Whether you are looking at the scenic monthly calendar on your kitchen wall or the personal digital assistant you keep in your back pocket, you'll probably find many celebrations marked. From national holidays to family birthdays, these celebrations usually have one thing in common. They are often about remembering or honoring an important person or event.

National holidays often remember and celebrate the lives of famous leaders, important victories in war, or the sacrifices of a country's defenders. Celebrations that honor national heroes help strengthen feelings of patriotism. The music sung and heard on such occasions is often familiar and brings back memories.

In the United States, music can play an especially important role in uniting people from many different cultures and celebrating the common ground of your American identity. You have read about how music can help honor your past and your cultural heritage. Music also helps you celebrate the present and look to the future. This includes the dreams that you share for your common future as well as your personal dreams.

LISTENING **CD 8:5**

Celebration Medley (montage)

This medley includes excerpts from some of the songs you'll hear throughout this unit: "Be Yours," "The Star-Spangled Banner," "The Singing Woods," "Batuque," and "Wide Open Spaces."

Listen to "Celebration Medley" and discuss what kind of celebration you think of when you hear each selection.

Music Journal

What person, event, or way of life would I most like to honor or celebrate in a song? If I could commission someone to write such a song, what would I tell the composer about the lyrics and the style of music that I think is most appropriate?

The Legacy of Liberty

Compared to many nations around the world, the United States of America is a relatively young country. Countless people have come to America as immigrants, and one of the first sights many saw when arriving in their new country was the Statue of Liberty in New York Harbor. On July 4, 1986, our nation celebrated the centennial of the statue. Composer John Williams was commissioned to write a **fanfare** for the occasion. A fanfare is a short, lively sounding of trumpets or other brass, played to honor an important person or to announce an important event.

music.mmhschool.com
Read more about the centennial celebration of the Statue of Liberty and other national celebrations.

The Statue of Liberty is a great symbol of freedom in the United States.

LISTENING CD 8:6

Liberty Fanfare (excerpt) by John Williams

Composer John Williams also conducts this performance of "Liberty Fanfare" by the Boston Pops Orchestra.

Listen to the recording of "Liberty Fanfare" while following the listening map below.

Listening Map for *Liberty Fanfare*

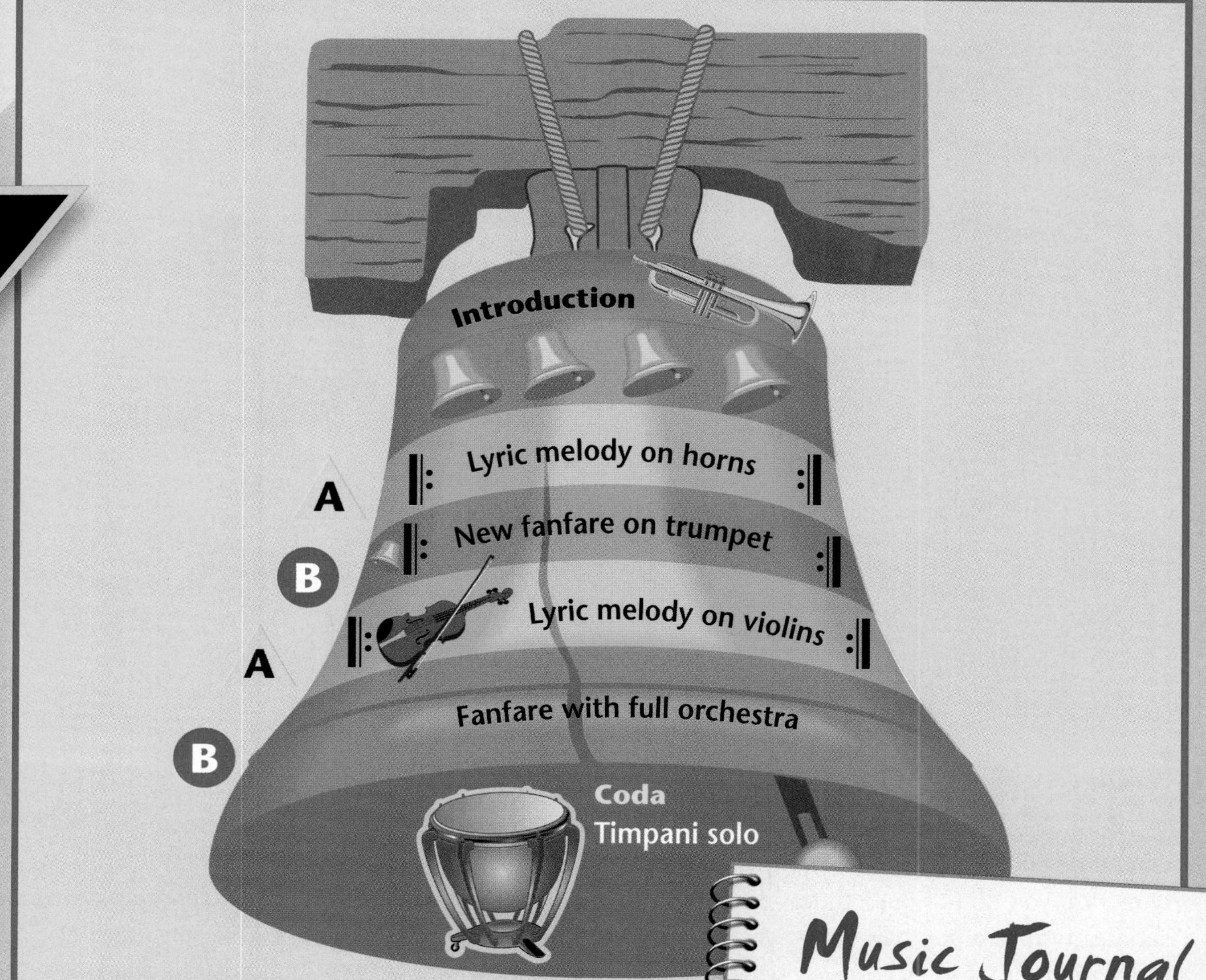

Music Journal

Using "Liberty Fanfare" as an example, how can I describe musical qualities that inspire patriotism?

One Song for All

In a time and place such as twenty-first century America, you do not need to travel far to learn about cultures other than your own. Your own background may in fact include several cultures. The 2000 U. S. Population Census reports are certainly evidence of this. So what happens when it's time to gather your extended family for a holiday celebration?

Such events certainly don't have to be a culture clash. "Be Yours" was written especially for families and friends with a wide variety of backgrounds who celebrate holidays together. The lyrics exclude no one. The message is a simple holiday wish that you can share with anyone.

Sing "Be Yours" along with the recording.

Describe the musical qualities that help convey the message of the lyrics.

Be Yours
CD 8:7
Words and Music by Mary Unobsky
May the warm-est smiles be yours; May the sweet-est dreams be yours. May the most
peace-ful heart in the world to-night be yours this hol-i-day.
May the kind-est words be yours; May the dear-est friends be yours. And may the
deep-est thoughts full of love and light be yours this hol-i-day. May it be a
spe-cial time when stars do shine on tra-di-tions old and new. You
know I want for you what you want for me, too.
May the rar-est wish be yours; May the bright-est hope be yours. And may the
joys this sea-son of pure de-light be yours this hol-i-day, Be
yours this hol-i-day.

Common Journeys

Just as Americans throughout our country's history have shared a common journey in search of freedom, specific cultural and religious groups also share their own common journeys. The songs and celebrations of these groups unite them with their ancestors' culture and faith and with people throughout the world who share their heritage today.

In some traditions, when people remember and celebrate their past, they relive the common experiences and journeys of their forbearers in faith. In celebrations of the Jewish Passover, for example, as the story of the Exodus (or escape) from slavery in Egypt is retold, people eat the same kinds of food that the Jewish people ate during the Exodus. In remembering and sharing in these experiences, Jewish people today are united with Jewish people who lived thousands of years ago.

LISTENING **CD 8:10**

Hashkivenu by Craig Taubman

Originally sung in Jewish homes as part of a family's bedtime prayers, the Hashkivenu prayer has become part of Friday evening Sabbath services around the world. The text, sung in Hebrew on this recording, is a prayer for peace, safety, and protection so that we will rise again with the morning's light. For younger children, it is an affirmation that it is safe to go to sleep. Composers have set this ancient text to many styles of music throughout the centuries.

Art Gallery

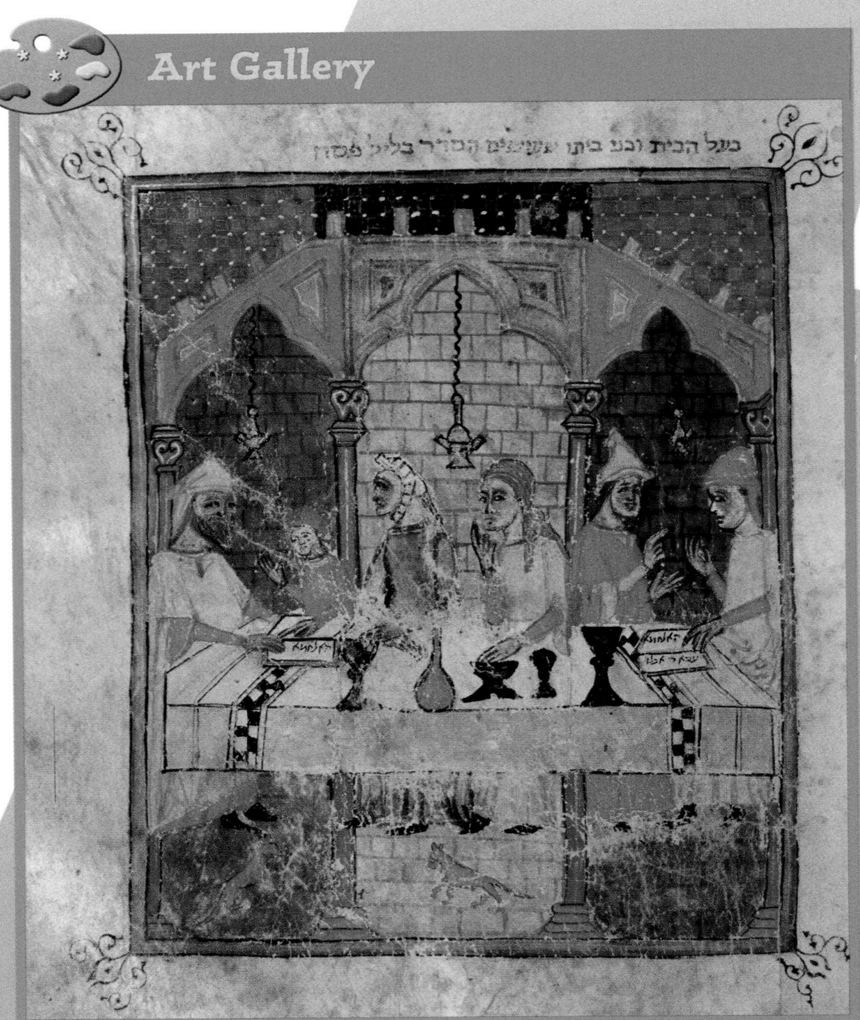

Untitled **(Passover Meal)**
Anonymous,
vellum,
Northern Spain, ca. 1350

For the many Americans who travel or move from one town, state, or region to another, memories are often associated with the places where they have journeyed. The classic song "Route 66," popularized by singer Nat King Cole, describes one person's journey along a historic highway that crosses many states in the southern United States.

LISTENING CD 8:11

Route 66 by Bobby Troup

Nat King Cole is accompanied by piano and string bass on this 1944 recording. In 1944 Cole's popularity was mostly with jazz-loving audiences.

Listen to "Route 66."

Describe the style of the vocal performance as well as the piano and string bass performances.

music.mmhschool.com
Learn more about the famous Route 66, the *road* as well as the *song*!

Your Creative Unit Project

Start a "musical family tree" that includes the music which has most inspired you. This should be music that helped shape your musical preferences as well as your understanding of who you are. Include songs that help you to honor your past, to celebrate who you are today, and that inspire your hopes and dreams for the future. These can be popular songs as well as songs that reflect your cultural, religious, and musical heritage. See how many generations you can represent in your musical family tree!

LESSON 2

Patriotic Inspiration

It's hard to deny the power of music to stir up feelings of patriotism and pride in your country. Nearly every country around the world has a **national anthem**, a song of praise that honors a particular nation. A national anthem is like a country's musical "motto" or theme song. It is carefully selected and is intended to stir emotions and foster loyalty. What do you remember about the national anthem of the United States? Can you name the national anthem of any other country?

National anthems often play an important role in sporting events. When an athlete wins the gold medal at the Olympics, his or her country's national anthem is played at the award ceremony. Most U.S. sports events begin with a performance of "The Star-Spangled Banner." It is considered a great honor for a performer to be chosen to sing the national anthem at events such as the annual Super Bowl game.

LOG ON

music.mmhschool.com
Take a look at the original handwritten notation for "The Star-Spangled Banner."

Free-skating gold medalist Sarah Hughes at the 2002 Winter Olympics in Salt Lake City, with bronze medalist Michelle Kwan

Art Gallery

Untitled by Unknown
The British attack on Washington, D.C., in August 1814

What are some events where you might hear the national anthem of the United States performed? What kinds of rules do people observe when the national anthem is performed? Can you think of any other songs whose performance requires a particular response from the listeners?

Although the United States officially declared its independence from Great Britain in 1776, the song now accepted as our national anthem was not written until 1814. Ironically, the melody is believed to have been written by the English composer John Stafford Smith. The lyrics penned by Francis Scott Key in 1814 describe a scene of battle that he observed during the War of 1812, not the Revolutionary War. Despite the song's popularity, it was more than a century before the song was officially made the national anthem in 1931.

Who could have imagined that a song written in the early nineteenth century, even a national anthem, would become a popular single in the early twenty-first century? In 1991, when the United States was fighting the Gulf War, Whitney Houston was chosen to sing our national anthem at Super Bowl XXV. Her inspiring recording became a major hit. Ten years later, shortly after the terrorist attacks in 2001, the song was re-released and became popular once again.

Our National Anthem

Read through the lyrics of "The Star-Spangled Banner." What do they tell you about the battle that Francis Scott Key witnessed?

Read the notation as you sing along with the recording. Notice the range of the melody, the distance between the highest and lowest notes.

Read the key signature and determine which notes are flatted.

Identify which of the following rhythm patterns appears at the beginning of "The Star-Spangled Banner."

The rhythm ♩. ♪ is called a dotted rhythm.

Sing "The Star-Spangled Banner" as notated. Then sing it changing the dotted rhythms to equal rhythms to feel the difference.

LISTENING CD 8:15

Freedom by Michael W. Smith

This selection is from Michael W. Smith's first instrumental album, released in 2000. Smith calls the album "the soundtrack to the movie in my mind." This title piece begins with an inspiring drum cadence, followed by piano, brass, strings, and a pennywhistle.

Michael W. Smith

Listen to "Freedom" and describe the feelings that it inspires.

Create or find spoken parts to be read over the music. These can be original or excerpts from speeches or poetry you know. Allow the music to be heard in between the spoken parts.

Create a listening map to guide other listeners through the musical experience of "Freedom."

Strike Up the Band

Can you imagine a parade without a band? Why do you think nearly every high school, college, and branch of the U.S. military service has a band? Bands can really get the emotions flowing by raising spirits and generating pride in the organizations they represent. As a result, bands are often the ensemble of choice for performing patriotic music.

Bands that play inside an auditorium or hall are usually called concert bands. One way to think of a concert band is as an expanded version of the wind and percussion sections of the orchestra.

Read and speak the following rhythms by saying these words:

down the street we're for ♪♪♪♪

marching for ♪♪

on for ♩

LISTENING CD 8:16

The Stars and Stripes Forever by John Philip Sousa

This performance by the Columbia All-Star Band demonstrates all the patriotic enthusiasm that Sousa must have imagined when he composed this piece.

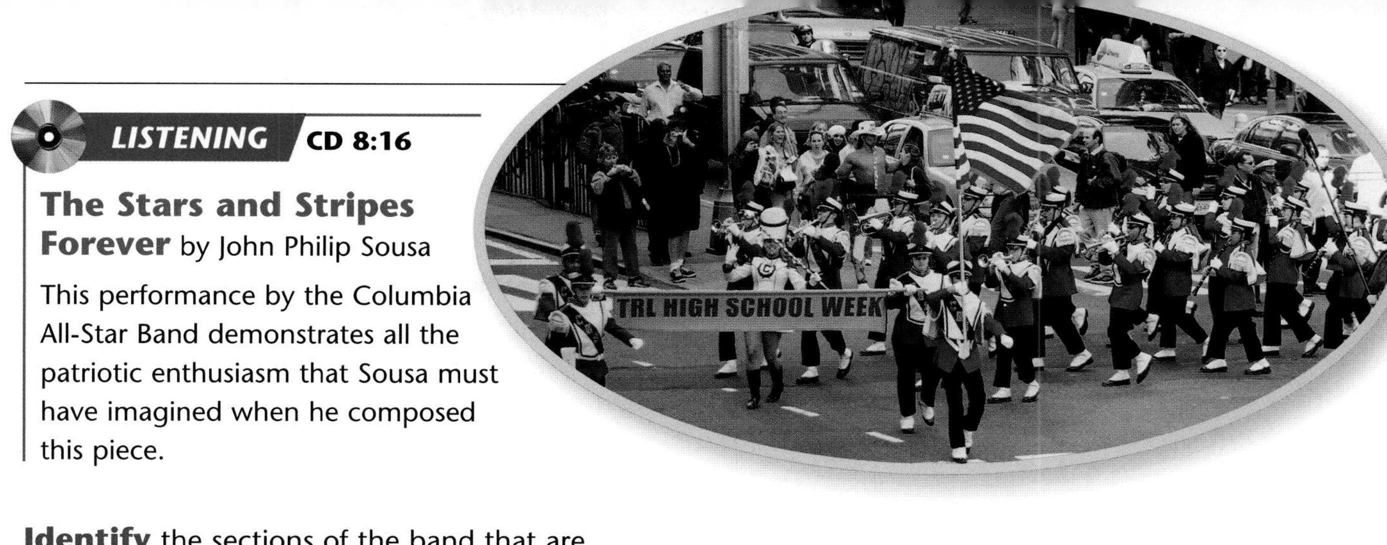

Identify the sections of the band that are featured in this recording of "The Stars and Stripes Forever."

Celebrating Identity

Music can be an important way for people to celebrate their identity as a community. It also enables them to share something about themselves with people outside their community. Sometimes a community's celebration is a private experience, but often the celebration occurs where outsiders can watch and listen. Can you think of private community celebrations you have attended or participated in? What about celebrations with an audience?

Music and other art forms are important expressions of the value and dignity of peoples and cultures. In the West Indies, drum music became an important cultural resource for freed slaves after their liberation in 1834. According to some accounts, freed slaves who wanted to join local celebrations were forced by poverty to make their own drums. They formed percussion ensembles using instruments made of bamboo tubes struck with sticks.

On the Caribbean island of Trinidad, musicians began to experiment with making instruments from old steel barrels left there after World War II. Drummers discovered that indentations and dents in the drums could produce a wide range of tones. The result was the steel pan drum, which became the center of a thriving musical culture that later spread throughout the West Indies and far beyond. Because the steel pan was developed from an everyday object and was used to create music, it is an example of a **found instrument**.

Making music as an ensemble can create a strong sense of community.

LISTENING CD 8:17

Jump in the Line by J. T. Taylor

J. T.'s Island Steel ensemble performs on steel drums or pans created from 55-gallon oil barrels. Some people find the sound of the steel drum soothing and relaxing, while others find it lively and festive. The steel drum is a key part of the calypso style that grew out of the folk music of Trinidad.

Perform the following rhythmic patterns as you listen to the recording of "Jump in the Line."

	1	2	3	4	5	6	7	8
1.	♪	𝄾	♪	𝄾	♪	𝄾	♪	𝄾
2.	𝄾	♪	𝄾	♪	𝄾	♪	𝄾	♪
3.	♪	♪	♪	♪	𝄾	𝄾	𝄾	𝄾
4.	𝄾	𝄾	𝄾	𝄾	♪	♪	♪	♪
5.	♪	♪	♪	𝄾	♪	♪	♪	𝄾
6.	♪	𝄾	𝄾	♪	♪	𝄾	𝄾	𝄾

Notice the multiple layers of rhythm patterns. This sounding of two or more rhythm patterns at the same time creates **polyrhythms**.

Music Journal

If I were going to make music with a found instrument, what would I use? How would I use it?

MIDI

See *Spotlight on MIDI* to further explore steel band music.

Tradition Meets Modern Music

"One-Eyed Ford" is a song that often accompanies social dancing at powwows, particularly among the Native American nations of the southern plains of the United States. It is an example of a more contemporary style of Native American music known as "49s." These frequently humorous songs often contain English lyrics mixed with **vocables**. Vocables are sung sounds that are not real words, much like scat singing.

The *one-eyed Ford* refers to a car with only one head light. Many years ago, the roads were not paved well and cars were often left with only one "eye" because the "other" eye got knocked out by loose rocks.

One-Eyed Ford
CD 8:18
Inter-tribal Native American 49 Song
Repeat song in higher keys
Solo
Group
we ya ha do we ya ha do we ya ha do we ya ha do
ya yo he ya he ya he ya ho hai ya
he ya ha he ya ha do we ya ha we ya ha do we ya ha do
ya yo he ya he ya he ya ho hai ya he ya ha he ya ha do
When the dance is o - ver, sweet-heart, I will take you home in my one-eyed Ford.
he ya he ya he ya ho hai ya he ya ha he ya ha - e
*Voices overlap

Sing "One-Eyed Ford" with the recording.

Play the following drum pattern on unpitched percussion instruments, except during the English words.

LISTENING CD 8:19

The Singing Woods by Brent Michael Davids

The Kronos Quartet, a nontraditional string quartet, commissioned Davids to create a composition that combines Native American and traditional European concert music.

Listen to "The Singing Woods" and discuss how the instruments imitate the sounds of the woods "singing."

Describe the parts of the composition that seem to reflect European musical characteristics.

Describe the parts of the composition that seem to reflect Native American musical characteristics.

Describe how the musical characteristics of "The Singing Woods" have been combined to create a new musical style.

Composer Brent Michael Davids narrates a 2001 performance of "The Last of James Fenimore Cooper."

RECORDED INTERVIEW CD 8:20

Brent Michael Davids

A member of the Mohican Nation, composer Brent Michael Davids is well-schooled in both classical music and the traditions of Native American music, which he learned from relatives on the reservation where he grew up. When the New Mexico Symphony Orchestra performed his 15-movement symphony "PauWau: A Gathering of Nations," the ensemble was joined by many performers who don't usually contribute to a symphony concert. These included a traditional powwow emcee, Native American dancers, and Davids on a special quartz crystal flute.

music.mmhschool.com
Read more about Brent Michael Davids' experimental music.

Music Journal

What other songs can I find that combine musical styles from two or more cultures or could be combined to define a new and unique style?

Brazilian Dance Music

In early twentieth-century Brazil, artists and composers began to blend the unique character of Brazilian folk music with a more "universal" language of music. They did this by experimenting with mixing the popular tradition of oral, or **nonwritten music**, into the European tradition of classical **written music**. Nonwritten music is passed from one person or generation to another through oral transmission, while written music uses notation, or written symbols, showing how to perform music.

LISTENING CD 9:1

Batuque by Oscar Lorenzo Fernândez

In 1930, Brazilian composer Oscar Lorenzo Fernândez wrote a suite for orchestra that used rhythms found in native folk dances. "Batuque," the last movement of the work, is filled with the polyrhythms of these dances. The word *batuque* simply means "samba rhythm."

Bahia Dancers in Pelourinho Salvador, Brazil

Listen to the recording of "Batuque," paying close attention to the layered rhythm patterns. How many different rhythms can you identify?

Clap each of the following rhythm patterns used to accompany the A section of "Batuque."

Perform these same rhythm patterns on unpitched percussion instruments as an accompaniment to the A section of "Batuque."

Meet the Musician

Oscar Lorenzo Fernândez (1897–1948) demonstrated musical talent from an early age. Born in Brazil's largest city, Rio de Janeiro, he entered Brazil's National Music Institute at the age of twenty. Although Fernândez composed many *classical* works, he was very proud of his Brazilian heritage. Brazilian folklore is always present in his work to acknowledge the culture in which he was raised. In 1940 a famous conductor of the time, Arturo Toscanini, directed a performance of "Batuque" in Rio de Janeiro. Toscanini was on tour with New York City's prestigious National Broadcasting Corporation (NBC) Symphony.

Music Inspires Dreams

Have you ever heard a song that so closely expresses something you have felt that it sounds as if you could have written the song yourself? Music surely inspires the dreams we have for our futures and gives us hope that anything is possible. It is certainly something to celebrate when music helps people through difficult times.

Many songs sung by enslaved Africans in nineteenth-century America used biblical stories to talk about their dream of one day being free. These spirituals often used the suffering and eventual freedom of Hebrew slaves from Egypt as a way to express the dreams of slaves in America.

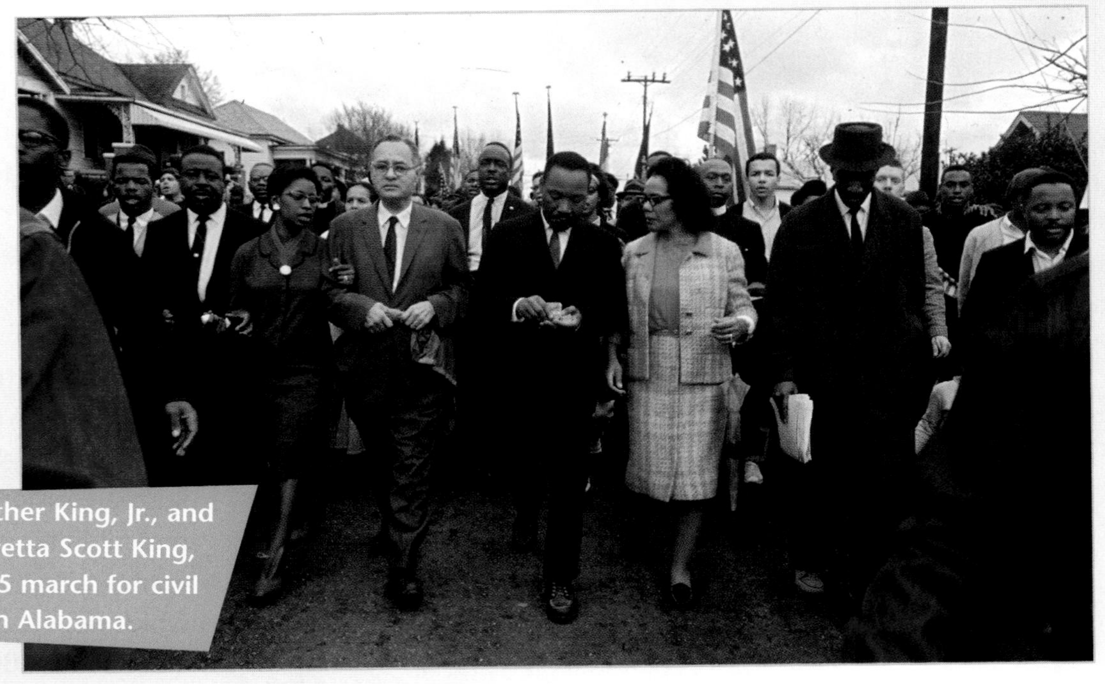

Dr. Martin Luther King, Jr., and his wife, Coretta Scott King, lead the 1965 march for civil rights in Alabama.

Although slavery was abolished in the mid-1800s, the lives of African Americans remained difficult well into the twentieth century. Dr. Martin Luther King, Jr., one of the best-known leaders of the 1960s civil rights movement, gave new voice to the dream of true freedom and equality. King delivered one of his most famous and important speeches during the March on Washington in 1963. It became known as the "I Have a Dream" speech because he repeatedly used that phrase.

Dr. King was assassinated during a 1968 visit to Memphis. Despite his untimely death, the dreams inspired by his words and courageous life continue to give people hope to this day.

In 1998 the mayor of Memphis commissioned a song for the thirtieth anniversary of Dr. King's death. Many songs were submitted. The song "The Gift" was chosen to be performed at the celebration.

The musical structure of "The Gift" uses a pattern of alternating between the soloist and other singers that is similar to **call and response**. This refers to a song form in which each phrase sung by a solo leader is then followed by a phrase sung by the group.

LISTENING CD 9:2

The Gift by Mary Unobsky and Alan Roy Scott

Teens from the Memphis, Tennessee, area ranging in age from 14 to 21 comprise this Echoes of Truth ensemble performing "The Gift." Teens who volunteer or work for Echoes of Truth come from challenging life circumstances. They need to show team spirit, a positive work ethic, and the desire to achieve at high levels in order to participate in the program. They work closely with teachers who help them achieve the highest possible standards of performance and creative expression.

Listen to the recording of "The Gift" and identify where call and response is used.

Another musical technique used in "The Gift" is called **modulation**, or transition from a section of music based on one scale to a section based on a different scale. Usually the second scale is higher than the first.

Listen to "The Gift" again and try to identify where modulation occurs.

music.mmhschool.com
Learn more about Dr. King and how communities throughout the country continue to celebrate his dream today.

The Life and Legacy of Rev. Dr. Martin Luther King, Jr.

1948	*Receives BA in sociology from Morehouse College*
1951	*Receives degree from Crozer Theological Seminary, enrolls in Boston University*
1953	*Marries BU music student Coretta Scott*
1954	*Becomes minister of Dexter Avenue Baptist Church, Montgomery, Alabama*
1955	*Receives PhD in systematic theology from Boston University*
	Leads boycott of segregated Montgomery buses, gains national reputation
1956	*U.S. Supreme Court ruling prompts Montgomery to desegregate buses*
1957	*King helps found Southern Christian Leadership Conference (SCLC)*
1963	*Delivers "I Have a Dream" speech during March on Washington; creates powerful image, builds momentum for civil rights legislation*
1964	*Receives Nobel Peace Prize*
1968	*Assassinated in Memphis during visit to support striking black garbage collectors; Rep. John Conyers introduces legislation for federal holiday to commemorate King*
1973	*Illinois is first state to adopt Martin Luther King, Jr., Day as a state holiday*
1983	*Martin Luther King, Jr., Day created by Congress*
1986	*Federal Martin Luther King, Jr., holiday goes into effect*
1999	*New Hampshire becomes last state to adopt a state Martin Luther King, Jr., holiday*

Acting with Courage

It's not enough just to dream about better days to come. You need to work hard to make your dreams come true. "Follow Your Dream" was inspired by the care, courage, confidence, and commitment of people like Dr. King. Dr. King's dream involved a special kind of commitment—the kind that motivates and inspires other people to pursue the same dream. This kind of dream can become reality only when pursued in cooperation with others.

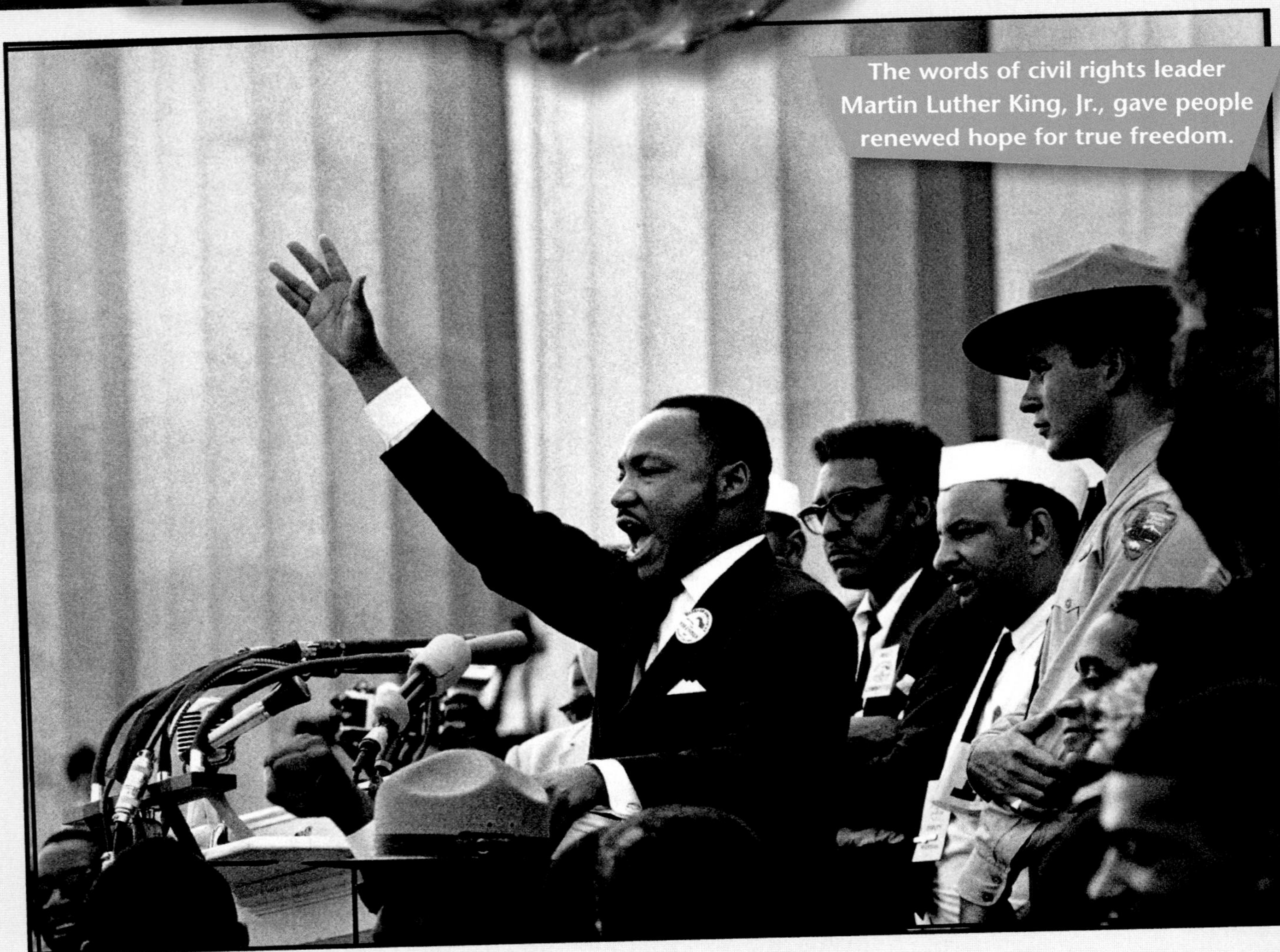

The words of civil rights leader Martin Luther King, Jr., gave people renewed hope for true freedom.

Follow Your Dream
CD 9:3
Words and Music by
Janet McMahan-Wilson and Ted Wilson
Freely
do
F♯m E F♯m E F♯m E F♯m E
Fol - low, fol - low, fol - low your dream wher -
A E
ev - er it may lead you.
F♯m E F♯m E F♯m E F♯m E
Fol - low, fol - low, fol - low your dream wher -
A E
ev - er peo - ple need you.
C♯m F♯m E A E F♯7 E
Heal a heart, hold a hand. It's time to start to take a stand, so
F♯m E F♯m E F♯m G♯m F♯m E
Last time do these two measures two more times
Fine
fol - low, fol - low, fol - low your dream.
1. It may
2. You may be
A F♯m Bm A
take you through the val - ley or to the moun - tain - top. Down the
sing - ing in the sun - shine or march - ing through the rain. When you're
G D G
crowd - ed streets and the lone - ly roads,
trav - el - ing to the prom - ised land,
1. B E A B
nev - er nev - er stop.
2. B E A B
D.C. al Fine
push right past the pain.

Finding Your Way

The Dixie Chicks know what it takes to follow a dream. This female trio from Texas has worked hard to develop its unique mix of bluegrass, country, and pop music and has found great success. One of the many honors the Dixie Chicks have received is a Grammy Award for Best Country album in 1998 with *Wide Open Spaces.*

The Dixie Chicks pose for a photo at The American Music Awards.

LISTENING **CD 9:8**

Wide Open Spaces by Susan L. Gibson

This song by Susan Gibson was made famous by the Dixie Chicks. No matter who is singing this song, the message remains the same. It's about what a young girl needs to pursue her dreams.

Listen to "Wide Open Spaces."

Analyze how the instrumentation reflects bluegrass, country, and popular styles.

Explain the meaning of the lyrics in terms of your own dreams.

MIDI

See ***Spotlight on MIDI*** for help in creating your own inspirational song.

Wide Open Spaces

by Susan Lauralee Gibson

Who doesn't know what I'm talking about?
Who's never left home who'd never struck out
To find a dream and a life of their own—
A place in the clouds, a foundation of stone.
Many precede and many will follow
A young girl's dream no longer hollow.
It takes the shape of a place out West
But what it holds for her, she hasn't yet guessed.

Refrain
She needs wide open spaces,
Room to make her big mistakes.
She needs new faces.
She knows the high stakes.

She traveled this road as a child.
Wide-eyed and grinning, she never tired.
But now she won't be coming back with the rest.
If these are life's lessons, she'll take this test.

(Refrain)

As her folks drive away, her Dad yells,
"Check the oil!"
Mom stares out the window and says,
"I'm leaving my girl."
She says, "It didn't seem like that long ago
When she stood there and let her own folks know."

(Refrain)

Looking Back

Celebrating with music means different things to different people. Together we celebrate the people and events from the past that have helped make us who we are today. We celebrate the heritage we share as well as the cultures that make us unique. We also celebrate our personal hopes and dreams and the hopes and dreams we work toward together. What role has music played in the celebrations of your own musical family history?

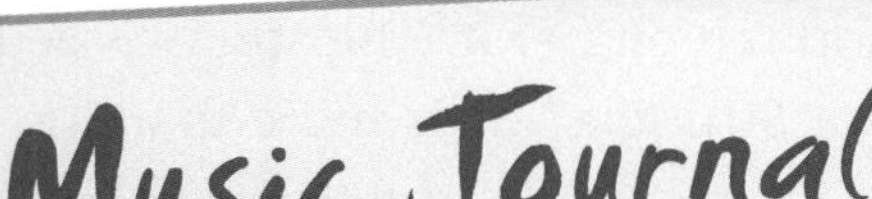

Which composer or performing artist who has played a role in celebrating my own family's musical history would I most like to interview? What kinds of questions would I ask? What kinds of answers would I hope to find?

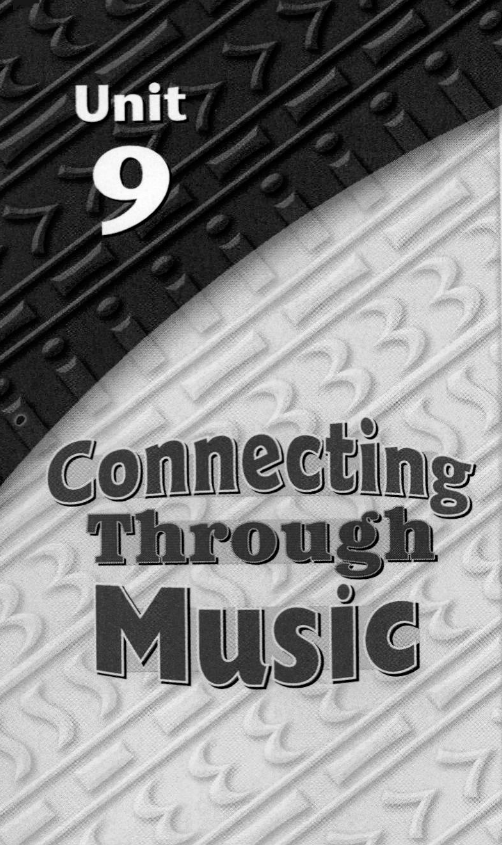

The Sounds of Freedom

Music draws people together in ways that nothing else can. As you have learned, it not only connects you with other people, it also connects you with your own deepest emotions. Music ties you to your cultural heritage and the things you feel most strongly about. The more in touch you are with these things, the more you can connect with others. For example, music has the power to draw together people who fight against injustice or care about the environment. A common zeal for music unites artists who create and perform in different styles. The same music even inspires people across generations and decades, forging a link from the past to the present, and from the present to the future.

One style of music that brings people together for a common cause is folk music. With its straightforward texts and simple melodies, folk music discusses everyday matters in such a way that once people hear the music, they quickly learn and remember it. The song "Freedom Is a Constant Struggle" does more than just tell a story. It rallies people together, especially people who struggle with issues of freedom.

This choir sang at the inauguration of President Nelson Mandela. The choir robes reflect the design and colors of the South African flag.

Sing the melody of "Freedom Is a Constant Struggle" with expression.

Freedom Is a Constant Struggle

CD 9:9

American Freedom Song

Am

1.-4. They say that free - dom is a con - stant

D7

(1., 4.) strug - gle. / (2.) sor - row. / (3.) cry - ing. They say that free - dom is a con - stant

Am

(1., 4.) strug - gle. / (2.) sor - row. / (3.) cry - ing. They say that free - dom is a con - stant

D7

strug - gle. O Lord,_ we've strug-gled too long.___
sor - row. O Lord,_ we've sor-rowed so long.___
cry - ing. O Lord,_ we've cried_ so long.___ We must be

Am

1., 2., 3. | 4.

free, We must be free. free.___

F D7 Am

___ We've strug-gled too long.___ We must be free.

music.mmhschool.com
Read more about the role of music in the struggle for civil rights.

A Timeless Rallying Song

In the 1960s, one song emerged as the anthem of the civil rights movement. "We Shall Overcome" is characteristic of what became known as "protest" or "message" songs. Inspired by the late Dr. Martin Luther King, Jr., and his preaching against the injustice and racial discrimination against African Americans, the song continues to unite people today.

Not only did Pete Seeger help write "We Shall Overcome," but he is one of many musicians who have performed it.

We Shall Overcome

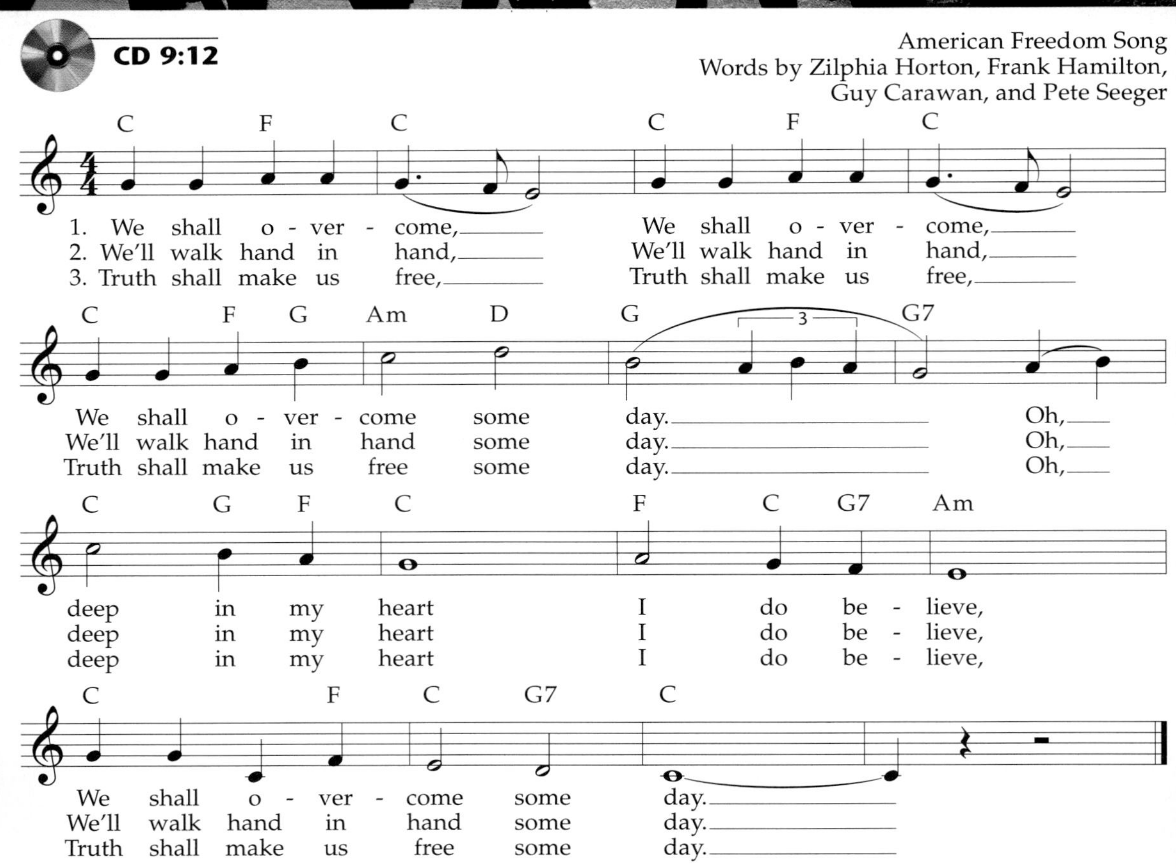
CD 9:12
American Freedom Song
Words by Zilphia Horton, Frank Hamilton, Guy Carawan, and Pete Seeger
C F C C F C
1. We shall o - ver - come, We shall o - ver - come,
2. We'll walk hand in hand, We'll walk hand in hand,
3. Truth shall make us free, Truth shall make us free,
C F G Am D G 3 G7
We shall o - ver - come some day. Oh,
We'll walk hand in hand some day. Oh,
Truth shall make us free some day. Oh,
C G F C F C G7 Am
deep in my heart I do be - lieve,
deep in my heart I do be - lieve,
deep in my heart I do be - lieve,
C F C G7 C
We shall o - ver - come some day.
We'll walk hand in hand some day.
Truth shall make us free some day.

Sing "We Shall Overcome" with the recording.

Discuss the song in terms of other forms of oppression with which you are personally familiar. How would you sing the song again without the recording, taking liberties to sing it more freely and expressively?

LISTENING CD 9:15

We Shall Overcome (Howard University Gospel Choir) by Zilphia Horton, Frank Hamilton, Guy Carawan, and Pete Seeger

Under the direction of Arphelius Paul Gatling III, this college-age ensemble from Washington, D.C., gives an inspiring performance of "We Shall Overcome."

Listen to "We Shall Overcome" performed by the Howard University Gospel Choir.

Compare this arrangement with the first recording you heard of "We Shall Overcome."

Describe the expressive qualities that help make the gospel choir version especially inspiring.

Identify where the key change occurs in the gospel choir version. Notice the **descant** that is sung above the melody after the modulation occurs. A descant is a counterpoint sung above the basic melody.

Rosa Parks, "mother" of the civil rights movement

Howard University Gospel Choir When Rosa Parks received the Congressional Gold Medal on June 15, 1994, the emotional climax of the ceremony came when the great opera singer Jessye Norman joined with the Howard University Gospel Choir to sing "We Shall Overcome." It was a fitting honor for the "mother" of the civil rights movement. President William Jefferson Clinton thanked them for their "wonderful, wonderful music." Founded in 1968, the choir is recognized as one of the finest choirs in the United States. The Howard University Gospel Choir has become world famous for its performances of African American spirituals and work songs, as well as choral works by composers of African descent.

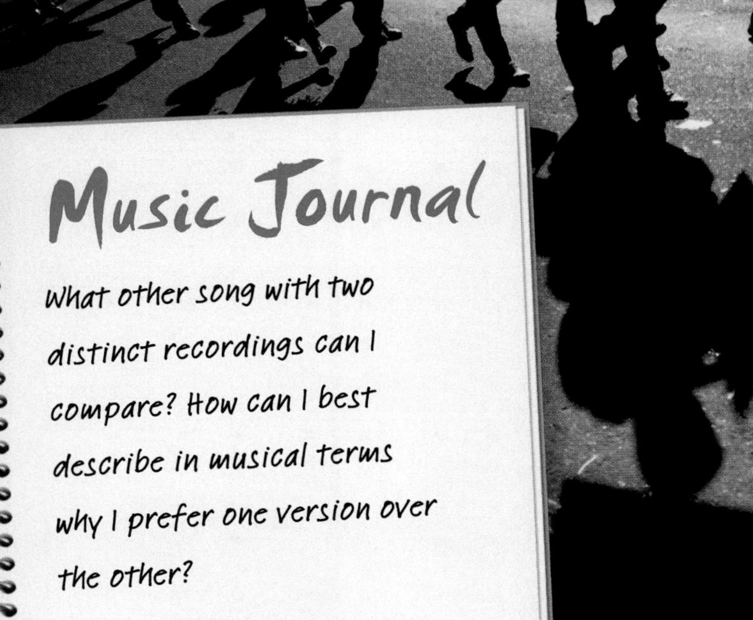

Music Journal

What other song with two distinct recordings can I compare? How can I best describe in musical terms why I prefer one version over the other?

Protest Music of South Africa

Voices speaking out against racial injustice in South Africa are among the most inspired in the world. For years South Africa's apartheid policy mandated racial segregation, which severely restricted the rights and suppressed the economic development of the nonwhite population. The South African people resisted and were backed by the world's most powerful countries, which imposed economic sanctions. Apartheid laws were finally repealed during the early 1990s through a series of reforms. Nelson Mandela is the leader who most fervently championed the struggle for liberation in South Africa.

THE LION SLEEPS TONIGHT

The beautiful singing with lush harmony that has become a trademark of South African protest songs, along with the conviction of the singers, makes this protest music especially effective. One of America's first encounters with this harmony was in the early 1960s when a traditional Zulu tribal song called "Mbube" (The Lion) was brought to America by a folk group called The Weavers. In the United States, the song is known as "The Lion Sleeps Tonight."

Sing each part of the accompaniment separately, then in four parts. Notice that the bass clef part consists of the roots for the I, IV, and V chords.

Sing through the entire song with the recording.

Sing the song using only the sung accompaniment or using guitar accompaniment.

Nelson Mandela visits a school in South Africa.

Meet the Musician

ON NATIONAL RADIO!

Name: Ben Pila
Age: 17
Instrument: Guitar
Hometown: Tampa, FL

Ben Pila never thought he would play classical guitar. "I started out in the world of heavy metal," he says. "I was into bands like Metallica, Ozzy Osbourne, Black Sabbath, and Led Zeppelin." He envisioned himself playing in a rock band one day.

Ben entered a high school for performing arts intending to study electric guitar, but was horrified to learn that the teacher he wanted to study with had been replaced. "The new teacher walked into the classroom carrying a classical guitar," recalls Ben. "I was like, 'Ugh, get me out of here!'"

A short time later Ben found out that Randy Rhoads, a guitarist who played with Ozzy Osbourne, wrote a classical piece influenced by a Bach flute suite. "I figured, if Randy Rhoads liked classical music I should at least give it a chance, so I learned the piece he ripped off!" Once Ben realized he could mix rock with classical music he began to enjoy playing classical guitar.

"Classical guitar is more of a challenge than electric guitar," says Ben. There are techniques that aren't used in rock guitar at all." As much as Ben loves playing classical guitar, every so often he still plugs in his electric guitar and rocks out.

RECORDED INTERVIEW

Listen to Ben's performance of "Sunburst" by Andrew York **(CD 10:1)** and his interview **(CD 10:2)** on the national radio program From the Top.

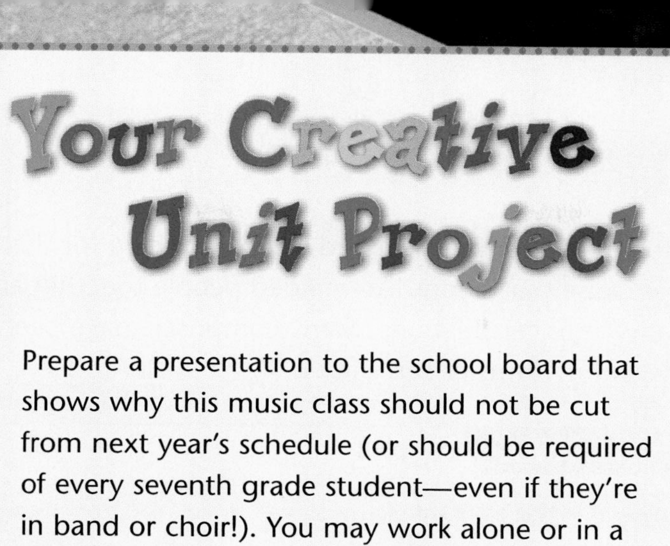

Your Creative Unit Project

Prepare a presentation to the school board that shows why this music class should not be cut from next year's schedule (or should be required of every seventh grade student—even if they're in band or choir!). You may work alone or in a group. Your project/presentation must be clear and focused with a manageable topic. The information presented should give the audience important and accurate facts and should be organized with details supporting the main ideas. You may use music and media to support your ideas and to hold the audience's attention. Your project/presentation is to show your personal understanding of the role of music in life in general. It should also give specific personal insights into music and its relevance to your life. You might also show how music has impacted your thinking about a career or how music impacts the economy. The final product can be in any form that represents or communicates what you have learned and why this class is valuable. The form could be a new musical composition, a play, a TV or radio show, a poem, a scrapbook or photo album with captions, a panel presentation, a videotape, a multimedia presentation, or a mural.

Music and the Environment

Like the quests for freedom and justice, concern for the environment is another cause that brings like-minded people together and inspires new, innovative musical creations. Many composers have been inspired by the sounds and rhythms of Earth itself.

LISTENING **CD 10:3**

Ocean Child by Paul Winter

In 1980, jazz saxophonist Paul Winter produced an album which paired recordings of various sea mammals with original compositions. He called the album *Earth: Voices of a Planet*. Winter uses the beauty of natural sounds to remind the listener of Earth's beauty and the fragility of endangered species. In his composition "Ocean Child," Winter combines recordings of Orca whales, also known as killer whales, that were taped in the Johnston Straits of British Columbia. The sounds in "Ocean Child" are understood to be a calf, or baby whale, and its parents communicating with one another.

Listen to "Ocean Child."

Describe what you think the piano accompaniment and soprano saxophone might represent in this composition.

LOG ON

music.mmhschool.com
Learn more about Paul Winter and his "sounds of nature."

LISTENING CD 10:4

The Moldau from *Má Vlast* by Bedřich Smetana

"Moldau" is actually the German word for *Vltava*, the Czech name for the river. "The Moldau" is a famous composition by the Czech composer Bedřich Smetana. In this **tone poem**, Smetana seeks to create a musical picture of the Moldau, a river that runs through the western Czech Republic. A tone poem is a work for orchestra that tells a story through music.

Listen to "The Moldau" and decide how accurately the music depicts the river in the photograph below. How does Smetana use the tone colors of the music to "paint" an image of the river?

LOG ON

music.mmhschool.com
Learn more about musical compositions that address environmental concerns.

Vltava (Moldau) River, Prague, Czech Republic

Music Journal

If I were to create or perform a piece of music about Earth, which composer's example would I be more likely to follow—Winter's or Smetana's? Why?

Meet Líbana

The members of Libana clearly show their joy in making music.

Music drawn from people's connection with Earth can be more than descriptive. Many musicians also use music to connect to other people and to share their passion for Earth. Libana is an ensemble that champions the joy of singing in the community at large while fostering respect for our natural environments. Their music includes a broad range of songs that draw from Native American, Eastern and Western European, African, Middle Eastern, and contemporary folk sources.

LISTENING **CD 10:5**

The Earth Is Our Mother (Libana)

Tap the rhythm pattern as you listen to Libana's rendition of "The Earth Is Our Mother." "The Earth Is Our Mother" has many versions in which different performing artists have added their own personal touches and distinctive lyrics.

Sing "The Earth Is Our Mother" in two-part harmony.

Improvise your own unpitched percussion accompaniment.

THE EARTH IS OUR MOTHER
CD 10:6
Adapted Native American
Harmony
Melody
The Earth_ is our Mo - ther, we must take care of Her. The
Earth_ is our Mo - ther, we must take care of Her.
Hey_ yan-na, ho_ yan-na, hey_ yan yan. Hey_yan-na, ho_ yan-na, hey_ yan yan.

Additional Verse:
Her sacred ground we walk upon with every step we take.
Her sacred ground we walk upon with every step we take.
Hey yanna, ho yanna, hey yan yan.
Hey yanna, ho yanna, hey yan yan.

Creating Environmental Awareness

In the later twentieth century, several composers addressed the quality of Earth's environment. Protest songs about the environment abounded in the 1970s and 1980s.

LISTENING **CD 10:10**

Stonehaven Sunset by John Denver

John Denver's "Stonehaven Sunset" addresses more than just environmental issues. Its poetic lyrics speak of very personal ways that people are affected by violence, war, and injustices. Denver calls us all to account for the role each of us can play in working toward a better quality of life. He inspires us to more deeply appreciate the beauty of the people and natural environments around us.

Listen to "Stonehaven Sunset" and discuss its lyrics.

Stonehaven Sunset

Words and music by John Denver

Stonehaven Sunset, the water's on fire;
My true love is singing, we kiss and conspire.
Sing a song for the ocean, a song for the sky,
A song for tomorrow, love, sweet by and by.
For the child who is coming and for dreams that come true,
Sing a song for each other, for me and for you.
Sing a song for all lovers, all the stars in the skies.
Sing of Stonehaven water home, Stonehaven Sunrise.

Stonehaven Sunset, the desert's on fire.
Christ on the cross again burns with desire.
They are shooting at random, though they aim at us all.
It's the children who rise up and children who fall.
All the angels are weeping; the sweetest of tears
Fall like rivers of mercy to wash all our fears.
Sing a song for Old Glory and a future that dies.
Sing of Stonehaven desert home, Stonehaven Sunrise . . .

. . . Stonehaven Sunset, the mountain's on fire.
My spirit is lifted, rising higher and higher.
All the prophets are laughing; they say, "We told you so."
It's one thing to play guessing games, another to know.
For the needs of the many are the sins of a few,
And the day is forthcoming when accounting is due.
Sing a song for sweet justice with a fire in her eyes.
Sing of Stonehaven mountain home, Stonehaven Sunrise.

First verse repeats.

Meet the Musician

John Denver (1943–1996) is one of the most loved songwriters of his generation. Born in Roswell, New Mexico, Denver was among the first performing artists from the West to tour mainland China in the early 1990s. Denver was surprised by how many people knew by heart the words to nearly all of his songs.

Denver's grandmother gave him his first acoustic guitar before he was a teenager. After playing in rock and roll bands during high school, Denver started playing in folk clubs in the Los Angeles area during college. One of the most successful recording artists ever, he also co-founded a non-profit environmental education and research center in 1976. Denver tragically died in a plane crash at the age of 53.

Honoring the Environment

In recent decades, composers have also addressed the destruction of natural habitats and defenseless animals. Libby Larsen's *Mass for the Earth*, composed for a classical style ensemble, is one example.

LISTENING **CD 10:11**

Gloria from *Mass for the Earth* by Libby Larsen

Music for a traditional Mass can include a variety of musical moods, from very somber to celebratory. In *Mass for the Earth*, Larsen adopts traditional texts to address people's relationship with Mother Earth. Larsen's text for the "Gloria" is from the poet Gerard Manley Hopkins, which begins "Glory be to God for dappled things . . ." and concludes with "Praise him." But Larsen's intent is not only to praise God. She also seeks to express reverence for Mother Earth to whom we owe reverence for all she gives to us. This performance by the Oregon Repertory Singers is conducted by Gilbert Seeley.

Listen to "Gloria."

Describe the mood of this excerpt and what musical qualities help express it.

Libby Larsen (b. 1950) studied music at the University of Minnesota. One of the most important composers in the United States since the 1980s, Larsen has composed for orchestra, opera, and theater as well as dance, choral, and vocal repertoire. She calls her *Mass for the Earth* a celebration of "a land which can be terribly beautiful and gentle, a land which can be harsh, but which is always giving and renewing."

LISTENING CD 10:12

Aideu Yoruban Folk Song

The lyrics of "Aideu" are a prayer addressed to Ochun. Ochun is one of many gods worshipped by the Yoruba people of West Africa, whose religion has been very influential in Brazil and Cuba. Traditions of nature worship and ancestor reverence, along with celebrations that feature drumming and dancing, are important in the lives of the Yoruba people.

The Cuban-Latin band Conjunto Céspedes is based in Oakland, California.

Listen to "Aideu" as you follow the listening chart.

Intro (with bells ringing)	$3\frac{1}{2}$ measures
Female vocal solo	
Phrase 1	8 measures
Phrase 2	8 measures
Phrase 3	8 measures
Female vocal duet	
Phrase 1	8 measures
Phrase 2	8 measures
Phrase 3	8 measures
Call	2 measures
Refrain	36 measures (4-measure phrase repeated 9 times)

Sing and play these parts for "Aideu." You may play the vocal parts on mallet instruments rather than sing them.

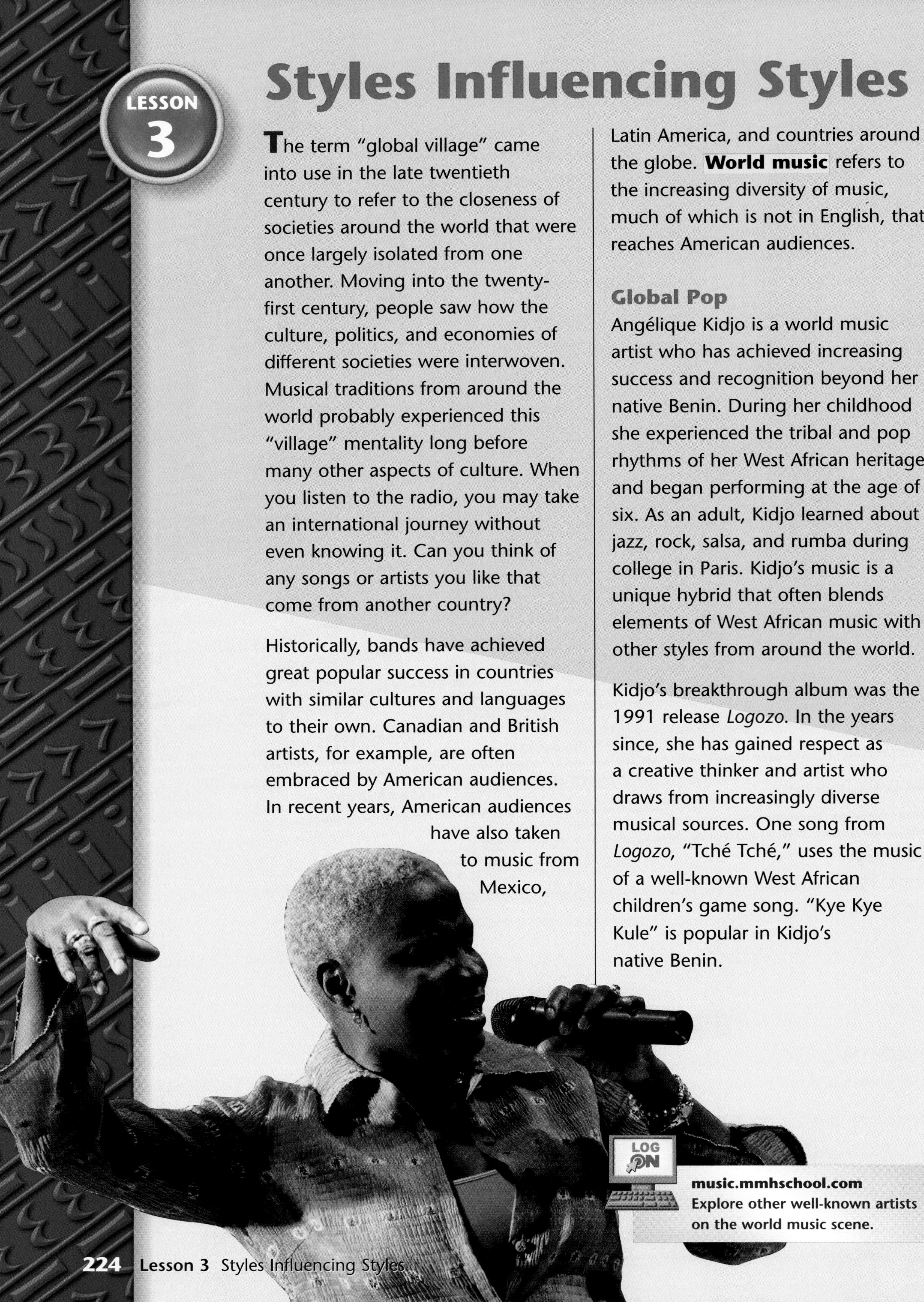

Styles Influencing Styles

The term "global village" came into use in the late twentieth century to refer to the closeness of societies around the world that were once largely isolated from one another. Moving into the twenty-first century, people saw how the culture, politics, and economies of different societies were interwoven. Musical traditions from around the world probably experienced this "village" mentality long before many other aspects of culture. When you listen to the radio, you may take an international journey without even knowing it. Can you think of any songs or artists you like that come from another country?

Historically, bands have achieved great popular success in countries with similar cultures and languages to their own. Canadian and British artists, for example, are often embraced by American audiences. In recent years, American audiences have also taken to music from Mexico, Latin America, and countries around the globe. **World music** refers to the increasing diversity of music, much of which is not in English, that reaches American audiences.

Global Pop

Angélique Kidjo is a world music artist who has achieved increasing success and recognition beyond her native Benin. During her childhood she experienced the tribal and pop rhythms of her West African heritage and began performing at the age of six. As an adult, Kidjo learned about jazz, rock, salsa, and rumba during college in Paris. Kidjo's music is a unique hybrid that often blends elements of West African music with other styles from around the world.

Kidjo's breakthrough album was the 1991 release *Logozo*. In the years since, she has gained respect as a creative thinker and artist who draws from increasingly diverse musical sources. One song from *Logozo*, "Tché Tché," uses the music of a well-known West African children's game song. "Kye Kye Kule" is popular in Kidjo's native Benin.

LOG ON

music.mmhschool.com
Explore other well-known artists on the world music scene.

Listen to "Kye Kye Kule." How is the song organized between the leader and the group? Why do you think this song would be easy for children to learn?

Play these percussion parts to accompany "Kye Kye Kule."

Bridging Cultural Gaps

One of the most striking effects in Angélique Kidjo's music is her combination of so many different musical styles. In recent years she has drawn not only on West African and Western European styles, but also on *Bahia* and other music from Brazil and Latin America. "Afirika" is a classic example of how Kidjo bridges the gap between and among different cultures in her music.

LISTENING **CD 10:14**

Afirika by Angélique Kidjo, Jean L. Hebrail, and Thomas E. Faragher

"Afirika" is from Kidjo's 2002 album *Black Ivory Soul* which features a multinational ensemble from Benin, France, Brazil, and the United States. Kidjo's inspiration for this album was her belief that music alone has the power to heal pain and bring people together. Her goal is to inspire people to think on a deeper level about poverty, freedom, and family.

Listen to "Afirika" and decide which body percussion pattern best fits the meter of the song.

Clap snap-snap   Clap snap-snap-snap

Identify musical styles of the various cultures.

Listen to the English lyrics and discuss what Kidjo means by "black ivory soul."

"Music is not only emotion and groove. It's something that speaks for a culture and its people."

—Angélique Kidjo

Mexican and Canadian Influences

Read the lists of musicians and performing groups from Mexico and Canada (or those who have roots in these countries) below. Which of these artists are you familiar with? What additions would you make to these lists? What contributions have these performers made to American culture and music? What other cultures or nations might you add in order to more broadly represent the many influences on the American music scene?

Music Journal

If I were introducing someone from another country to the music of my culture, which music and performing artists would I highlight to help that person appreciate all that the music of my culture offers?

Canadian Performers

Crash Test Dummies
Robert Goulet
The Guess Who
Heart
Diana Krall
k.d. Lang
Gordon Lightfoot
Sarah MacLachlan
Joni Mitchell
Alanis Morissette
Our Lady Peace
Steppenwolf
The Tragically Hip
Shania Twain
Rufus Wainwright
Neil Young

Mexican Performers

Carlos Santana
Lola Beltrán
Los Fabulosos Cadillacs
Molotov
Maná
Tierra Caliente
Café Tacuba
Los Jaguares
El Tri
Los Tigres del Norte
Luis Miguel
Natalia Lafourcade
Thalía
Tatiana

American-born Mexican Performers

Selena (born in Lake Jackson, TX)
Los Lobos (born in Los Angeles, CA)
Herb Alpert (born in Los Angeles, CA)
Flaco Jiménez (born in San Antonio, TX)
Ritchie Valens (born in Pacoima, CA)
Los Kumbia Kings (born in Texas)

Pieces of Africa

In 1992 the Kronos String Quartet album *Pieces of Africa* topped both Billboard's classical and world music charts at the same time. This album has sold more than 300,000 copies!

Why was this album so successful? The Kronos Quartet moved well beyond the traditional role of a string quartet as small chamber ensemble playing compositions of classical composers. *Pieces of Africa* drew the quartet into collaboration with seven composer-performers from all over the continent of Africa. Each of these indigenous composers created a piece of music for string quartet. Voices and traditional African instruments combined with the string quartet to form new tone colors and textures.

In *Pieces of Africa*, the traditional four-movement form associated with the string quartet was replaced with eight movements, each based on a different story or literary idea.

Movement I was written by Dumisani Maraire, of the Manyika province in Zimbabwe. The title of this movement is "Mai Nozipo," which means "Mother Nozipo."

LISTENING **CD 10:15**

Mai Nozipo by Dumisani Maraire

"Mai Nozipo" portrays the life of the composer's mother, who died in 1989. Maraire describes the organization of "Mai Nozipo" as follows:

Part 1: His life with his mother on Earth, which was "very long and full of caring and happiness"

Part 2: Sadness, portraying her death

Part 3: Happiness again, celebrating that "my mother is well, she cares for and looks after me and all her children still on Earth and she now lives her new life in the world of spirits or in heaven"

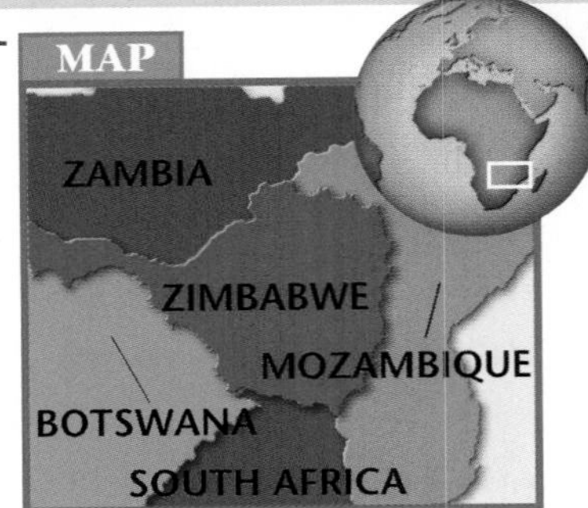

Learn to play this four-measure musical question and answer from Part 1 of "Mai Nozipo."

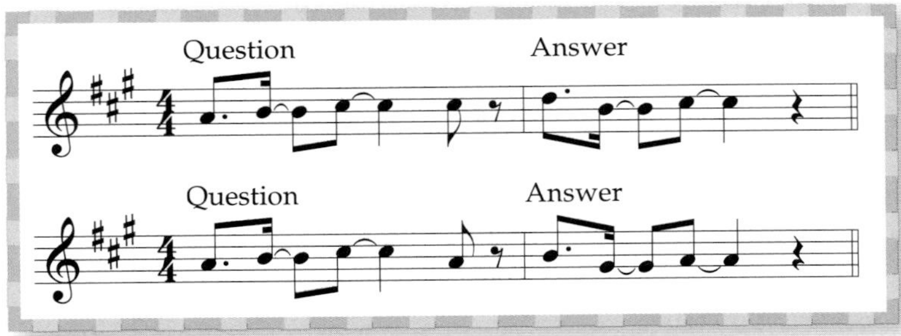

Decide how the pitch at the end of the first answer has a different function from the pitch at the end of the second answer.

Analyze the listening map of "Mai Nozipo."

Listening Map for *Mai Nozipo*

Part 1 Question-Answer repeated 10 times
Shona drum and string bows on wood - 4 measures
String bows on wood -12 measures
String bows on wood with hosho (shaker) and strings enter - 4 measures
Question- Answer returns - softly

Part 2 (Sadness portraying Mother Nozipo's death)
Slower, softer, less active rhythmically
Fragments of question-answer present

Part 3 (Return to Happiness portraying that Mother Nozipo is well in heaven)
Question-Answer returns as in Part 1

Meet the Musicians

When he formed the **Kronos Quartet** in 1973, David Harrington aimed to "tell the whole story, if possible." For more than three decades, Kronos has been breaking musical barriers and going where no string quartet has ever gone before. The quartet's repertoire ranges from Béla Bartók to Jimi Hendrix, from Franz Liszt to Thelonious Monk, from Hildegard von Bingen to Frank Zappa. Their many collaborators have included Indian tabla master Zakir Hussain, poet Allen Ginsberg, the Mexican band Café Tacuba, and the Throat Singers of Tuva. "There are strange things in the air today," says Harrington, "and musicians are responding the only way they can—through music."

LOG ON

music.mmhschool.com
Explore the unique experimental music world of The Kronos Quartet.

Connecting with Tomorrow

People connect to others in many different ways. Describe what you think is happening in each vignette in the illustration below.

Through the course of each day, we encounter and interact with other people. Because people are social in nature, we generally enjoy the companionship of others. True, there are times when we want or need to be alone. However, overall we value sharing ourselves, our ideas, and our thoughts with other people. We enjoy learning more about our lives by connecting with the lives of others. Think about the different ways you interact with other people and groups.

"Music expresses that which cannot be said and on which it is impossible to be silent."

—Victor Hugo

Music is a form of human communication. It can be an important way to share something about ourselves. Through music, we can express more than just words. We connect with people on a deeper level.

In the game charades, people attempt to communicate a written phrase or idea without words. Select a word or topic from the following list and communicate it to others without using words. Identify additional musical words and phrases, and play the game again.

Heavy	Staccato	Raining	It's time to take a bath.
Presto	Slow	Tall	The train is leaving!

Describe how not using words challenges your communication skills.

Music Journal

Some music has words that are sung and some music doesn't. When does music with words communicate better than music without words? Why? When does music without words communicate more effectively? Why?

music.mmhschool.com
Read what people are saying about the music of the future.

Connection Challenges Tradition

Regardless of where or when we live, the arts help us better understand one another. They can also expand our own self-understanding.

Some artists and composers create art which is viewed as strange or different by people at the time it is created. It can take years, or even decades, before it is valued for its contributions to people's lives.

Pablo Picasso (1881–1973) was a Spanish painter and sculptor, considered by many to be the greatest artist of the twentieth century. He was a unique inventor of forms and innovator of styles and techniques. Picasso was one of the most prolific artists in history, having created more than 20,000 art works.

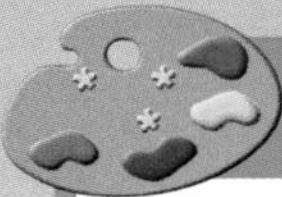

Art Gallery

This unnamed sculpture by Pablo Picasso stands in the Daley Plaza in downtown Chicago, IL.

LISTENING **CD 10:16**

St. Matthew Passion (J. S. Bach) and *The Rite of Spring* (Igor Stravinsky) (excerpts)

Today the music of German church musician-composer Johann Sebastian Bach (1685–1750) is considered among the most profound music ever composed. In his lifetime, however, Bach and his music were viewed as merely adequate. Eighty years after his death, his *Saint Matthew Passion* was performed for the first time.

German composer Felix Mendelssohn (1809–1847) once conducted the *St. Matthew Passion.* That performance created renewed interest in Bach's music, interest which continues today.

Now regarded as a ground-breaking twentieth-century masterpiece, Stavinsky's *The Rite of Spring* initially caused

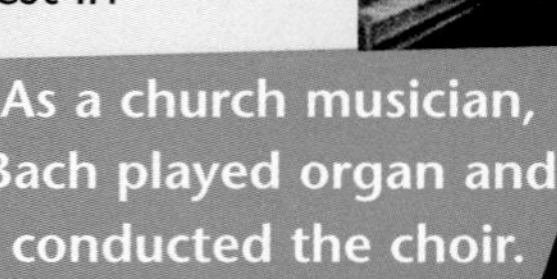

As a church musician, Bach played organ and conducted the choir.

quite a stir. "Well, it started with shouts, catcalls, and whistles from the audience. Then some fistfights in the aisles soon turned into a riot!" This statement describes a 1913 riot in Paris, France, at the Théâtre des Champs-Élysées. This famous ballet house was the site of the first performance of *The Rite of Spring* (Le Sacre du Printemps). Russian composer Igor Stravinsky (1881–1972) and choreographer Vaslav Nijinsky were presenting their new ballet—and people were rioting!

Listen to excerpts from J. S. Bach's *Saint Matthew Passion* and Igor Stravinsky's *The Rite of Spring*. Identify some of the musical characteristics which contributed to the pieces' being overlooked and considered by some critics to be controversial.

Igor Stravinsky

music.mmhschool.com Read more about J. S. Bach and other Baroque era composers who are still widely performed today.

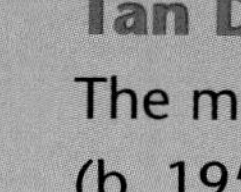

Tan Dun

The music of Chinese composer Tan Dun (b. 1957) is performed throughout the world by today's leading orchestras and ensembles. Like Bach, he has composed music using text from the Gospel of Saint Matthew. Unlike Bach, however, Tan Dun uses unusual instruments—including seventeen transparent water bowls, various percussion instruments, and electronically processed sounds of exotic, ancient string instruments as well as the violin and cello.

LISTENING CD 10:17

Water Cadenza from *Water Passion After St. Matthew*

by Tan Dun

Listen to "Water Cadenza" from *Water Passion After Saint Matthew.*

Discuss how you think listeners may have initially responded to this music.

Tan Dun

Music Journal

What do I think might help to ensure that Tan Dun's music will connect with people in five hundred years, as he hopes?

Connecting to Tomorrow

French author Jules Verne (1828–1905) is one of the most famous science fiction authors in the world. His well-known 1870 book *20,000 Leagues Under the Sea* describes a submarine, the *Nautilus*, which runs on a mysterious power source. In 1886 two Englishmen created an electric-powered submarine, and in 1955, a nuclear-powered submarine was launched. Both took the name *Nautilus*. Jules Verne connected with the world of tomorrow through his writing. He shared his ideas, thoughts, and feelings with other people. Imagine being able to connect with the world of tomorrow!

Writer Jules Verne

In 1977, the United States launched the robot spacecrafts *Voyager I* and *Voyager II*. Designed to explore the outer regions of our solar system, the spacecrafts are still traveling away from Earth at a speed of 1 million miles per day! Even more amazing is that they are still sending information back to Earth about what they are encountering.

Attached to each spacecraft in an aluminum case is a small, gold-coated copper phonograph record. On the record are examples of music from the people of Earth. Scientist Carl Sagan urged the inclusion of music on the spacecraft because "We are feeling creatures." By including music we make "a creditable attempt to convey human emotions." Part of the mission of *Voyagers I* and *II* is to try to connect with tomorrow, to share ourselves with others regardless of when they might find us.

If you could share something with people of tomorrow, what would it be? Music is a powerful way to share our human feelings and emotions. It can calm us, wake us up, and serve to help us touch the most sensitive aspects of our humanness. When we share with others through our music, we open ourselves up for new and exciting insights into life. We touch the future of our lives and of others.

Music Journal

If I were to create a "time capsule of music" to be opened ten years from now, what musical selections, composers, performing artists, and personal reflections would I include to represent both my present experience and my predictions about what our experience of music will be over the next ten years?

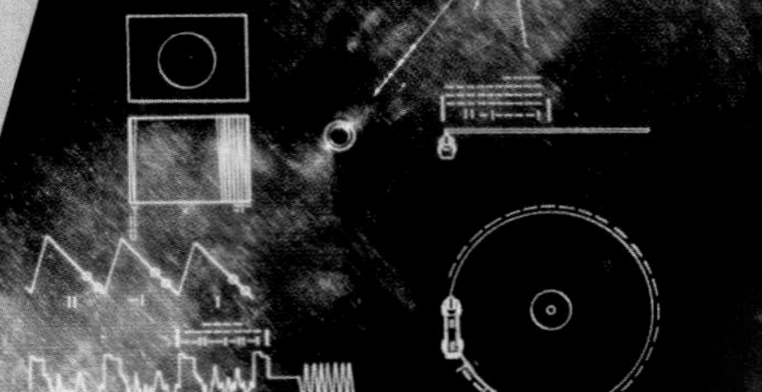

(right) Cover of the *Voyager 1* and *2* "Sounds of Earth" records

Looking Back

Look back through this unit to review some of the ways that music helps us make connections with people who share a passion for social and environmental issues as well as with people of various cultures around the world. What are some other ways that music helps you make connections? What have you learned in this unit and throughout this course about the value of music as part of your education as a middle school student and as a human being?

MTI's BROADWAY junior

RAGTIME
THE MUSICAL

Mini musicals specifically designed for classroom study and presentation, featuring scenes and songs from the musical Ragtime.

Book by Terrence McNally

Music by Stephen Flaherty

Lyrics by Lynn Ahrens

Based on the novel *Ragtime* by E. L. Doctorow

Musical Numbers

Ragtime

Success

Henry Ford

The Night That Goldman Spoke

Atlantic City

Ragtime Epilogue & Finale

Ragtime School Edition,
North Shore Music Theatre at Dunham Woods © 2003, Joshua Weisgrau

Libretto/Vocal Book

NARRATOR: Based on the Pulitzer Prize-winning novel by E. L. Doctorow, the musical *Ragtime* explores the influence of this particular form of music on American culture. Like many of the social and political changes facing the country, ragtime music was a revolutionary departure from the popular music that came before it.

About the Script

CHARACTER NAMES are colored **RED**

DIALOGUE is colored **BLUE**

STAGE DIRECTIONS are colored ***GREEN***

(Begin song introduction.)

NARRATOR: In 1902, the melting pot of influences that would make up the new century were colliding—especially in New York. The "well-to-do" built beautiful homes in New Rochelle and it seemed for some years thereafter their days would be sunny and warm.

Ragtime

CD 11:1
Music by Stephen Flaherty
Words by Lynn Ahrens
A little faster
People of New Rochelle:
mp
12
The skies were blue and ha - zy, rare-ly a storm, bare-ly
16
a chill. La - la - la - la - la! The af - ter - noons were la - zy,
Pt. 1
People of New Rochelle:
19
ev - ry - one warm, ev - ry - thing still. La - la - la - la - la! And there was
Pt. 2
People of New Rochelle:
22
dis - tant mu - sic, sim - ple and some - how sub - lime,
25
giv - ing the na - tion a new syn - co - pa - tion. The peo - ple called it Rag - time!
div.

(The following section of dialogue is underscored.)

NARRATOR: In Harlem, men and women of color forgot their troubles and danced and reveled to the music of Coalhouse Walker, Jr. This was a music that was theirs and no one else's.

(The IMMIGRANTS come forward, poorly clothed and undernourished.)

TATEH: Tateh, along with other immigrants from all over the globe, poured into New York's Ellis Island—escaping to the promise of freedom and opportunity.

GIRL: Houdini! Look, it's Houdini!

(HOUDINI appears with a flourish. The crowd applauds.)

HOUDINI: Harry Houdini was one immigrant who made an art of escape. He was a headliner in the top vaudeville circuits.

(HOUDINI'S MOTHER points with pride.)

HOUDINI'S MOTHER: Ich bin die Mutter des grossen Houdinis!

HOUDINI: He made his mother proud. But for all his achievement, he knew he was only an illusionist. He wanted to believe there was more.

(CROWD silently applauds. The moment is broken as HOUDINI is enveloped by his crowd of admirers.) (Song continues.)

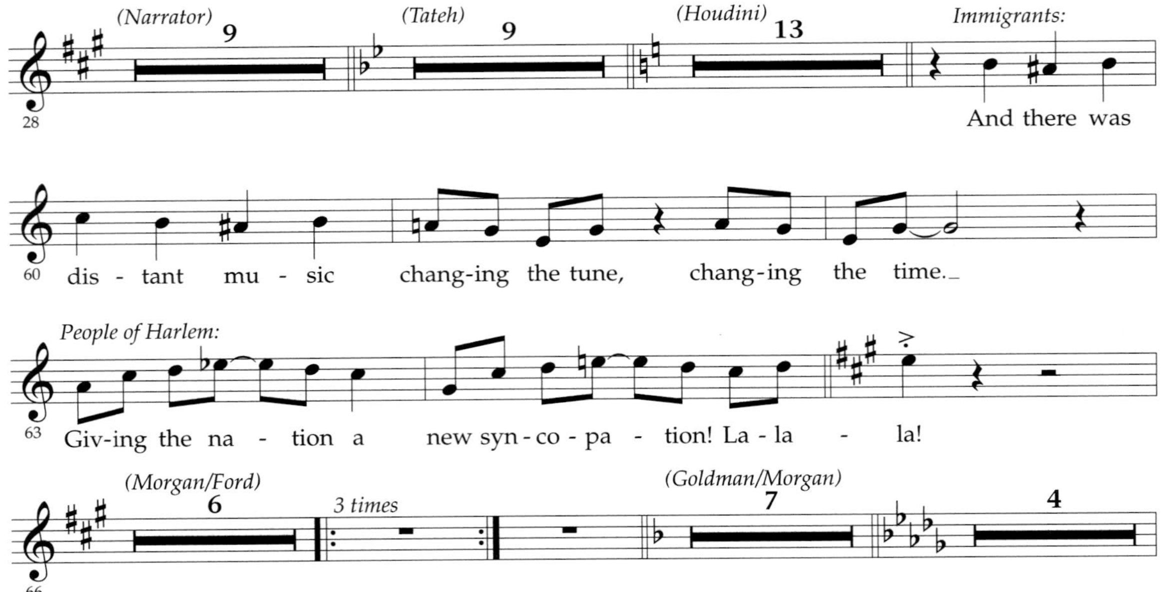

(The following section of dialogue is underscored.)

J.P. MORGAN: Certain people make a country great.

HENRY FORD: They can't help it.

J.P. MORGAN: At the very apex of the American pyramid—

HENRY FORD: —that's the very tip-top!

J.P. MORGAN: Like Pharaohs reincarnate, stood J.P. Morgan.

HENRY FORD: And Henry Ford.

J.P. MORGAN: All men are born equal.

HENRY FORD: But the cream rises to the top.

(EMMA GOLDMAN steps forward.)

EMMA GOLDMAN: Certain people were not treated as equal as others.

J.P. MORGAN: Someone should arrest that woman!

(J.P. MORGAN and HENRY FORD move away.)

EMMA GOLDMAN: One of them was Emma Goldman. She rallied for equal opportunities for all. She hoped it wouldn't take another century to realize her American dream. And though it seemed that no one was listening to her, Goldman knew it was only 1906 … *(Song continues.)*

Ragtime, School Edition, North Shore Music Theatre at Dunham Woods © 2003, Joshua Weisgrau

All
85 And there were nine-ty-four years_ to go!
f
88 And there was dis-tant mu-sic, skip-ping a beat, sing-ing
Pt. 1 All
91 a dream. La - la-la-la - la! A strange in - sis-tant mu-sic
Pt. 2 All sub. p
94 put-ting out heat, pick-ing up steam. La - la-la-la - la! The sound of
accel.
97 dis-tant thun-der sud-den-ly start - ing to climb.
f
101 It was the mu - sic of some-thing be-gin - ning, an er-a ex-plod - ing, a
104 cen-tu-ry spin - ning in rich-es and rags_ and in rhy-thm and rhyme._ The
107 peo-ple called it Rag - time! Rag - time! Rag - time!
112 Rag - time!

TATEH: When immigrants first set foot on American soil there was a true feeling of hope in the air. But we found out that the streets were not all paved with gold. The gold would have to be mined. Tateh was willing to work hard to realize his American dream.

(TATEH and IMMIGRANTS file through ELLIS ISLAND.)

Success

CD 11:2

Music by Stephen Flaherty
Words by Lynn Ahrens

4
Tateh:
Here in A-mer - i - ca an - y - one at all can suc-ceed.
Immigrants:
mp
— A-mer - i - ca! We're in A-mer - i - ca!
Tateh:
Do what you do,— and the world
— will come to you, gua - ran - teed!—
Immigrants:
mp
A-mer - i - ca! We're in A-mer - i - ca!
Tateh:
I may be just a mak - er of art, but here you could start with less
and make a suc - cess!—
Tateh:
9

(The following dialogue is underscored.)

(TATEH begins to set up his cart and to address people on the street.)

TATEH: Step right up and have a silhouette made by a real artist! With ordinary paper, a pair of scissors and some glue I will give you a thing of such beauty! A life-like portrait of someone you love. Silhouettes of your favorite celebrity.

(Song continues.)

Tateh:
28
E - ve - lyn Nes - bit! Hey, look! She's on her vau - de - ville stage.
32
Har - ry Hou - di - ni! He prac - ti - c'lly es - capes from the page.
36
On - ly a nick - el. Don't walk a - way! Some - day, these will im - press
40
when I'm a suc - cess!
Immigrants:
Look at the sil - hou - ettes
44
here in the te - ne - ments, bent o - ver sew - ing or danc - ing or ar - gu - ing.
47
Thou - sands of sil - hou - ettes, thou - sands of sto - ries to tell.
50
Tateh:
Look at them, ev - 'ry - one, such op - por - tu - ni - ty!
53
Right on the cor - ner of Or - chard and Riv - ing - ton.
55
We'll make our sil - hou - ettes. Think how they'll sell!
Immigrants:
We'll
57
join the pa - rade of A - mer - i - cans all do - ing well!
rall.
a tempo
f
Suc -
61
cess!
Tateh & Immigrants:
Suc - cess
Morgan: (spoken)
I'm J. P. Mor - gan, my friends, the

65 wealth-i - est man_ on this earth! *Immigrants:* Suc - cess! *J.P. Morgan:* You im - mi-grants,

68 look up to me,_ and you'll see what mo - ney is worth! *Immigrants:* Suc -

71 cess! *Morgan:* One day, your im - mi-grant sweat might get you the whole_ U.

74 *rit.* S.! *Houdini:* And if you're trapped and fail-ure seems im - mi-nent,

77 think of Hou-di - ni, that fab - u - lous im - mi-grant! Break those chains with

80 all you pos-sess!_ *All:* This is A-mer - i - ca! This is the land_ of suc -

83 *a tempo* cess!________ Suc - cess!!________ *(Emma:)* **4**

(The following dialogue is underscored.)

EMMA GOLDMAN: The angry, fetid tenements of the Lower East Side were worse than anything immigrants had suffered in Europe. Still, they searched for the land of opportunity.

NARRATOR: Meanwhile, industry was booming, and one of the top innovators was Henry Ford. He didn't just manufacture the first automobiles—he made them the American Dream. He saw the assembly line not as another sweatshop, but as an expression of that dream.

(The CAST reconfigures and become workers in HENRY FORD'S factory. As they sing they become an assembly line—each with an individual job to do.)

Henry Ford

CD 11:3

Music by Stephen Flaherty
Words by Lynn Ahrens

Henry Ford:
See my peo-ple? Well, here's my theo - ry of

7 what this coun - try is mov - in' t'ward. Ev - 'ry work-er, a cog in mo-tion. Well,

11 that's the no - tion of Hen - ry Ford.

17 One man tight-ens and one man ratch-ets and one man reach-es to pull one cord.

21 Car keeps mov-ing in one di - rec-tion. *All:* A gen - u - flec - tion to Hen - ry Ford!

25 Hal - le - lu - jah! Praise the mak - er of the Mod - el

31 T! *Henry Ford:* Speed up__ the belt! Speed up the belt, Sam! *All:* Hal - le - lu - jah!

35 *Buyer:* Yes__ I'll take her!_ *All:* Sure a - maz - in' how far some fel - las can

39 see!________________ *Henry Ford:* Speed up__ the belt! Speed up the belt, Sam!

43 Speed up__ the belt! Speed up the belt, Sam! *All:* Speed up the, speed up the,

46 speed up the, speed up the belt!

49 Mass pro-duc-tion will sweep the na-tion, a sim-ple no-tion, the world's re-ward.

Henry Ford:

53 E-ven peo-ple who ain't too cle-ver can learn to tight-en a nut for-ev-er, at-

All:

57 tach one ped-al or pull one lev-er, for Hen-ry Ford!

61 Hen-ry Ford! Hen-ry Ford! Hen-ry Ford!

Henry Ford: *All:*

66 Grab your gog-gles! And climb

Buyer:

71 a-board! Come on a-board!

EMMA GOLDMAN: This is not the America we came here for. None of us did. None of us!

(The CHORUS becomes STRIKERS, shouting at a rally.)

EMMA GOLDMAN: But there is hope, my friends. Eight weeks ago these same workers—Italians, Poles, Belgians, Russian Jews—with one voice said "No!" to the mill owners and went on strike. They are holding firm and we must support them.

The Night That Goldman Spoke
CD 11:4
Music by Stephen Flaherty
Words by Lynn Ahrens
All:
It was win - ter in New York as the snow be - gan to fall and the
Work-men's Hall had not a seat to spare, when a young man ducked in - side just to
warm him - self, was all. The night that Gold - man spoke at U - nion Square.
(Emma)

(The following dialogue is underscored.)

EMMA GOLDMAN: What is happening in Lawrence, Massachusetts, is happening everywhere. Let us at last make this the land of opportunity for all people and not just the owners. We cannot rest!

(Song continues.)

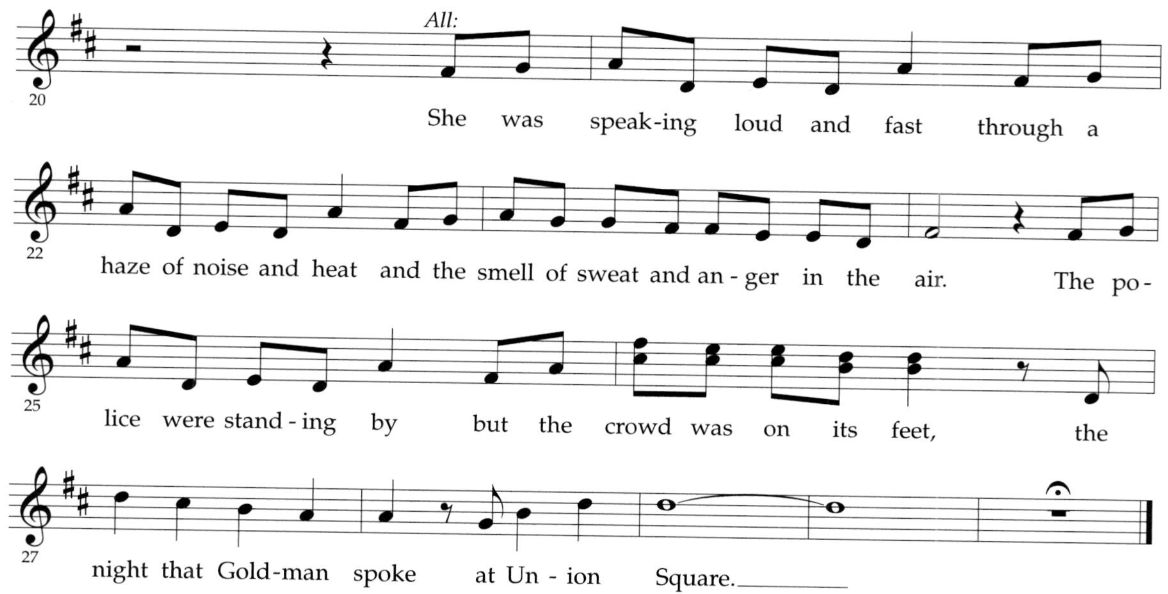

All:
She was speak-ing loud and fast through a
haze of noise and heat and the smell of sweat and an - ger in the air. The police were stand - ing by but the crowd was on its feet, the
night that Gold-man spoke at Un - ion Square.

WORKERS: Strike! Strike! Strike!

NARRATOR: The strike in Lawrence became famous. The press called it the Children's Crusade. Public indignation grew. The mill owners were not slow in calling in the militia to protect their property.

WORKERS: Strike! Strike! Strike! Strike!

NARRATOR: In another world of America the "well-to-do" were concerning themselves with pleasure—entertainment dished out to them by Coalhouse Walker, Harry Houdini, and something new called "the movies."

(The CHORUS becomes vacationers in Atlantic City, a place of amusement.)

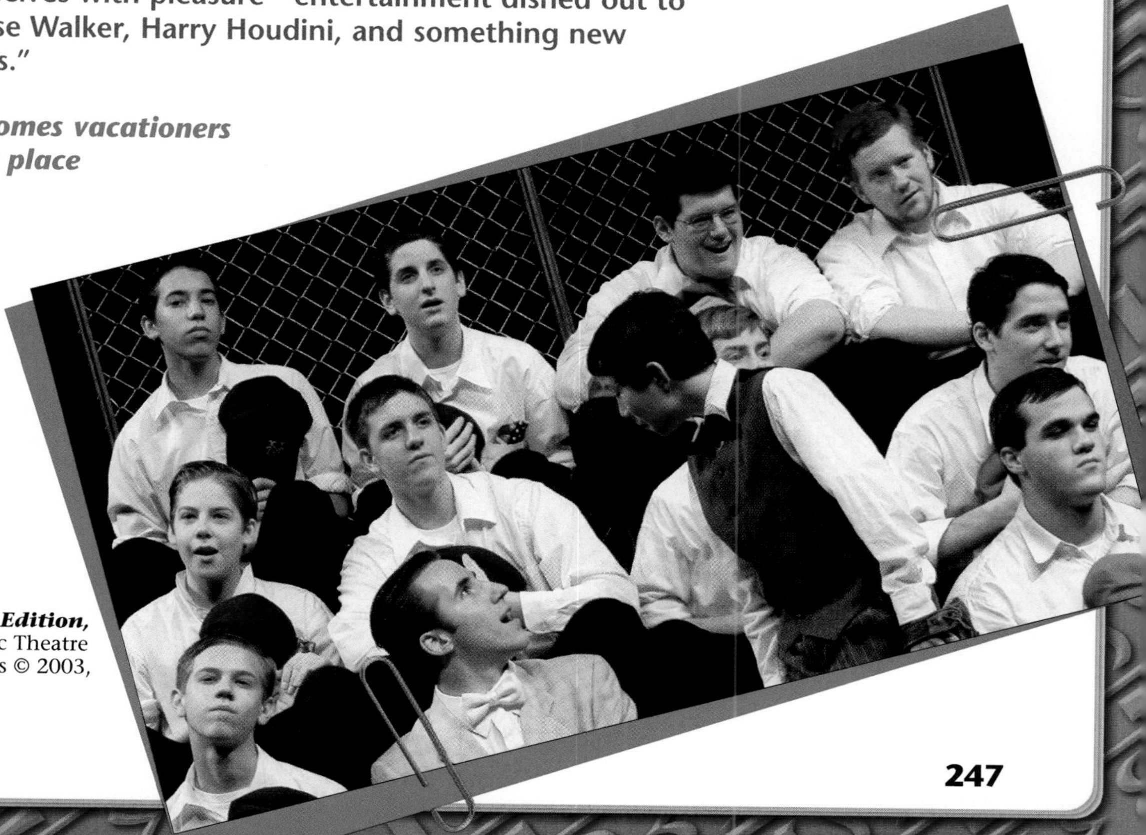

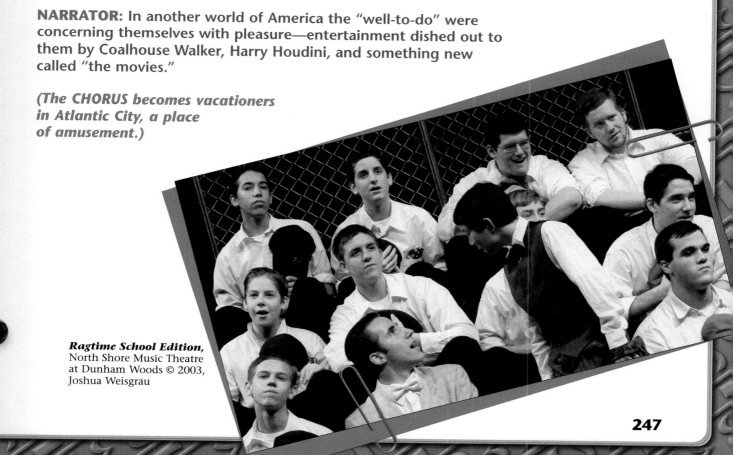

Ragtime School Edition, North Shore Music Theatre at Dunham Woods © 2003, Joshua Weisgrau

Atlantic City

CD 11:5

Music by Stephen Flaherty
Words by Lynn Ahrens

(Out of the crowd comes a MOVIE DIRECTOR. He is typical of the silent era: jodhpurs, white silk shirt, riding boots, megaphone.)

DIRECTOR: Cut! That was wonderful, Mr. Houdini. It is a dream come true to work with an artist of your magnitude. *Danke.*

HOUDINI: *Danke* yourself, Baron.

DIRECTOR: Take five, ladies and gentlemen.

(HOUDINI exits. The DIRECTOR takes off his hat and turns towards the audience. He is TATEH.)

DIRECTOR'S ASSISTANT: Baron. Here's the schedule for tomorrow. And your leading lady is unhappy with her lines.

TATEH: Tell our leading lady no one is going to hear her lines! This is a silent movie! Actors! Where is Mary Pickford when I need her?

NARRATOR: The era of Ragtime had run out, as if history were no more than a tune on a player piano. But we did not know that then.

EMMA: The signs of the coming world war were everywhere. Emma Goldman was arrested again, of course, but this time she would be deported, as well.

HOUDINI: Harry Houdini was hanging upside down high over Times Square when the Archduke Franz Ferdinand was assassinated in Sarajevo. Thirty days later the world would be at war.

TATEH: One afternoon, watching his children play, Tateh had an idea for a movie: a bunch of children, rich, poor—all kinds—a gang of kids getting into trouble, getting out of trouble, but together despite their differences. He was sure it would make a wonderful movie—a dream of what this country could be. He would be first in line to see it.

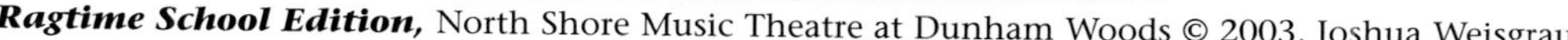

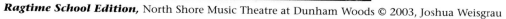

Ragtime School Edition, North Shore Music Theatre at Dunham Woods © 2003, Joshua Weisgrau

Ragtime Epilogue & Finale

CD 11:6

Music by Stephen Flaherty
Words by Lynn Ahrens

accel.
14 climb.___ It was the mu - sic of some-thing be-gin - ning, an
18 e - ra ex-plo - ding, a cen-tu - ry spin - ning in rich-es and rags_ and in
21 rhy-thm and rhyme._ The peo-ple called it Rag - time! Rag -
24 time!___ Rag - time!___ Rag - time!___

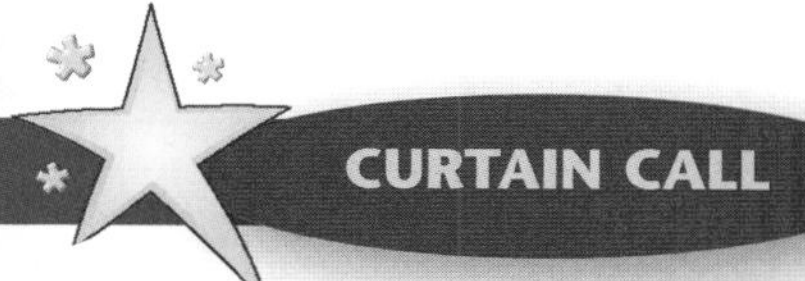
CURTAIN CALL

Meet the
Musicians

Lynn Ahrens and Stephen Flaherty

Besides *Once on This Island*, Lynn Ahrens and Stephen Flaherty cowrote the score to the Broadway smash hit, *Ragtime*. Ragtime won four 1998 Tony Awards including Best Score and Best Musical. The two have been working together for many years and have written several Broadway musicals, including *Lucky Stiff, My Favorite Year,* and *Seussical*. Ahrens and Flaherty also wrote the score for the animated film *Anastasia*. Ms. Ahrens is well known for the songs she wrote for the television series *Schoolhouse Rock!* Mr. Flaherty is a graduate of the Cincinnati College Conservatory of Music.

Playing the Guitar

STANDARD TUNING

E A D G B E

D

D7

Dm

E

E7

3-string Em

Em

Easy F

F

Easy F♯m

Easy G

G

Easy G7

G7

Easy Gm

A

A7

A7 alt.

3-string Am

Am

B

3-string B7

Easy B7

Easy Bm

Easy C

4-string C

C

Playing the Keyboard

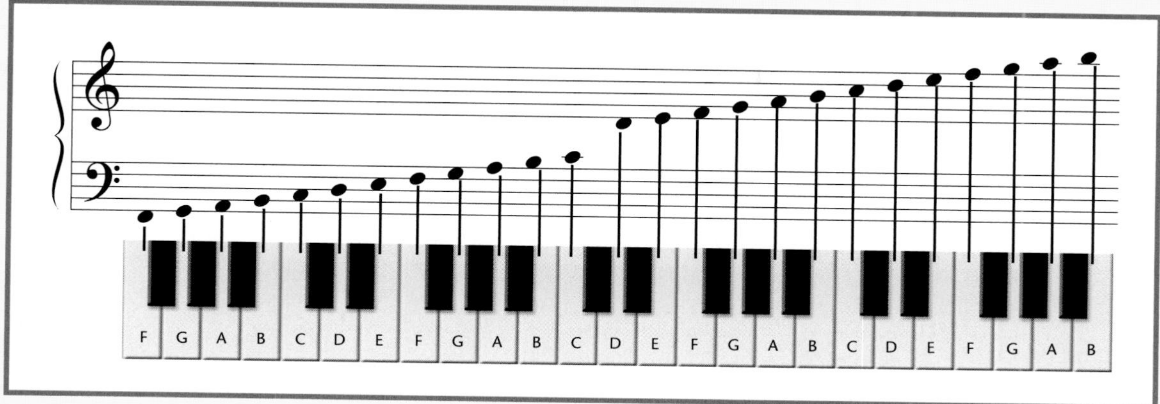

Posture, Hand Position, and Fingering

Sitting slightly forward on the bench, with feet resting on the floor or in position to use floor pedals, provides the best support for playing the keyboard or piano. Position your knees just under the front edge of the keyboard. Forearms should be stretched forward just enough so that there is no tension in the elbows.

Hands should be relaxed at the wrists and fingers slightly curved at the middle joint. Wrists should be parallel to the keyboard. When you are reading notation that indicates fingering, number *1* indicates the thumb of each hand.

The Keyboard

The keyboard has sets of white and black keys. Center yourself in front of the keyboard and find each set of *two* black keys up and down the keyboard. C is always the white key to the left, D is the white key in the middle, and E is the white key to the right of the two black keys. Middle C is the C that is closest to the center of the keyboard.

Each set of *three* black keys is a reference point for finding F, G, A, and B. F is always the white key to the left, G and A are the white keys in the middle, and B is the white key to the right of the three black keys.

Right and Left Hands

Notation for keyboard or piano is written on a staff that includes both the treble and bass clefs. Pitches in the treble clef are usually played with the right hand. Pitches in the bass clef are usually played with the left hand.

Major and Minor Triads

To play a major triad, find the root of the chord. The other two pitches in the triad will be four half steps up from the root and then three half steps. To play a C major triad with your right hand, your thumb will be on C, your third finger on E, and your fifth finger on G. To play a C chord with your left hand, your fifth finger will be on C, your third finger on E, and your thumb on G.

To play a minor triad, find the root of the chord. The other two pitches in the triad will be three half steps up from the root and then four half steps. To play a C minor triad with your right hand, your thumb will be on C, your third finger on E-flat, and your fifth finger on G. To play a C minor chord with your left hand, your fifth finger will be on C, your third finger on E-flat, and your thumb on G.

Practice forming and playing other major and minor triads.

Playing the Recorder

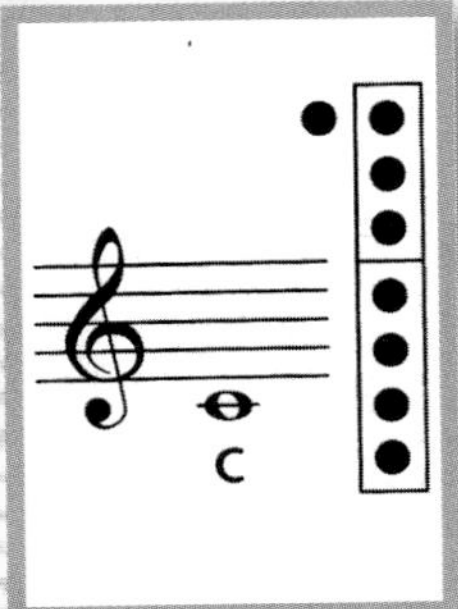

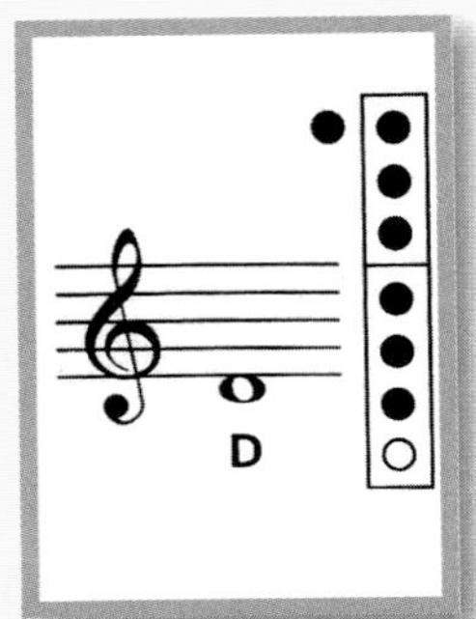

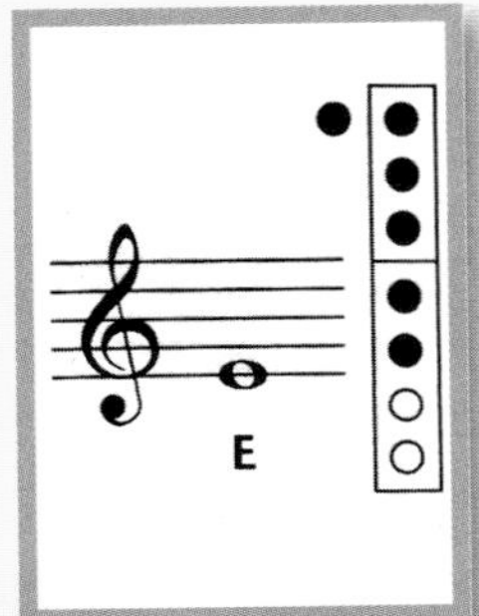

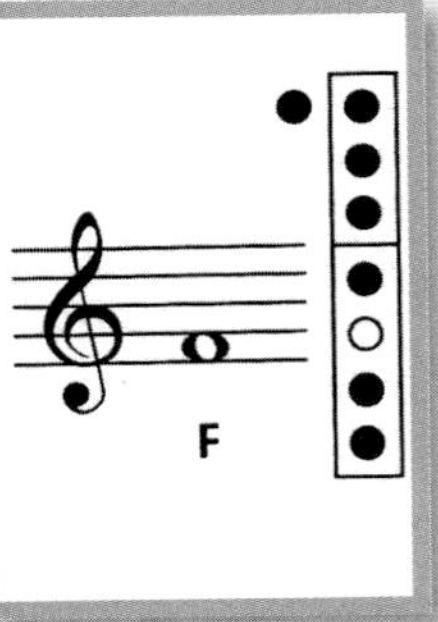

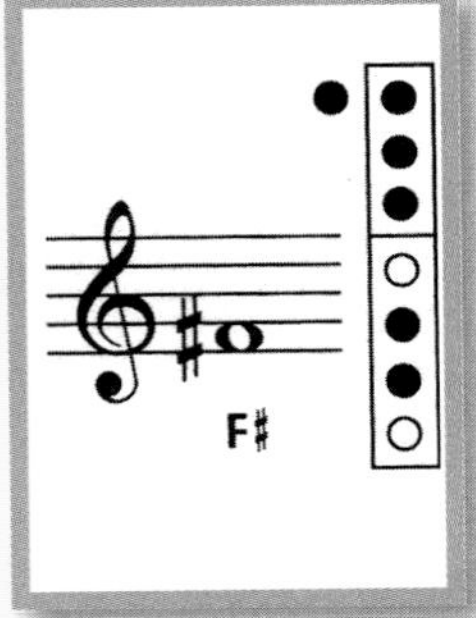

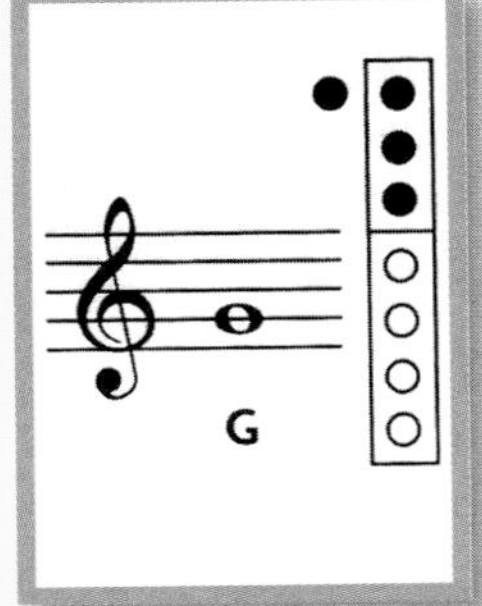

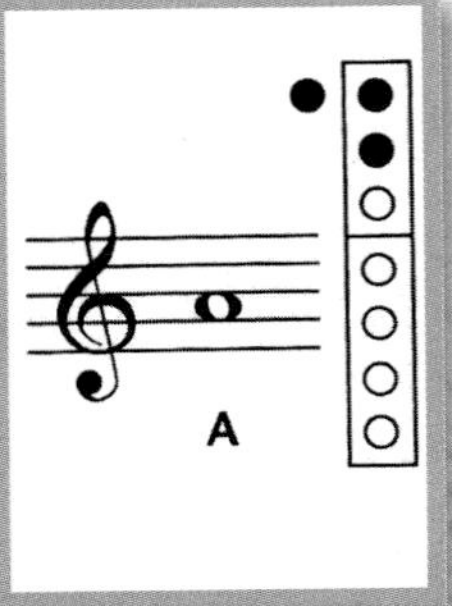

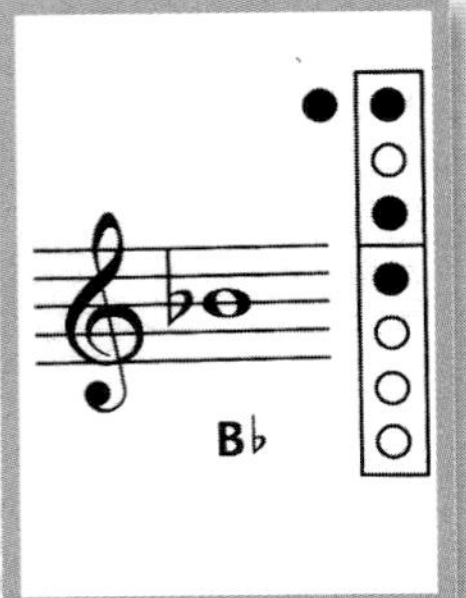

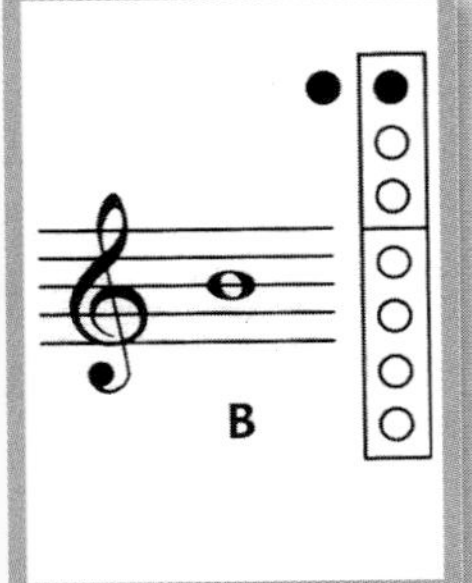

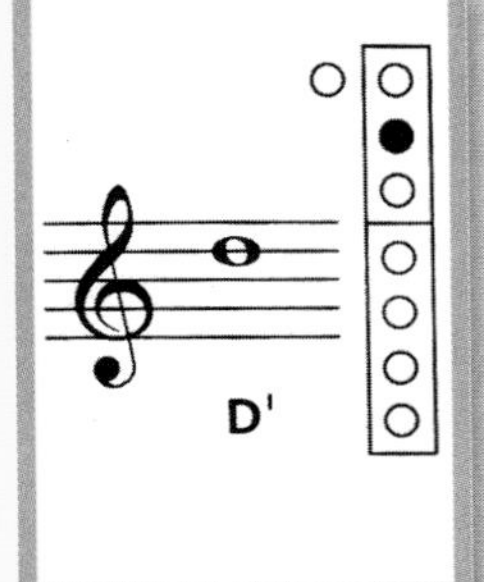

Glossary of Instruments

accordion a keyboard instrument that is a kind of portable organ with keys, metal reeds, and a bellows. The bellows forces air past the reeds to produce sound. It is often played while standing and held by straps over the shoulders, **CD 13:10**

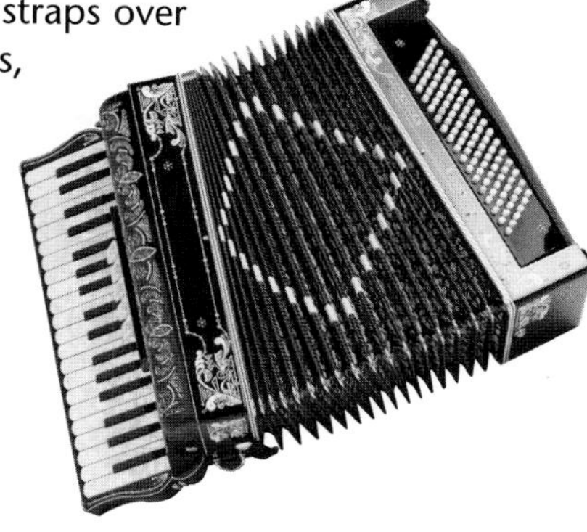

B

bagpipe a woodwind instrument that is made of a leather bag and pipes, played by blowing air through a blowpipe into the bag and then pressing the bag so that the air is forced out through the pipes, **145 CD 13:11**

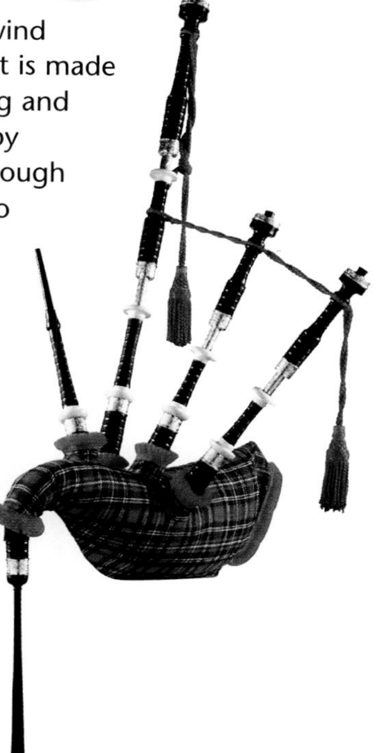

banjo a string instrument that has a round body, a long neck, and usually five strings. It is played by plucking or strumming, **CD 13:20**

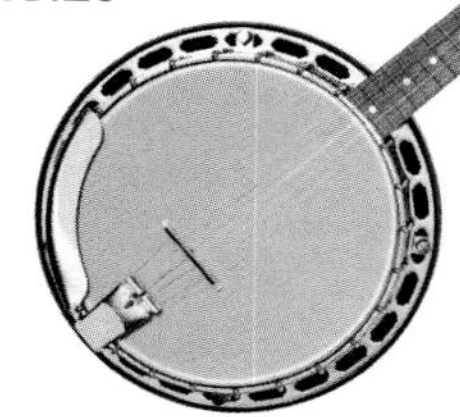

bass drum a very large percussion instrument that gives a deep, booming sound when struck, **39 CD 12:32**

bassoon a low-pitched woodwind instrument with a long wooden body attached to a smaller, curved metal tube with a double reed. It is played by blowing into the reed while covering fingerholes along the body. It is sometimes part of a woodwind quintet, **38 CD 12:15**

C

cello the second-largest instrument in the orchestral string family. It is held between the knees and played by bowing or plucking the strings. It is sometimes part of a string quartet or quintet, **48 CD 12:6**

clarinet a woodwind instrument that uses a single reed and is played by blowing into the mouthpiece while covering fingerholes along the body. It is sometimes part of a woodwind quintet, **38 CD 12:12**

conga a Latin American percussion instrument that has a low-pitched sound when struck and is usually played in pairs tuned a fifth apart, **64 CD 13:30**

cymbal a metal, percussion instrument shaped like a plate that is played by hitting one against another or striking it with a stick or mallet to make a clashing sound, **39 CD 12:37**

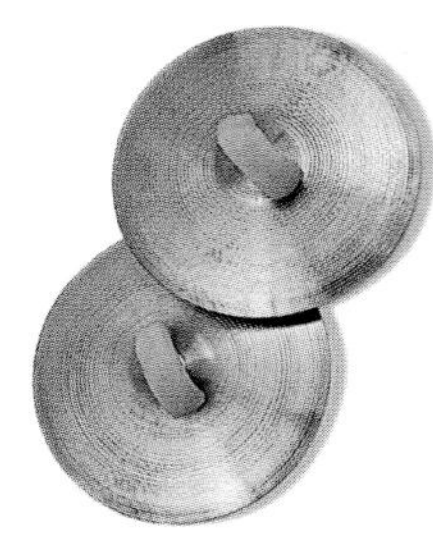

D

djembe a West African percussion instrument that is a drum usually made from pottery or wood and played with the hands, **CD 13:2**

double bass the largest instrument in the orchestral string family, held upright and played by bowing or plucking the strings, **CD 12:7**

F

flute a long, thin, woodwind instrument that is played by blowing across a hole at one end while covering holes along the body with fingers. It is sometimes part of a woodwind quintet, **38 CD 12:10**

French horn a brass instrument that is played by the buzzing of lips into the mouthpiece while pressing keys with fingers. It is sometimes part of a brass or woodwind quintet, **CD 12:20**

G

güiro a Latin American percussion instrument that is made from a gourd and has a bumpy surface that is scraped with a stick to make a sound, **CD 13:33**

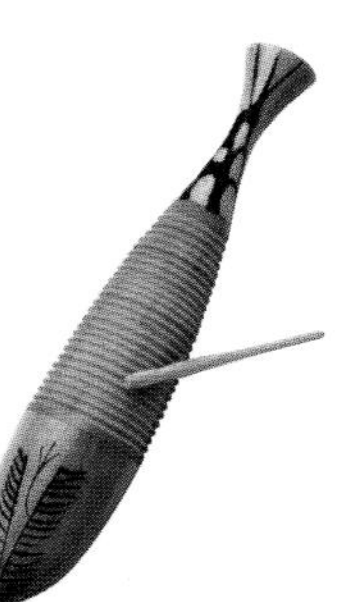

guitar a string instrument with a long neck and usually six strings, played by strumming, plucking, or picking, **8 CD 13:13**

H

harp one of the oldest and largest instruments of the string family, in which the strings are set in an upright triangle-like frame with a curved top. It is played by plucking or occasionally strumming the strings with fingers, **48 CD 13:15**

K

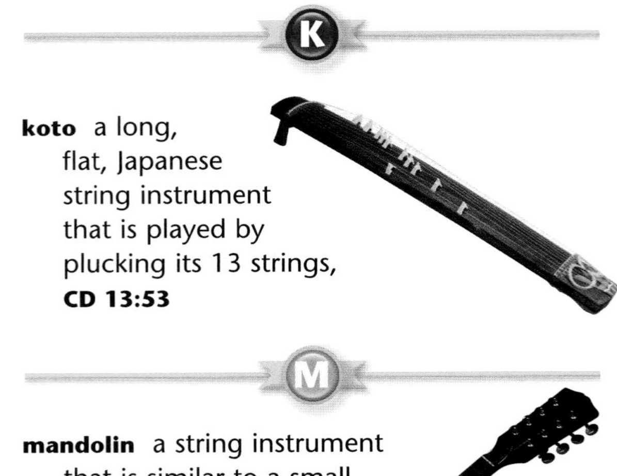

koto a long, flat, Japanese string instrument that is played by plucking its 13 strings, **CD 13:53**

M

mandolin a string instrument that is similar to a small guitar but has a more elaborately shaped body and eight metal strings, **CD 13:16**

maracas a Latin American percussion instrument that is made from a gourd and is played by shaking, which produces a rattling sound. They are usually played in pairs, **148 CD 13:35**

O

oboe a high-pitched, double-reed woodwind instrument that is played by blowing into the reeds while covering fingerholes along the body. It is sometimes part of a woodwind quintet, **38 CD 12:13**

P

piano a keyboard instrument in the percussion family that is played by pressing keys on the keyboard. Its sound is produced by hammers hitting stretched strings, **6 CD 12:41**

piccolo a small woodwind instrument, similar to the flute, but plays higher pitches, **CD 12:11**

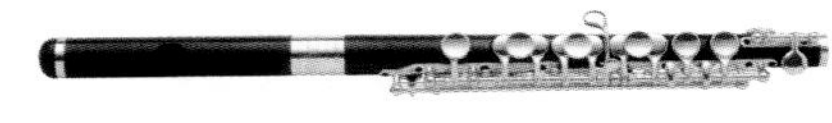

S

saxophone a woodwind instrument that is played by blowing into the mouthpiece while pushing keys along the body with fingers, **6 CD 12:16**

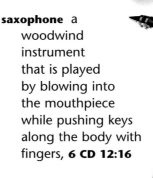

shekere an African percussion instrument that is a hollow gourd covered with a net of beads or seeds, **CD 13:8**

slit drum a percussion instrument that is found in Africa, Asia, and Oceania and is formed by hollowing a tree trunk through a slit on one side, **CD 13:9**

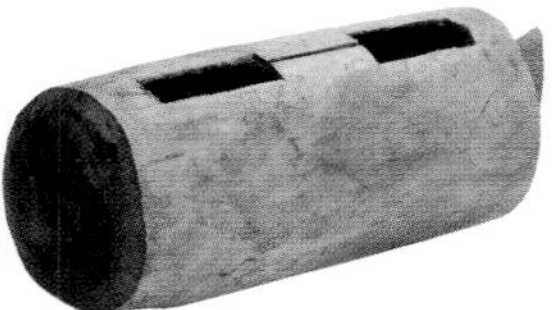

snare drum a percussion instrument with wires or strings stretched along the bottom. When the top of the drum is struck, the wires vibrate and give the drum a loud, slightly rattly sound, **CD 12:35**

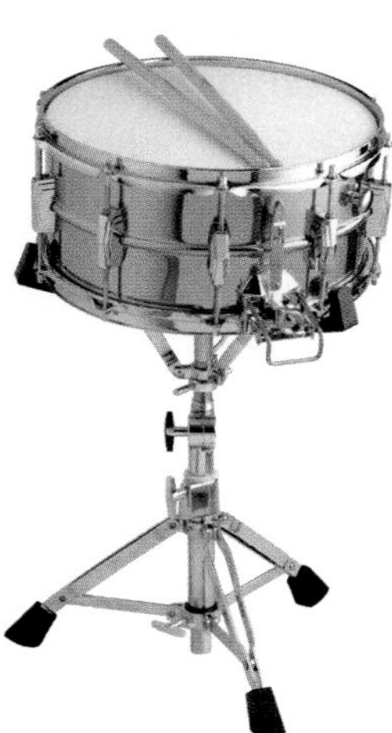

spoons common household objects that are used as percussion instruments by holding two together and striking them against the body. Musicians sometimes use an instrument created by fastening two spoons together with a wooden handle, **CD 13:23**

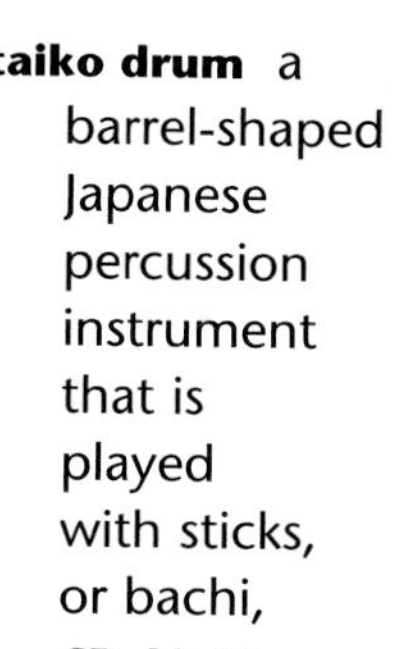

T

taiko drum a barrel-shaped Japanese percussion instrument that is played with sticks, or bachi, **CD 13:51**

tambourine a percussion instrument that is a small, hand-held drum with metal disks attached loosely around the rim. It is played by either shaking or tapping with the hand, **39 CD 12:36**

timpani also known as kettledrums, a set of percussion instruments consisting of two or more large kettle-shaped drums played with mallets, **CD 12:26**

trombone a large, low-pitched instrument in the brass family, played by the buzzing of lips into the mouthpiece while moving the slide in or out. It is sometimes part of a brass quintet, **6 CD 12:21**

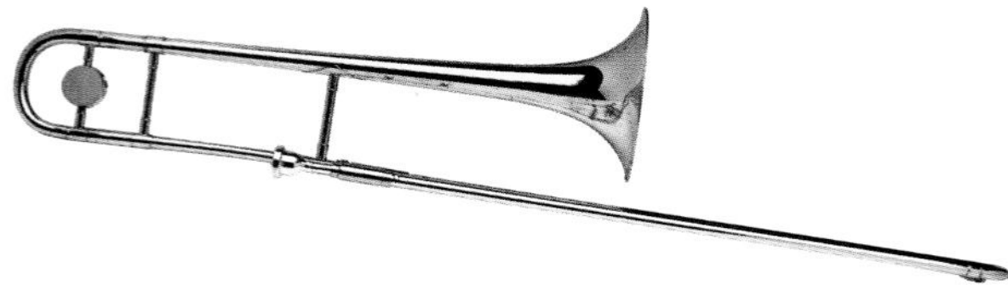

trumpet the smallest, highest-pitched instrument in the brass family, played by the buzzing of lips into the mouthpiece while pressing keys with fingers. It is often used to play a fanfare to honor important people or to announce an important event, and is sometimes part of a brass quintet, **CD 12:18**

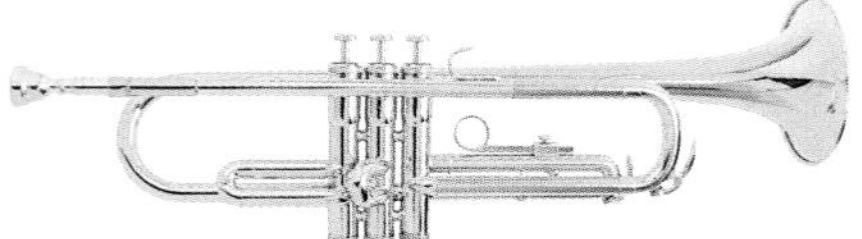

tuba the largest, lowest-pitched instrument in the brass family, played by the buzzing of lips into the mouthpiece while pressing keys with fingers. It is sometimes part of a brass quintet, **54 CD 12:22**

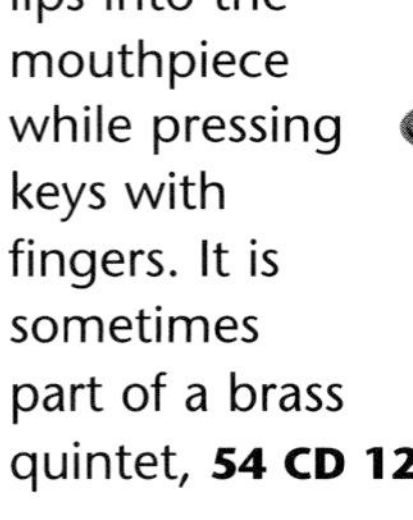

V

viola a string instrument midway between the violin and the cello in size, played by being held under the chin and bowing or plucking the strings. It is sometimes part of a string quartet or quintet, **48 CD 12:5**

violin the smallest of the orchestral string instruments, played by being held under the chin and bowing or plucking the strings. It is sometimes part of a string quartet or quintet, **6 CD 12:4**

X

xylophone a percussion instrument that is made up of one or two rows of wooden bars of different lengths, played by hitting the bars with mallets, **166 CD 12:30**

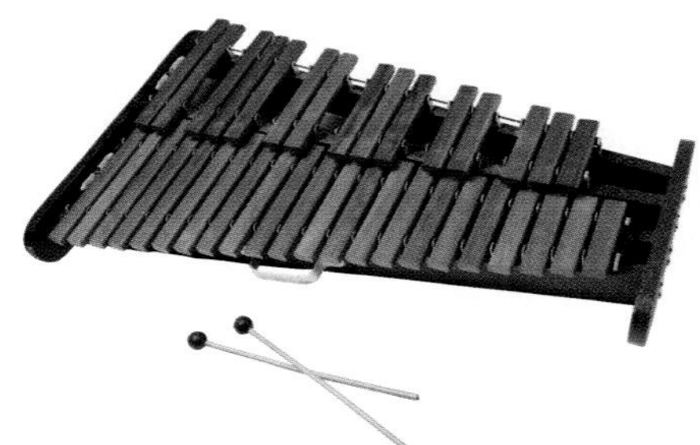

Glossary of Terms

AB form (binary form) a form of music that has two sections—the A section and the B section, **61**
accidentals a sharp (♯), flat (♭), or natural (♮) sign that raises or lowers a note in a measure, **135**
acoustics the characteristics of a space that determine the quality and control of sound waves within that space, **94**
aerophones instruments that produce sound through a vibrating column of air, including the woodwind and brass families as well as pipe organs, **167**
anticipation the use of a nonaccented beat in the measure before a phrase begins, to introduce the phrase, **138**
art song a type of music written for solo voice and instrumental accompaniment, usually keyboard, **124**
atonality the absence of a tonal center and equal emphasis on all twelve tones of the chromatic scale, **126**

Baroque period the era of music development from about 1600 to about 1750, **108**
binary form (AB form) a form of music that has two sections—the A section and the B section, **61**
blues a style of American music characterized by flatted notes and a jazz rhythm, often slow and syncopated, **17**
borrowed chords chords taken from a different but related scale, **135**
brass musical instruments made of brass or other metal, including the trumpet, trombone, French horn, and tuba, **36**

call and response a form in which a phrase sung by a solo leader is followed by a similar phrase, sung by a group, **205**
chord three or more pitches sounding together, **15**
chordophones instruments that produce sound when a string or chord is struck, rubbed, or plucked, **167**
choreographer a person who creates a pattern of dance movements to go with music, **158**
concert etiquette behavior appropriate for attending a concert-hall performance, such as listening attentively and avoiding speaking or using cell phones, **102**
concertino a small group of soloists within a larger group, **112**
concerto music contrasting an orchestra with solo performers, **112**
contemporary currently most popular in a particular time and place, **6**
contrast new or different musical ideas from those already heard, **36**
copyright laws give composers the exclusive right to publish their compositions, **81**

descant an accompanying melody that is sung above the main melody of a song, **213**
dissonance the sounding of a combination of pitches that creates harmonic tension and sounds incomplete, **126**

electrophones instruments that generate sound from electricity, **167**
entrada a festive, marchlike section that begins a musical composition, **113**

fanfare a short showy tune for trumpets or brass, played to honor important people or to announce an important event, **186**
folk music a type of popular music that is usually characterized by simple lyrics about everyday life and a simple instrumental accompaniment, **69**
form the overall structure and design of a musical composition, **12**
found instrument an instrument developed from an everyday object, **198**

gamelan the traditional instrumental ensemble of Indonesia, made up of gongs, metallophones, rhythmic drums, flutes, and string instruments, **100**
garage bands small rock bands formed by teens who practice and perform in garages, **14**
glissando the continuous movement from one pitch to another, **162**

homophony music having several harmonic parts that sound together, **110**
hymns four-part songs of praise used in religious services, **144**

idiophones simple, solid instruments that produce sound by being struck, scraped, or shaken, **167**
incidental music the music that is performed during a play to accompany the action onstage, **122**

katadjait (throat songs) a style of singing and musical expression resulting from the influences of cultures in Northern Canada, **176**

march a form of music characterized by a strong steady beat, the use of accents, and repeated and contrasting sections, usually performed by a band, **37**
measure a set of beats between bar lines, **20**
melodic contour the shape of a melody, **156**
membranophones instruments that produce sound by striking or rubbing a skin or membrane stretched across a resonating air chamber, **167**

minimalism a compositional style that emphasizes repetition of short rhythmic and melodic patterns, **130**

mixed meter a rhythm pattern in which the meter or time signature changes, **57**

modulation the transition from a section of music based on one scale to a section based on a different scale, **205**

monophony music having a single, unaccompanied melodic line, **110**

motive a short musical phrase that is repeated throughout a song, **28**

music critics writers who share opinions on music through published reviews online, in newspapers and magazines, or on television and radio, **25**

musicology the study of music, specializing in fields other than performance and composition, **127**

national anthem a song of praise that honors a particular nation, **192**

nonwritten music music passed from one person to another through oral transmission, **202**

oratorios dramatic musical compositions, usually settings of religious texts, performed by soloists, chorus, and orchestra, **110**

orchestra a large instrumental ensemble that usually includes members of the string, woodwind, brass, and percussion families, **48**

ostinato a repeated melodic or rhythmic pattern, **72**

percussion musical instruments that are struck to produce a sound, including the drum, cymbal, xylophone, tambourine, and piano, **36**

phasing a technique in which one pattern is performed over and over for the duration of a piece of music, while the same pattern is begun in unison but shifts the downbeat over one beat with each repetition, until with the final repetition players are in unison again, **130**

pipe organ a large instrument with sets of pipes corresponding to keys on several manuals of keyboards, producing sounds through air compression, **108**

polyphony music having two or more independent melodic lines sounding together, **110**

polyrhythms combinations of two or more different rhythm patterns played at the same time, **199**

popular music the music that is most liked and accepted by the people of a generation, **6**

programmatic representing or suggesting a story or series of events, **112**

ragtime a style of American popular music having melodies with syncopated rhythms performed over a steady beat, **22**

rap music a style of rhythm-and-blues music that includes a rhythmic vocal line spoken or sung over an instrumental accompaniment, **70**

ritornello a section of a baroque concerto played by all the players after a series of melodic lines played by smaller groups, **112**

rondo a musical form that uses alternating repetitions of the main theme with two or more contrasting sections, such as ABACA, **36**

root the pitch on which a chord is built, **29**

scale an ordered series of pitches, **135**

steady beat the underlying beat or pulse, **5**

string section of musical instruments that are made of wood and have strings that are bowed or plucked, including the violin, viola, cello, bass, harp, and guitar, **48**

strophic form a form in which the music is repeated with each new verse or stanza of text, **124**

style a set of musical qualities that are characteristic of a culture, individual, or historical period, **3**

suite a musical composition consisting of a succession of short pieces, **102**

syncopated placing emphasis on beats that are not normally accented, giving a catchy, uneven sound, **17**

ternary form a form of music that has three parts with repetition following one contrast (ABA), **82**

texture the way in which melody and harmony are combined to create layers of sound, **135**

throat songs (katadjait) a style of singing and musical expression resulting from the influences of cultures in Northern Canada, **176**

toccata a freestyle composition for organ or piano characterized by the use of full chords and running passages; often used as the prelude of a fugue, **108**

tone color the unique sound of an instrument or voice, **5**

tone poem a work for orchestra that tells a story through music, **219**

tutti the full orchestral ensemble, **112**

vocables sung syllables that have no specific meaning, **200**

vocal range the pitch distance between the lowest and highest notes that can be sung or played by a performer, **40**

voiced sounds sounds produced in music by a singer that are not actually sung, **174**

woodwinds musical instruments historically made of wood, including the flute, oboe, clarinet, bassoon, and saxophone, **36**

world music diverse music from around the world, much of which may not be in English, that reaches American audiences, **224**

work songs songs that have a strong rhythm that helps workers move together as they work, **146**

written music music that uses notation, or written symbols, to show how to perform the music, **202**

zydeco a blend of blues, jazz, French, African, and Caribbean musical styles, **89**

Music Theory Handbook

① BEAT

Beat is a steady pulse. Beats are organized into recurring patterns that define meter.

② METER

Meter is a pattern of strong and weak beats. All meters can be simplified to duple or triple meter. Other meter types are called combined or mixed, compound, asymmetrical or irregular, and nonmetric.

Duple and Triple Meter

Duple meter is a group of two beats in a strong-weak pattern.

< < < <
1 2 1 2 1 2 1 2

Triple meter is a group of three beats in a strong-weak-weak pattern.

< < <
1 2 3 1 2 3 1 2 3

Time Signatures

Time signatures are sets of numbers (written as fractions) used at the beginning of a piece of music (placed to the right of the key signature)

a. to indicate the number of beats in each measure, and

b. define the note that represents the basic beat.

Duple Meter: 2 4 2
4 4 2

Triple Meter: 6 3 9
8 4 8

For instance, in the first example there are two beats per measure with a quarter note receiving one beat. In the last example, there are nine beats per measure with an eighth note receiving one beat. If the upper number of the meter signature is divisible by two, but not divisible by three, the meter is duple meter. If the upper number of the meter signature is divisible by three, then the meter is triple meter.

Combined and Compound Meters

Combined or mixed meter is the mixture of duple and triple meters. The beat continues as a steady pulse, with alternating accented beats according to the meters. Combined meter signatures are shown in the measure of meter change.

< < < <
1 2 1 2 3 1 2 1 2 3

Compound meters have two or more groups of triple meter.

6 9 12
8 8 8

Asymmetrical Meters and Nonmetric Music

Asymmetrical or irregular meter is the unequal pairings of beats in a meter.

These meters can be:

5 5 7 11
4 8 8 8

Nonmetric refers to music with no fixed groups of beats, no time signature, and no measure bars. Plainsong, or chant, is nonmetric. It is also used in twentieth-century music.

NOTES AND RESTS

Notes and rests are musical symbols. Each note represents the duration of a musical sound or pitch—the length of time value in beats. Silence, or the absence of sound, is indicated by a symbol called a rest. The note and rest names indicated are in relationship to the longest commonly used note value, the whole note.

The value is indicated by the *meter signature*, designating the type of note that receives the basic beat. In the following example, the quarter note represents the basic beat.

Name	Note	Rest	Value	Relative Duration
Whole			4 beats	
Half			2 beats	
Quarter			1 beat	
Eighth			1/2 beat	
Sixteenth			1/4 beat	

Dotted Notes

Dotted notes and rests have augmentation dots added to lengthen their durations. The dot is added to the right of the note or rest, and it adds half of the original note or rest value.

The example below shows how the dotted half note relates to combinations of half and quarter notes.

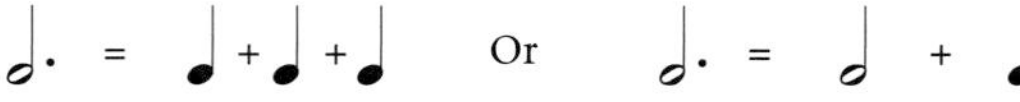

Other Combinations of Notes

Notes may be grouped in a variety of ways. When playing these combinations, internalizing a counting system may help. Here are suggestions for text, as related to a pizza.

In this example, the quarter note represents the basic beat. Each combination of notes receives one beat.

RHYTHM

Rhythm is a combination of long and short sounds and silence played over a beat. Rhythm in a song or vocal piece is determined by the text. In an instrumental piece, rhythm is determined by the specific notation durations chosen by the composer. When a rhythm (usually two to eight counts) is repeated over and over, it is called an *ostinato.*

PITCH

Sounds are vibrations that travel through the air. Vibrations are heard as sound when they reach our ears. The speed of the vibrations affects the sound or the pitch of the sound. Pitch is based on how high or how low a sound is heard. The faster the vibration, the higher the pitch. A pitch vibrating 440 times per second is heard as the absolute pitch A, the A above middle C on a keyboard instrument. It is called A-440 and is used as a baseline note for tuning instruments.

Notating and Measuring Pitch

In Western musical culture, absolute pitches are labeled with seven alphabetical letters: A-B-C-D-E-F-G, often called the *musical alphabet.* The musical alphabet repeats as the pitch ascends, or gets higher. When the pitch descends, the letters are reversed. Relative pitches using solfège, *do-re-mi-fa-so-la-ti-do,* correspond to the musical alphabet.

The *staff* is a system of five horizontal lines and four spaces between the lines. It is used to show how high and low the pitches are.

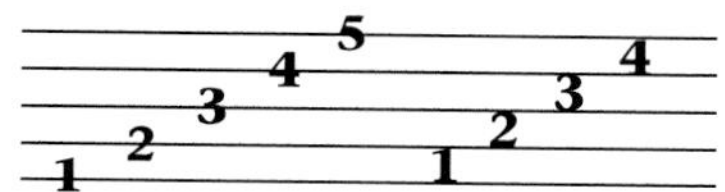

Clef signs placed on a staff assign absolute pitch names to specific lines and spaces. The two clefs most commonly used are: G clef, or treble clef; and F clef, or bass clef.

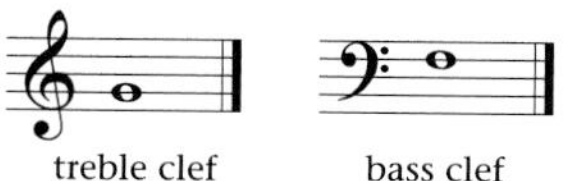
treble clef bass clef

When connected together with a bracket on the left side, it is called a *grand staff.* See below. The second measure separates and names the line and space notes.

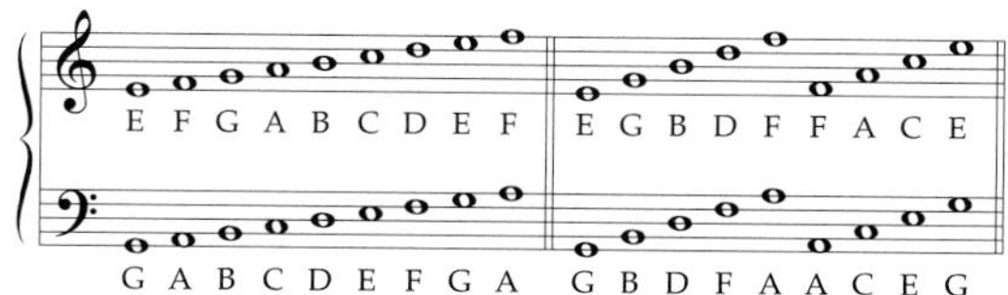

Each clef is named for the pitch it indicates on the staff. The G clef marks the pitch G on the second line of a staff, where the clef sign passes through the second line four times.

When the F clef is used, it designates the fourth line of a staff as the pitch F. The center of the C clef indicates the pitch C below A-440, called middle C. When the C clef marks the third staff line as C, it is called an alto clef. When the C clef marks the fourth staff line as C, it is called the tenor clef. Clefs are used to keep a range of notes on the staff.

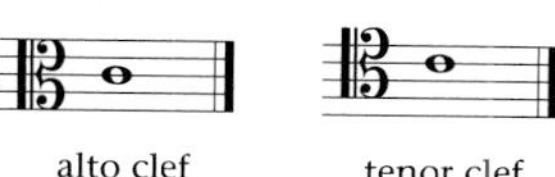
alto clef tenor clef

Organizing Pitches

The *octave* is divided into twelve equal parts or pitches. A *semitone* (also called half tone or half step) is the smallest interval in Western musical tuning. It corresponds to the difference between two adjacent keys on a piano, or between two frets on a guitar. A *whole tone* (also called tone or whole step) is equal to two semitones. In the example below, look at the half steps and whole steps.

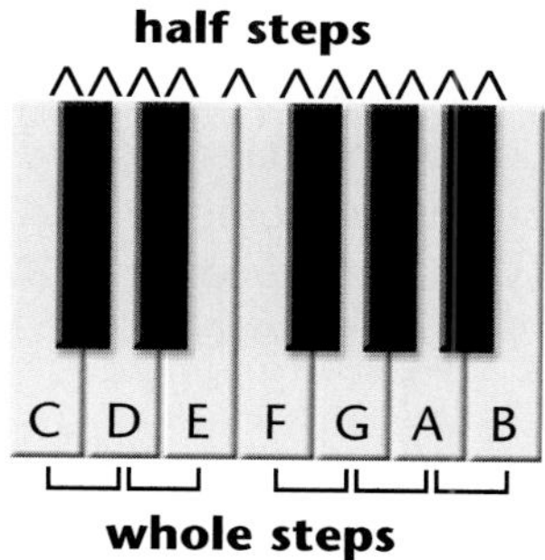

A *sharp sign* (♯) raises the pitch by one half step and a *flat sign* (♭) lowers the pitch by a half step. Pitches that sound the same but have different names are called *enharmonic pitches.* See the black keys on the example below.

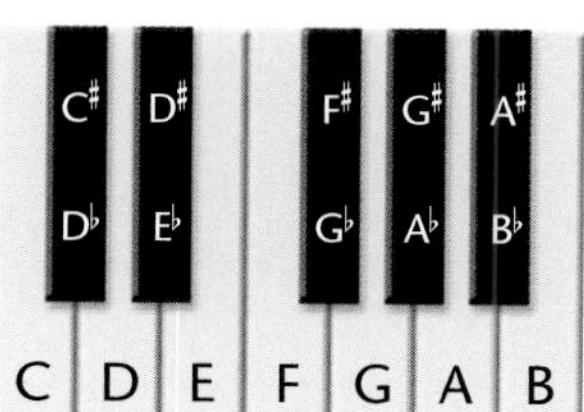

6 SCALES

A *scale* is a group of pitches organized in ascending pitch order. Each scale uses a certain number of pitches, which are organized in specific patterns. The patterns create the same type of scale when started on any pitch. The scale patterns are frequently described as ascending orders of half steps and whole steps. *Solfège syllables (do-re-mi-fa-so-la-ti)* are frequently used to represent the scale patterns. Each syllable represents a pitch in the scale. Singing musical patterns and melodies with solfège is a useful tool for musicians. It helps to improve a musician's sense of relationships between tones in musical patterns.

The Major Scale

The *major scale* is the most familiar scale in Western music culture. A major scale contains seven different pitches that can be repeated in the continuation of the scale beyond one octave. The ascending pattern is shown in the following example using a musical keyboard, letter names, and solfège. The major scale pattern is whole-whole-half-whole-whole-whole-half, beginning from any starting pitch. The half steps occur between scale steps 3 and 4, or *mi* and *fa,* and between steps 7 and 8, or *ti* and *do.*

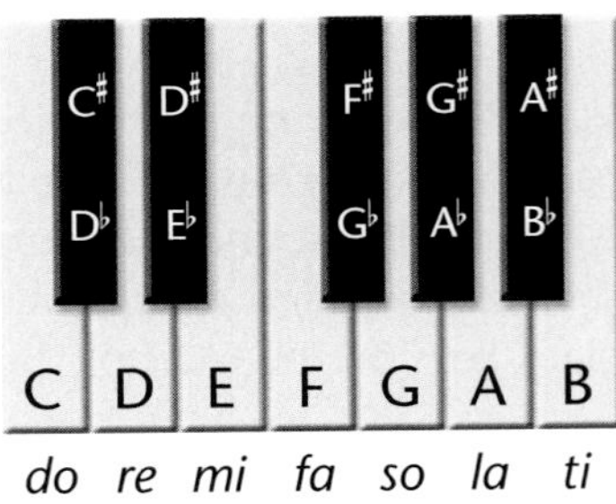

The Minor Scale

The *minor scale* is also a familiar scale in Western music. There are three patterns of minor scales. They are natural minor, harmonic minor, and melodic minor. All three scales share similar patterns for the first five scale tones. The differences in the scale patterns are the sixth and seventh scale tones. The example below shows the different sequence of whole steps and half steps for each minor scale. The melodic minor scale is the only scale that uses two different patterns, one for going up the scale and another for coming down the scale. The ascending pattern is shown and the descending pattern is just like the natural minor pattern.

Other Scales

Modal scales originated with early Greek civilization. They are called Ionian, Dorian, Phrygian, Lydian, Mixolydian, Aeolian, and Locrian. The Ionian scale later became the major scale and the Aeolian became the minor scale. Pentatonic scales have five pitches: *do-re-fa-so-la*. They are common in the folk music of cultures around the world, including Eastern Europe, Asia, North and South America, and Africa.

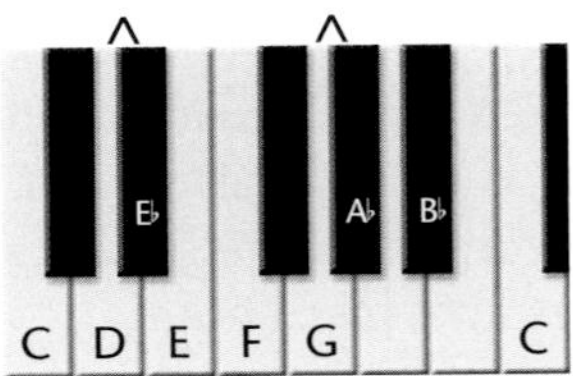

natural minor (Aeolian)

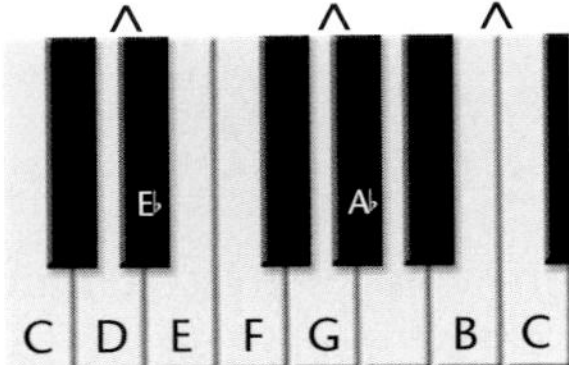

harmonic minor

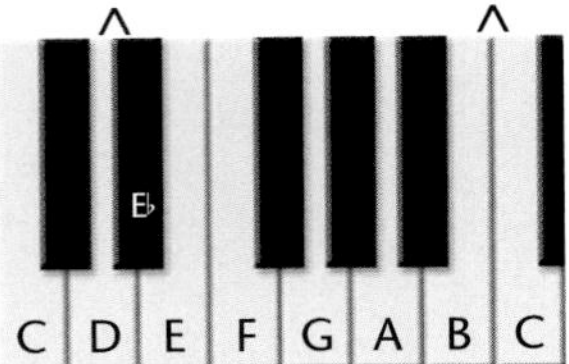

melodic minor (ascending)

INTERVALS

An *interval* is the distance between two pitches. Musicals intervals are primes (unisons), 2nds, 3rds, and so on. To count an interval between two pitches, include each letter name of the two pitches and all letter names between them. Sharps and flats do not affect this general measurement. For example, the distance between B up to the next higher E is a 4th.

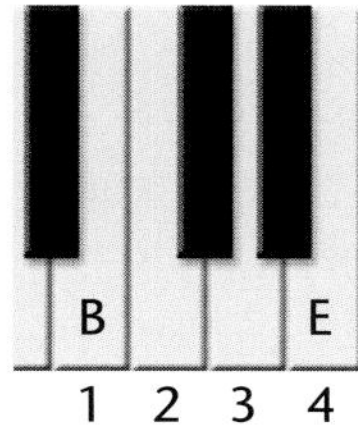

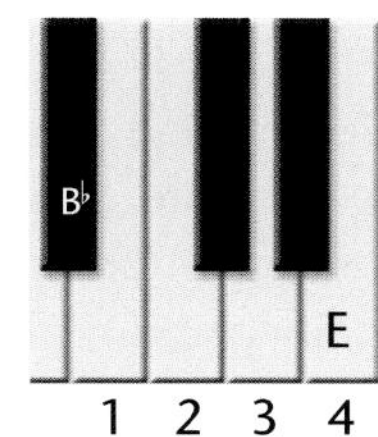

Counting intervals between two notes on the staff is similar to counting them with letter names. On the staff, count each line or space that the two notes are on, and count all lines and spaces between them.

Prime 2nd 3rd 4th 5th 6th 7th 8va Octave

Intervals and Their Quality

As shown above, intervals measure the general distance between two pitches. They also measure quality. When you measured the intervals between B and E, and between B♭ and E, you found that both were 4ths. However, they are not the same exact size.

P4

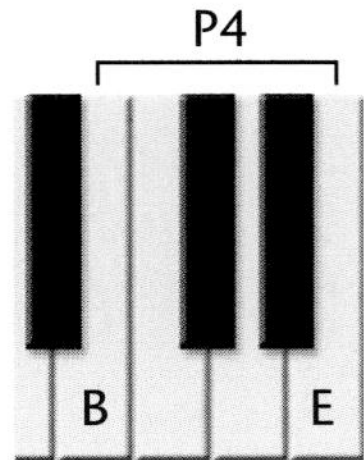

A4

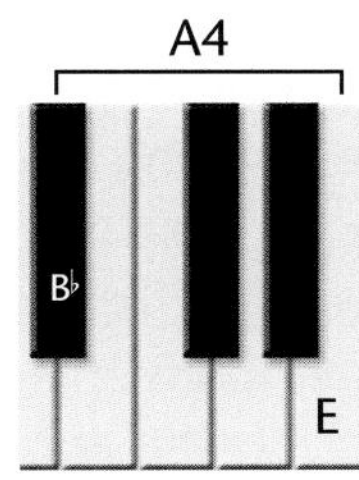

They are not the same "quality" 4ths. P4 indicates "perfect" 4th. A4 indicates "augmented" 4th.

Intervals from middle C to high C are shown in the example below. Count the number of whole steps and half steps in each interval.

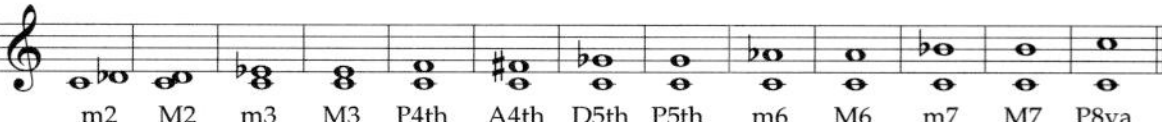

Modifying Intervals

It is possible to modify intervals.
Follow these rules:

1. If the bottom note of a perfect or major interval is lowered a semitone (or the top note is raised), the interval has been *augmented.*
2. If the bottom note of a perfect or minor interval is raised a semitone (or the top note is lowered), the interval becomes *diminished.*
3. If the bottom note of a minor interval is lowered a semitone, the interval becomes *major.*
4. If the bottom note of a major interval is raised a semitone, the interval becomes *minor.*

SCALES AND TONAL CENTERS

A *scale* is a group of pitches organized in ascending and descending order. The order of pitches always follows the order of letter names: A-B-C-D-E-F-G. The pitches of a scale are called *degrees,* that is, the first pitch of a scale is called the first degree, and so on. Each type of scale uses a particular order of semitones and wholetones.

The first degree of a scale is called *tonic.* It is "home base." A melody or harmony can go away from tonic but eventually will come back to *tonic.*

Each pitch in a scale has a name. The names come from their relationship to tonic. *Tonic* is the tonal center of a piece of music. In the following example the tonic is in the center of the scale rather than at the beginning. This shows how the other notes relate to tonic. The fifth note of the scale is the *dominant* because it is a P5 interval above tonic. The fourth note of the scale is the *subdominant* (below the dominant) because it is a P5 below the tonic. The other note names also show their relationships to tonic.

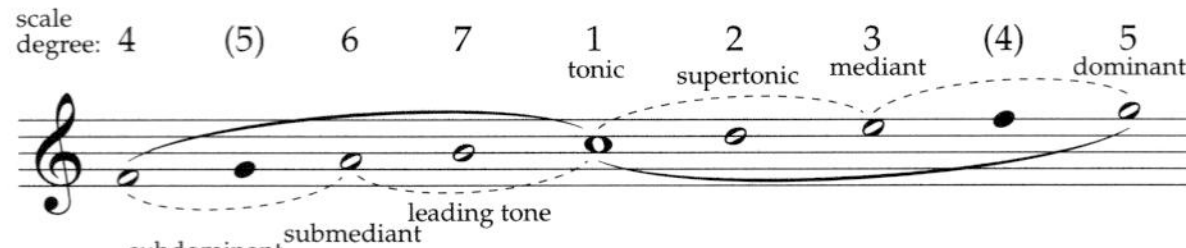

KEYS AND KEY SIGNATURES

Key is a general term used to identify the pitches used in a piece of music. *Key signatures* are numerical fractions that are placed at the beginning of each staff, between the clef and the meter signature, and are generally used to avoid writing so many accidentals.

Basically, it tells you which notes are to be played as a sharp or flat in the song.

Scales with sharps in their key signatures are he following

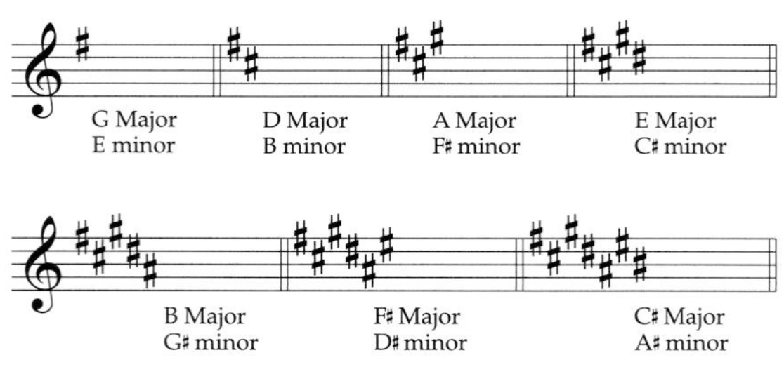

Scales with flats in their key signatures are the following

Different keys that share the same key signature are called *relative keys* (See examples above). For example, the key signatures of F major and D minor share the same key signature of one flat. They also share the same group of pitches, but they do not share the same tonic or "home base" note. The scales of relative keys overlap. The first note of the minor scale is the sixth note, or *la*, of the major scale. Therefore, we often refer to the minor scale as *la*-based. The first note of the major scale is the third note of the minor scale. See the following example.

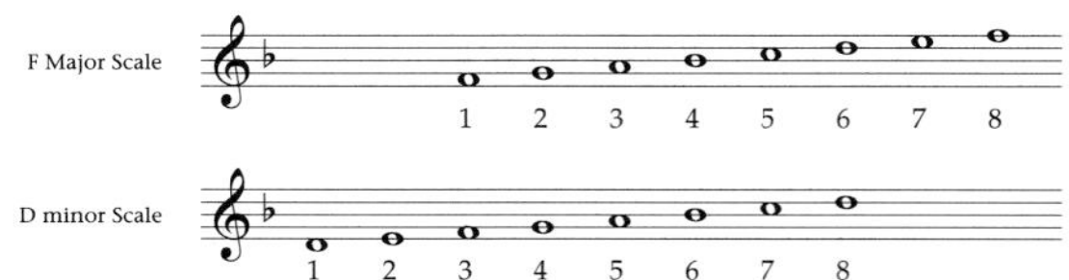

As the number of sharps or flats increases in the key signature, the names of the keys form a series of P5 intervals. This pattern is called the *circle of 5ths*. The circle of 5[ths] is a convenient way to see, learn, and think about the keys and key signatures.

Starting clockwise from the top C, each new letter represents a new scale, a fifth above the one before it. The inside circle tells you how many flats or sharps are in the key.

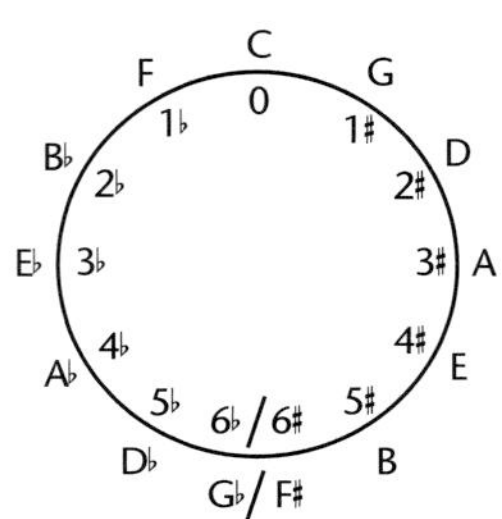

HARMONY

Triads

The simultaneous sound of tones is called *harmony*. Groups of three or more pitches that sound together are called *chords*. In traditional harmony, chords are built on intervals of 3rds. Chords made of three pitches and written as two consecutive thirds are called *triads*. Triads may be in root position, first inversion, or second inversion.

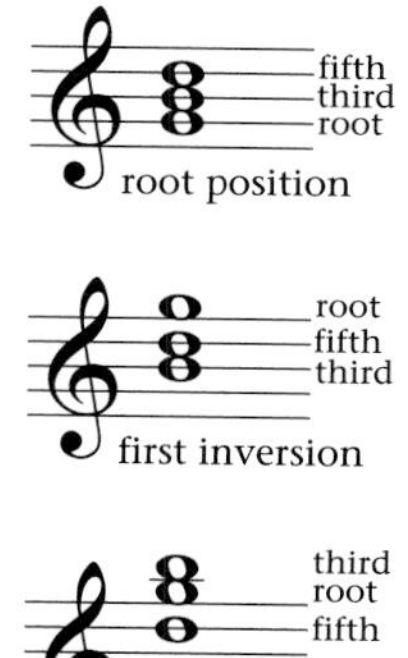

Qualities of Triads

There are four types, or qualities, of triads. These are major, minor, diminished, and augmented. A *major triad* uses a M3 and a P5. A *minor triad* contains a minor 3rd and perfect 5th above the root. A *diminished triad* also has a minor 3rd above the root, but the quality of the 5th is diminished. An *augmented triad* is built with a major 3rd and an augmented 5th.

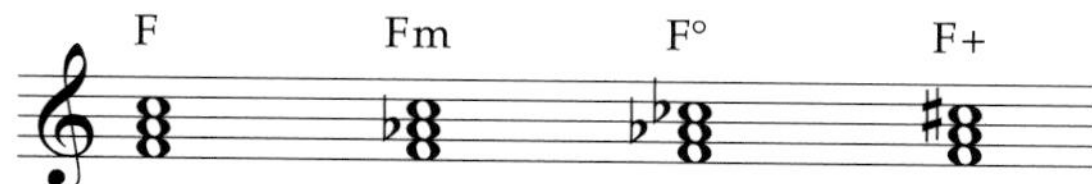

Chords are also labeled with chord symbols above the staff. Chord symbols indicate the root of the chord by pitch name and the quality of the chord. All symbols use uppercase letters. Other symbols are added to show the quality of the chord. In major keys there are three major triads, three minor triads, and one diminished triad.

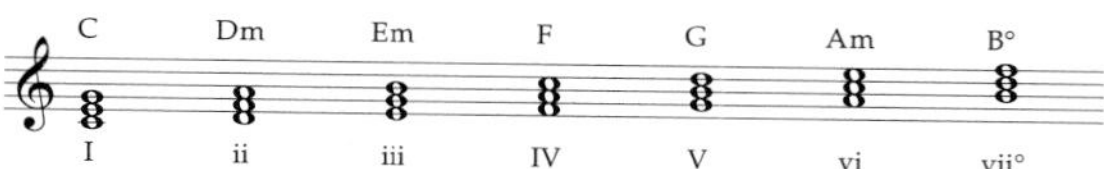

Minor keys have several possible chord qualities, as there are three forms of minor scales. Frequently used chord qualities are shown below.

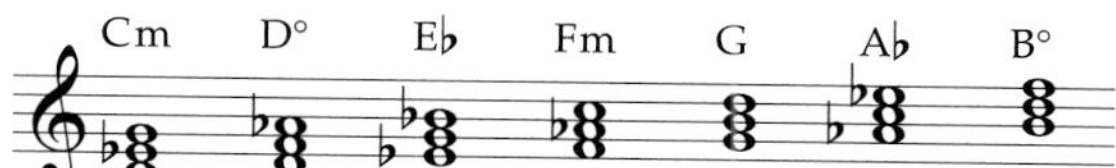

Seventh and Secondary Chords

A *seventh (7th) chord* is a four-note chord that combines a triad with an interval of a 7th above the root. Below are the five most commonly used 7th and chords: major 7th, dominant 7th, minor 7th, half-diminished 7th and the diminished 7th chords.

- A major 7th chord combines a major triad and a major 7th.
- A dominant 7th chord combines a major triad with a minor 7th.
- A minor 7th chord combines a minor triad with a minor 7th.
- A half-diminished chord, minor 7♭5, combines a diminished triad with a minor 7th.
- A diminished chord combines a diminished triad with a diminished 7th.

The qualities of 7th chords in a major key are shown here:

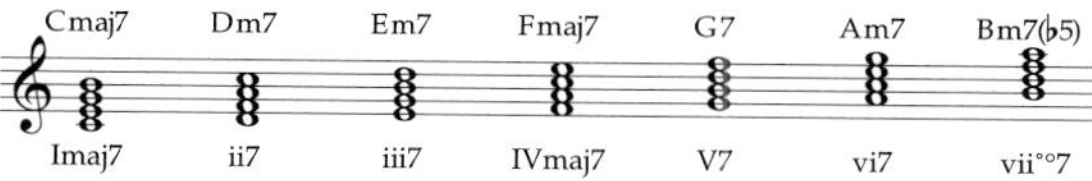

The 7th chords commonly used in minor keys are shown here:

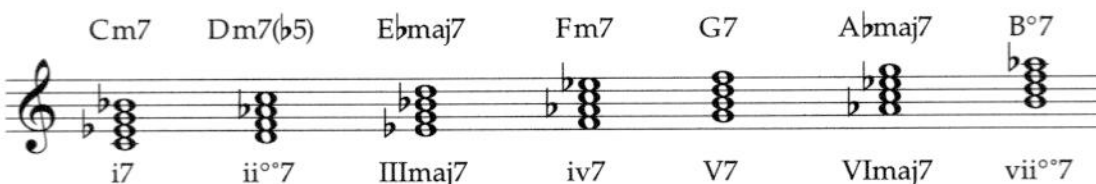

Primary chords in major keys are tonic, subdominant, and dominant. These chords collectively contain the notes in the major scale. See below.

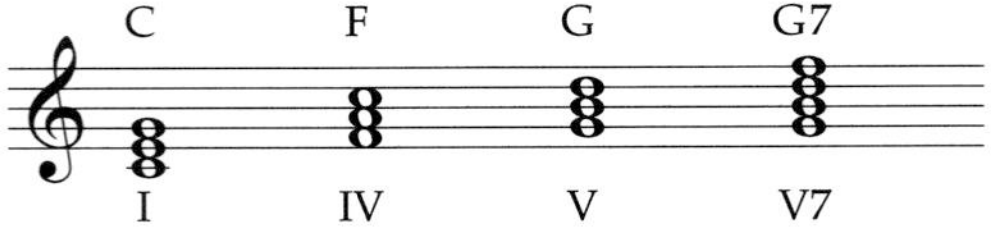

Every pitch in a simple melody can be harmonized with one of these chords. See below.

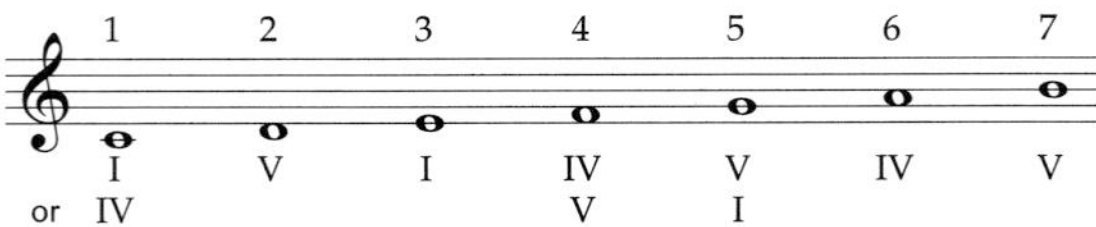

The other chords in a major key are *secondary chords.* Secondary chords substitute for primary chords to add interesting contrast to the music.

Primary chord:	**I**	**IV**	**V7**
Secondary chord:	**iii or vi**	**ii or vi**	**vii°**

The *primary chords in minor* are also tonic, subdominant, and dominant; but the quality of the tonic and subdominant chords is minor. This makes the minor tonality distinctive from the major tonality.

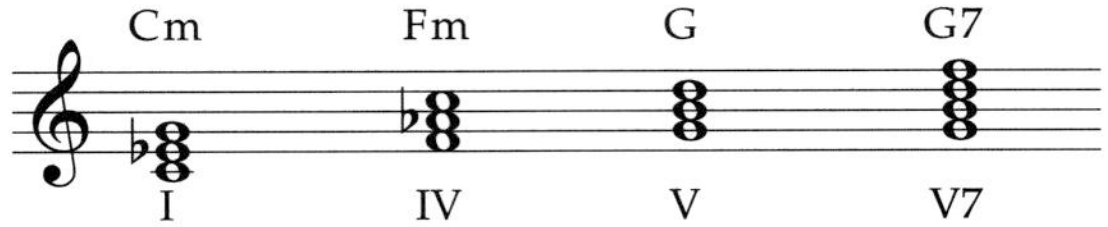

Folk music is typically limited to triads, the dominant 7th, and occasionally, minor 7th chords. Other styles, such as jazz, regularly use all types of 7th chords.

A *chord progression* is the order of chords played in a song. The *12-bar blues* is a simple chord progression used in most blues songs and is the basis for many rock, pop, and jazz tunes. Each number or letter represents one measure.

Numbers	Chords	7th chord example
I-IV-I-I	**(A-D-A-A)**	**A7-D7-A7-A7**
IV-IV-I-I	**(D-D-A-A)**	**D7-D7-A7-A7**
V-IV-I-V	**(E-D-A-E)**	**E7-D7-A7-E7**

Time Line

Composer	Dates	Year	Event
Michael Praetorius	1571–1621	1620	Mayflower lands at Plymouth Rock
Thomas Weelkes	1576–1623	1643	Louis XIV becomes king of France at age 5
Jean Baptiste Lully	1632–1687	1666	Newton discovers Law of Gravity
Johann Pachelbel	1653–1706		
Henry Purcell	1659–1695		
Antonio Vivaldi	1678–1741		
Johann Sebastian Bach	1685–1750		
George Frideric Handel	1685–1759		

1600

1700

Composer	Dates	Year	Event
Franz Joseph Haydn	1732–1809	1707	United Kingdom of Great Britain formed
Wolfgang Amadeus Mozart	1756–1791	1769	James Watt patents his steam engine
Ludwig van Beethoven	1770–1827	1775	American Revolution begins
Franz Schubert	1797–1828	1776	American Declaration of Independence
		1783	American Revolution ends
		1789	French Revolution; George Washington is elected first U.S. president

1800

Composer	Dates	Year	Event
Fanny Mendelssohn Hensel	1805–1847	1803	Louisiana Purchase
Felix Mendelssohn	1809–1847	1804	Lewis and Clark expedition
Frédéric Chopin	1810–1849	1807	Robert Fulton builds first commercial steamboat; London streets lighted by gas
Robert Schumann	1810–1856	1812	War of 1812
Richard Wagner	1813–1883	1825	Erie Canal opens
Johannes Brahms	1833–1897	1838	Daguerre takes first photographs
Georges Bizet	1838–1875	1844	First telegraph message transmitted
Modest Mussorgsky	1839–1881	1846	First use of ether as an anesthetic
Peter Ilyich Tchaikovsky	1840–1893	1848	First Women's Rights Convention; California Gold Rush
Edvard Grieg	1843–1907	1860	Civil War begins; Abraham Lincoln is elected sixteenth U.S. president
Nicolai Rimsky-Korsakov	1844–1908	1863	Gettysburg Address; Emancipation Proclamation
John Philip Sousa	1854–1932	1865	Abraham Lincoln assassinated
Cécile Chaminade	1857–1944	1869	First American transcontinental railroad
Edward Elgar	1857–1934	1876	Alexander Graham Bell invents telephone
Giacomo Puccini	1858–1924	1877	Thomas Edison invents phonograph
Claude Debussy	1862–1918	1879	Edison invents incandescent light bulb
Scott Joplin	1868–1917	1886	Statue of Liberty unveiled in New York Harbor
James Weldon Johnson	1871–1938	1889	Eiffel Tower in France is completed
Ralph Vaughan Williams	1872–1958	1895	Wilhelm Roentgen discovers X-rays
W.C. (William Christopher) Handy	1873–1958		
Arnold Schönberg	1874–1951		
Charles Ives	1874–1954		
Béla Bartók	1881–1945		
Manuel M. Ponce	1882–1948		
Igor Stravinsky	1882–1971		
Huddie Ledbetter	1885–1949		
Ferdinand ("Jelly Roll") Morton	1885–1941		
Gertrude ("Ma") Rainey	1886–1939		
Sergei Prokofiev	1891–1953		
George Gershwin	1898–1937		
Duke Ellington	1899–1974		
Irving Berlin	1899–1989		

1899

1900

Louis Armstrong **1900–1971**
Harry Partch **1901–1974**
Glenn Miller **1904–1944**
Harold Arlen **1905–1986**
Dmitri Shostakovich **1906–1975**
Art Tatum **1909–1956**

1901 Guglielmo Marconi transmits wireless telegraph signals across Atlantic Ocean
1902 Pierre and Marie Curie discover radium
1903 Wilbur and Orville Wright make first successful airplane flight
1904 First sound moving picture
1905 Albert Einstein offers Theory of Relativity
1906 San Francisco earthquake and fire
1908 Model T Ford produced
1909 Robert Peary and Matthew Henson reach North Pole

1910

Robert Johnson **1911–1938**
John Cage **1912–1992**
Benjamin Britten **1913–1976**
Lester Flatt **1914–1979**
Billie Holiday **1915–1959**
Frank Sinatra **1915–1998**
Milton Babbitt **1916–**
Ella Fitzgerald **1917–1996**
Thelonious Monk **1917–1982**
Leonard Bernstein **1918–1990**

1910 Discovery of the South Pole; discovery of protons and electrons
1912 *Titanic* disaster
1914 Panama Canal opens; World War I begins
1917 Russian Revolution
1918 World War I ends

1920

Charlie Parker **1920–1955**
Judy Garland **1922–1969**
Katsutoshi Nagasawa **1923–**
Earl Scruggs **1924–**
Paul Desmond **1924–1977**
Pierre Boulez **1925–**
Miles Davis **1926–1991**
John Coltrane **1927–1967**
Karlheinz Stockhausen **1928–**
Rosemary Clooney **1928–2002**
Burt Bacharach **1928–**
George Crumb **1929–**

1920 First commercial radio broadcast; 19th Amendment gives women right to vote
1925 Grand Ole Opry starts radio broadcasts from Nashville
1926 First talking picture, *Don Juan*, premieres on Broadway
1927 Charles Lindbergh's flight across the Atlantic; first television transmission; New York's Cotton Club begins broadcasting Duke Ellington's Band on radio
1928 Sir Alexander Fleming discovers penicillin; *Billboard Magazine* begins publishing music charts
1929 New York stock market crash; Great Depression begins

1930

Claude Bolling **1930–**
Stephen Sondheim **1930–**
Isao Tomita **1932–**
John Williams **1932–**
Willie Nelson **1933–**
Krzysztof Penderecki **1933–**
Elvis Presley **1935–1977**
Terry Riley **1935–**
Philip Glass **1937–**
Judy Collins **1939–**

1931 U.S. Congress designates "The Star-Spangled Banner" as the national anthem
1932 Franklin D. Roosevelt is elected president
1933 Nazi Revolution in Germany
1935 George Gershwin's *Porgy and Bess* opens
1936 Woody Guthrie hired by the Department of the Interior to perform folk songs around the country
1938 Orson Welles broadcasts "War of the Worlds"
1939 World War II begins; Glenn Miller Band's "In the Mood" becomes the band's biggest hit ever

1939

1940

Trevor Nunn 1940–
John Lennon 1940–1980
Ringo Starr 1940–
Joan Baez 1941–
Bob Dylan 1941–
David Fanshawe 1942–
Aretha Franklin 1942–
Paul McCartney 1942–
George Harrison 1943–2001
Mick Jagger 1943–
Joni Mitchell 1943–
Keith Richards 1943–
Vangelis 1943–
Eric Clapton 1945–
James C. Pankow 1947–
Elton John 1947–
Andrew Lloyd Webber 1948–
Stephen Schwartz 1948–
Stevie Nicks 1948–
Billy Joel 1949–
Bruce Springsteen 1949–

1940–42 Duke Ellington records "Take the A Train"
1941 Pearl Harbor is bombed; U.S. enters World War II
1943 *Oklahoma!* opens at the St. James Theatre
1944 Aaron Copland composes *Appalachian Spring*
1945 World War II ends; the first digital computer is completed
1946 Dizzy Gillespie innovates beyond Be-bop and popularizes Afro-Cuban/Latin jazz
1948 Nation of Israel is founded
1949 People's Republic of China is born

1950

Peter Gabriel 1950–
Libby Larsen 1950–
Stevie Wonder 1950–
Dewey Bunnell 1952–
Gloria Estefan 1957–
Madonna 1958–
Mary Chapin Carpenter 1958–

1950 Korean War begins
1951 The first computer to be commercially available and to store data on magnetic tape is built
1952 First hydrogen bomb explodes at Enewetok, Marshall Islands
1953 Francis Crick and James Watson present their double-helix model of the DNA molecule; IBM releases its first mainframe computer; Korean War ends; Rosa Parks is arrested in Alabama
1954 Dr. Jonas Salk develops polio vaccine; Texas Instruments creates a new generation of transistors using silicon; TV Dinners are introduced in the U.S.; "Rock Around the Clock" tops the music charts; Elvis Presley records "That's All Right, Mamma" at Sun Studios
1957 The Soviet Union launches the world's first artificial satellite
1959 Fidel Castro becomes premier of Cuba; Buddy Holly is killed in a plane crash

1959

1960

Amy Grant	**1960–**
Wynton Marsalis	**1961–**
Axl Rose	**1962–**
Clint Black	**1962–**
Garth Brooks	**1962–**
Jon Bon Jovi	**1962–**
Sheryl Crow	**1962–**
Tori Amos	**1963–**
Diana Krall	**1964–**
Lenny Kravitz	**1964–**
Moby	**1965–**
Shania Twain	**1965–**
Martina McBride	**1966–**
Tim McGraw	**1967–**
Faith Hill	**1967–**
Harry Connick, Jr.	**1967–**
Sarah MacLachlan	**1968–**
Will Smith	**1968–**

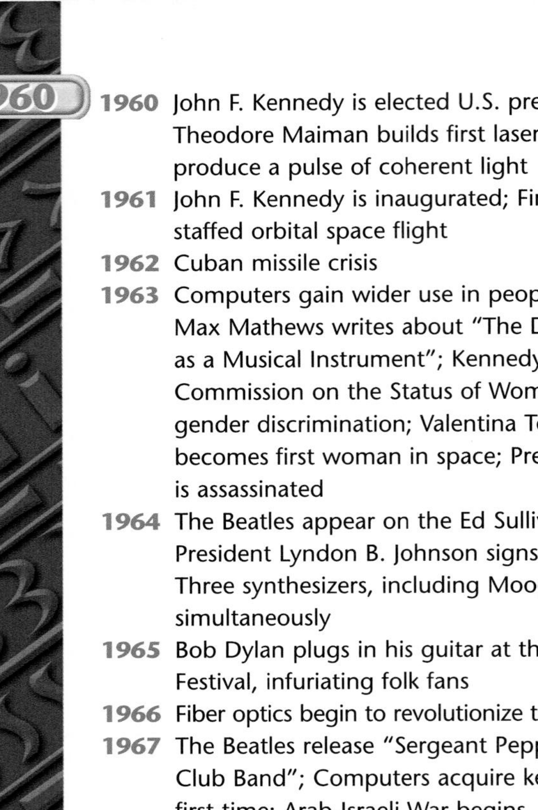

1960 John F. Kennedy is elected U.S. president; Theodore Maiman builds first laser to successfully produce a pulse of coherent light

1961 John F. Kennedy is inaugurated; First successful staffed orbital space flight

1962 Cuban missile crisis

1963 Computers gain wider use in people's daily lives; Max Mathews writes about "The Digital Computer as a Musical Instrument"; Kennedy endorses Commission on the Status of Women's report on gender discrimination; Valentina Tereshkova becomes first woman in space; President Kennedy is assassinated

1964 The Beatles appear on the Ed Sullivan Show; President Lyndon B. Johnson signs Civil Rights Act; Three synthesizers, including Moog's, are invented simultaneously

1965 Bob Dylan plugs in his guitar at the Newport Folk Festival, infuriating folk fans

1966 Fiber optics begin to revolutionize telecommunications

1967 The Beatles release "Sergeant Pepper's Lonely Hearts Club Band"; Computers acquire keyboards for the first time; Arab-Israeli War begins

1968 Martin Luther King, Jr. and Robert F. Kennedy are assassinated; The computer mouse debuts

1969 Neil Armstrong walks on the moon; Woodstock Music & Arts Festival draws half a million fans to a farm in upstate New York; The Who's rock opera *Tommy* is introduced

1970

Macy Gray	**1970–**
Mariah Carey	**1970–**
Beck	**1970–**
Alison Krauss	**1971–**
Ricky Martin	**1971–**
Robbie Williams	**1974–**
Ruben Studdard	**1978–**
Norah Jones	**1979–**
Aaliyah	**1979–2001**

1970 Jimi Hendrix and Janis Joplin die

1975 Vietnam War ends; Bruce Springsteen releases *Born to Run*

1977 Elvis Presley dies; *Saturday Night Fever* becomes a best-selling album

1979 Sony introduces the Walkman

1980

Beyoncé Knowles	**1981–**
Josh Groban	**1981–**
Jonny Lang	**1981–**
Kelly Clarkson	**1982–**
Mandy Moore	**1984–**
Charlotte Church	**1986–**

1980 John Lennon is murdered in New York City

1985 "We Are The World" is recorded; Worldwide Live Aid concert benefits Ethiopian famine victims

1987 Video CD format created

1990

Electronic mail becomes a primary means of personal and business communication

2000

Downloading music from the Internet has a negative impact on recording sales

Just Keep Goin' On, Words and Music by Dan J. Smith. Copyright © Never Say Never Songs. International Copyright Secured. All Rights Reserved.

Land of a Thousand Dances, Words and Music by Chris Kenner. © 1963, 1970 (Renewed 1991) EMI LONGITUDE MUSIC. All Rights Reserved. International Copyright Secured. Used by Permission.

Lead Man Holler, Words and Music by Irving Burgie. Copyright © 1956; Renewed 1984 Cherry Lane Music Publishing Company, Inc. (ASCAP), Lord Burgess Music Publishing (ASCAP) and DreamWorks Songs (ASCAP). Worldwide Rights for Lord Burgess Music Publishing and DreamWorks Songs Administered by Cherry Lane Music Publishing Company, Inc. International Copyright Secured. All Rights Reserved.

The Lion Sleeps Tonight (Wimoweh) (Mbube), Lyrics and Revised Music by George David Weiss, Hugo Peretti and Luigi Creatore. © 1961 FOLKWAYS MUSIC PUBLISHERS, INC. Renewed 1989 by GEORGE DAVID WEISS, LUIGI CREATORE and JUNE PERETTI. Assigned to ABILENE MUSIC, INC. c/o THE SONGWRITERS GUILD OF AMERICA. All Rights Reserved.

Mardi Gras Mambo, Words and Music by Frankie Adams, Ken Elliot and Lou Welsh. Copyright © 1996 by Arc Music Corporation. International Copyright Secured. All Rights Reserved. Used by Permission.

The Night That Goldman Spoke, From MTI's Broadway Junior Broadway for Kids RAGTIME Junior. Music by Stephen Flaherty. Lyrics by Lynn Ahrens. Copyright © 1996, 1997 WB Music Corp., Pen and Perseverance and Hillsdale Music, Inc. All Rights Reserved. Used by Permission.

Old Time Rock & Roll, Words and Music by George Jackson and Thomas E. Jones III. © 1977 MUSCLE SHOALS SOUND PUBLISHING CO., INC. All Rights Reserved. Used by Permission.

Papa Oom Mow Mow, Words and Music by Al Frazier, Carl White, John Harris and Turner Wilson, Jr. © 1962 (Renewed 1990) BEECHWOOD MUSIC CORP. and ATLANTIC MUSIC CORP. All Rights Reserved. International Copyright Secured. Used by Permission.

Park Rap 1, Words and Music by Chris Judah-Lauder. All Rights Reserved.

Park Rap 2, Words and Music by Chris Judah-Lauder. All Rights Reserved.

Peace in This House, Words and Music by Mac Huff. Copyright © 2001 by HAL LEONARD CORPORATION. International Copyright Secured. All Rights Reserved.

Ragtime, From MTI's Broadway Junior Broadway for Kids RAGTIME Junior. Music by Stephen Flaherty. Lyrics by Lynn Ahrens. Copyright © 1996, 1997 WB Music Corp., Pen and Perseverance and Hillsdale Music, Inc. All Rights Reserved. Used by Permission.

Ragtime Epilogue & Finale, From MTI's Broadway Junior Broadway for Kids RAGTIME Junior. Music by Stephen Flaherty. Lyrics by Lynn Ahrens. Copyright © 1996, 1997 WB Music Corp., Pen and Perseverance and Hillsdale Music, Inc. All Rights Reserved. Used by Permission.

Seasons of Love from RENT, Words and Music by Jonathan Larson. © 1996 FINSTER & LUCY MUSIC LTD. CO. All Rights Controlled and Administered by EMI APRIL MUSIC INC. All Rights Reserved. International Copyright Secured. Used by Permission.

Sixteen Tons, Words and Music by Merle Travis. Copyright © 1947 by Unichappell Music Inc. and Elvis Presley Music. Copyright Renewed. All Rights Administered by Unichappell Music Inc. International Copyright Secured. All Rights Reserved.

Stonehaven Sunset, Words and Music by John Denver. Copyright © 1990 Cherry Mountain Music (ASCAP) and DreamWorks Songs (ASCAP). Worldwide Rights for DreamWorks Songs Administered by Cherry Lane Music Publishing Company, Inc. International Copyright Secured. All Rights Reserved.

Success, From MTI's Broadway Junior Broadway for Kids RAGTIME Junior. Music by Stephen Flaherty. Lyrics by Lynn Ahrens. Copyright © 1996, 1997 WB Music Corp., Pen and Perseverance and Hillsdale Music, Inc. All Rights Reserved. Used by Permission.

Tears in Heaven, Words and Music by Eric Clapton and Will Jennings. Copyright © 1992 by E.C. Music Ltd. and Blue Sky Rider Songs. All Rights for E.C. Music Ltd. Administered by Unichappell Music Inc. All Rights for Blue Sky Rider Songs Administered by Irving Music, Inc. International Copyright Secured. All Rights Reserved.

Twist and Shout, Words and Music by Bert Russell and Phil Medley. Copyright © 1964 Sony/ATV Songs LLC and Sloopy II Music. Copyright Renewed. All Rights on behalf of Sony/ATV Songs LLC Administered by Sony/ATV Music Publishing, 8 Music Square West, Nashville, TN 37203. International Copyright Secured. All Rights Reserved.

We Go Together from GREASE, Lyric and Music by Warren Casey and Jim Jacobs. © 1971, 1972 WARREN CASEY and JIM JACOBS. © Renewed 1999, 2000 JIM JACOBS and THE ESTATE OF WARREN CASEY. All Rights Administered by EDWIN H. MORRIS & COMPANY, A Division of MPL Music Publishing, Inc. All Rights Reserved.

We Shall Overcome, Musical and Lyrical Adaptation by Zilphia Horton, Frank Hamilton, Guy Carawan and Pete Seeger. Inspired by African American Gospel Singing, members of the Food and Tobacco Workers Union, Charleston, SC, and the Southern Civil Rights Movement. TRO - © Copyright 1960 (Renewed) and 1963 (Renewed) Ludlow Music, Inc., New York, NY. International Copyright Secured. All Rights Reserved Including Public Performance For Profit. Used by Permission. Royalties derived from this composition are being contributed to the We Shall Overcome Fund and The Freedom Movement under the Trusteeship of the writers.

Wide Open Spaces, Words and Music by Susan Gibson. © 1997 PIE EYED GROOBEE MUSIC/Administered by BUG MUSIC. All Rights Reserved. Used by Permission.

CREDITS

Illustration Credits: Elizabeth Britton: 124–125. Viviana M. Diaz: 230–231. Patrick Kelly: i. Dave Klug: 249. Carl Salter: 106–107. Remy Simard: 32–33.

Photography Credits: All photographs are copyright of Macmillan/McGraw-Hill (MMH) except as noted below.

Allan Landau for MMH: iv-vii: trombone, 15: inset, t., 21: b., 24: c.r., b., 30-31: t., 35: t.r., 60: b.l., 61: b.l., 72-73: bkgd., 113: c.r., 165: t.r., 259: l., b.l., 260: t.l. Jade Albert for MMH: cover, i: b.r. Shane Morgan for MMH: 101: b.r.

iv-vii: Chinese wood blocks, congas, cowbell, electric keyboard, side drum, tuba, wood blocks, PhotoDisc, Inc.; decorated drum, French horn, silver drum, Corbis. 1: b.l. PhotoDisc, Inc.; b.c. Music Theatre International. 2: l./ Boutard David/Corbis/Kipa; b.c. Roger Ressmeyer/Corbis. 2-3: b. Denis O'Regan/ Corbis. 3: c.r., t. Corbis; t.r. PhotoDisc, Inc. 4; t.l. Bettmann/Corbis; b.l. AFP/Corbis. 5: t.r. PhotoDisc, Inc. 6: t. Jonathan Nourok/PhotoEdit, Inc.; l. Myrleen Ferguson Cate/PhotoEdit, Inc.; c. Charles Gupton/ Corbis; c.r. Corbis. 7: c. Bettmann/Corbis. 8: b.l. Corbis; b.r. PhotoDisc, Inc. 9: b.r. PhotoDisc, Inc. 10: b. Paul SChutzer/Time Life Pictures/Getty Images. 11: t.r., b. Bettmann/Corbis. 13: t. Annie Griffiths Belt/ Corbis. 14: b. Lawrence Manning/Corbis. 16: c.l. Corbis; b.l. Bettmann/Corbis; b.r. Christie's Images/ Corbis/Romare Bearden Foundation/licensed by VAGA, NY. 17: t.r. David Redfern/Redferns. 18-19: bkgd. PhotoDisc, Inc. 20: r. Corbis. 21: r. Tony Freeman/PhotoEdit, Inc. 22: b. Melissa Farlow/Aurora; b.r. Bettmann/Corbis. 23: t.r. Robert Milne. 25: t. Sarah Zupko. 26: l. PhotoDisc, Inc.; b. SW Productions/Brand X Pictures. 27: c.l. David Boutard/ Corbis/Kipa; c.r. David Redfern/Redferns Music Picture Library; br. Lawrence Manning/Corbis. 28: c.r. Donald Huff. 31: c.r. Redferns Music Picture Library. 35: b.l. Andy Lyons/Getty Images. 36: b.l. Odile Noel/ Lebrecht Music & Arts Photo Library; c.l. Odile Noel/Redferns Music Picture Library; t.l. Nigel Luckhurst/Lebrecht Music & Arts Photo Library. 37: t.r. Bettmann/Corbis; bkgd. Patrick Ward/Corbis; b.r., b.c., c.r., b.l. PhotoDisc, Inc.; t. Roger Mastroianni. 38: 1., 2., 4., 5. PhotoDisc, Inc. 38-39: bkgd. Patrick Ward/Corbis. 39: c., b.l., t.r. PhotoDisc, Inc.; t.r. courtesy of Sonor Instruments, a division of Hohner, Inc.; b.c. PhotoDisc, Inc. 40-41: bkgd. David Young-Wolff/PhotoEdit, Inc. 42: t.l. PhotoDisc, Inc.; c.r. cropwalk.org. 42-43: bkgd. Corel. 43: b.c.l. Paul McMahon; t.l. Tony Freeman/PhotoEdit, Inc.; b.l. Crop Walk; c. William Whitehurst/Corbis; t.r., c.r. MetaCreations/Kai Power Photos. 44: b. Sergei Karpukhin/AP Photo; t. PhotoDisc, Inc. 44-45: c. PhotoDisc, Inc. 45: t.r. Sergei Karpukhin/AP Photo; b.r. PhotoDisc, Inc. 46: t.l. Getty Images. 47: b. Odile Noel/Redferns Music Picture Library. 48: b.l. Reuters/ NewMedia, Inc./Corbis; b.r. Ulrike Welsch. 48-49: bkgd. Phil Banko/Corbis. 50: t.l. Charles Gupton/ Corbis. 51: t.r. Dennis MacDonald/PhotoEdit, Inc. 52: b.l. Hulton-Deutsch Collection/Corbis. 53: c. Petr Morgan/Reuters/Corbis; l. PhotoDisc, Inc.; t.r. Alastair Grant/AP Photo; b.r. Dennis MacDonald/PhotoEdit, Inc. 54: c. Peter Turnley/Corbis; b.l. David Butow/ Corbis/Saba. 54-55: b. Keren Su/Corbis. 55: t.r. Charles Gupton/Corbis. 56: b. M. Yamashita/Woodfin Camp & Associates, Inc.; t.l. Chieko Aoki/HAGA/The Image Works, Inc. 57: t.r. Reuters/Guang Niu/Corbis; b. Carl & Ann Purcell/Corbis. 58: b. Joe Sohm/The Image Works, Inc.; t.l. Bob Daemmrich/The Image Works, Inc. 59: bkgd. Corel. 60: t. Jerry Cooke/Corbis. 62: b.l. Marilyn "Angel" Wynn/Nativestock; c.r. Jules T. Allen/Corbis. 62-63: t.c. Myrleen Ferguson Café/ PhotoEdit, Inc. 63: t.r. Nativestock. 64: b.r. Hilarie Kavanagh/Getty Images; t.r. Paul J. Sutton/Corbis; b.l., c.l. PhotoDisc, Inc. 66: t. Jason Lauré. 67: t.r. Michael Nicholson/Corbis. 68: t.r. Chip Forelli/Getty Images; c.r. Tom & Dee Ann McCarthy/Corbis; b. Kelly/ Mooney Photography/Corbis. 69: c.r. Dave G. Houser/Corbis; b.l. Tony Savino/The Image Works, Inc. 70: t.r. Corbis. 71: t.r. Whacky Music, Inc.; b.l. Tony Freeman/PhotoEdit, Inc. 74: l. Ebet Roberts Photography. 74-75: b.c.Kerrick James; t.c. Tommy Hindley/ProSport/Topham/The Image Works, Inc. 75: t.r. AFP/Corbis. 76: l. PhotoDisc, Inc. 76-77: bkgd. Kelly/Mooney Photography/Corbis. 78: bkgd. Kelly/ Mooney Photography/Corbis. 79: b.r. Tommy Hindley/ProSport/Topham/The Image Works, Inc.; t.l. Bob Daemmrich/The Image Works; t.r. Peter Tumley/ Corbis. 80: c.l. Everett Collection; l. Michael S. Yamashita/Corbis. 80-81: b. Everett Collection. 81: t.r. Richard T. Nowitz/Corbis. 82-83: bkgd. PhotoDisc, Inc. 83: t.r. Mark Lennihan/AP/Wide World Photos. 84: c.l. David Redfern/Redferns. 85: t. Walt Disney Pictures/The Kobal Collection; b. Corbis. 86: l. Hugh Sitton/Stone/Getty Images. 86-87: t.c. Robbie Jack/ Corbis. 87: b. UPPA/Topham/The Image Works. 88: b. Lynda Richardson/Corbis; t.l. Redferns Music Picture Library. 89: t.l. Michael Siluk/The Image Works; t.r. Hinata Haga/HAGA/The Image Works; c., b.r. PhotoDisc, Inc.; b.l. Lynda Richardson/Corbis. 90: c. Robert Landau/Corbis; b.l. Doug Wilson/Corbis. 90-91: bkgd. Jose Fuste Raga/eStock Photo/PictureQuest. 92: b. Barry Gutierrez/Rocky Mountain News; t.l. Operation Respect. 93: bkgd. PhotoDisc, Inc. 94-95: bkgd. Yann Arthus-Bertrand/Corbis. 95: b.r. T. J. Florian/Photo Network/PictureQuest. 96: t.r. Christopher Berkey/AP/Wide World Photos; b.l. Reuters/Corbis. 96-97: bkgd. SuperStock. 97: r. Reuters/Corbis. 98: r. Ebet Roberts; bkgd. PhotoDisc, Inc.; b.l. The Post and Courier, Mic Smith/AP/Wide World Photos. 98-99: c. PhotoDisc, Inc. 99: r. Fin Costsello/Redferns Music Picture Library. 100: c.l. Rudi Von Briel/Index Stock Imagery; c.r. Art on File/Corbis; b.l. Lucy Nicholson/Reuters NewMedia, Inc./Corbis; b. L. Clarke/Corbis. 101: t.l. Lindsay Hebberd/Corbis; b.r. Artville. 102: bkgd. Bettmann/Corbis. 103: b.l. Bettmann/Corbis. 104: bkgd. Nik Wheeler/Corbis. 105: t.r. Michael Siluk/The Image Works; b.r. Reuters/ Corbis. 105: l. Morton Beebe/Corbis. 106: b.l., b.c.r., b.c.l. Archivo Iconografico, S.A./Corbis; b.r. Lebrecht Music & Arts Photo Library. 107: b.r. Corbis; b.l. Archivo Iconografico, S.A./Corbis; b.c.l., b.c.r. Lebrecht Music & Arts Photo Library. 108: t.l. Archivo Iconografico, S.A./Corbis; t.r. G. Salter/Lebrecht Music & Arts Photo Library; r. Ruggero Vanni/Corbis. 110: l. Archivo Iconographico, S.A./Corbis. 111: b. Brian Branch-Price/AP/Wide World Photos. 112: c.r. Bettmann/Corbis; c. Toby Wales/Lebrecht Music & Arts Photo Library. 112-113: bkgd. Lebrecht Music & Arts Photo Library. 113: t.r. Bettmann/Corbis. 114: t.r., b. Mimmo Jodice/Corbis; b.l., b.r. Archivo Iconografico, S.A./Corbis; b.c.l. Lebrecht Music & Arts Photo Library. 115: t.r. Bettmann/Corbis; b. Jose Fuste Raga/Corbis. 116: l. Harvey Lloyd/Getty Images; t.r. Lebrecht Music & Arts Photo Library. 118: t.l. Archivo Iconografico, S.A./Corbis. 120: b.c., b.l. Lebrecht Music & Arts Photo Library. 121: b.r. Francis G. Mayer/Corbis. 122: t.l. Lebrecht Music & Arts Photo Library; b.c. S. Lauterwasser/Lebrecht Music & Arts Photo Library; r. Private Collection/Lebrecht Music & Arts Photo Library. 123: bkgd., r. Corbis. 125: t.r. Colouriser/Lebrecht Music & Arts Photo Library. 126: t.l. Bettmann/Corbis; t.r. Lebrecht Music & Arts Photo Library; b.l., c. Bettmann/Corbis. 127: t.r. Corbis. 128: t.r. Frank Trapper/Corbis; t.l. Jeff Moore/Zuma Press. 128-129: bkgd. PhotoDisc, Inc. 130: b.r., t.l. Betty Freeman/Lebrecht Music & Arts Photo Library. 131: b.r. Private Collection/Lebrecht Music & Arts Photo Library; c.l. Harvey Lloyd/Getty Images; c. Jeff Moore/Zuma Press. 132: l. Richard Morrell/Corbis; b. David Stoecklein/Corbis. 133: b.l. Jose Luis Pelaez, Inc./Corbis; r. Gary Houlder/Corbis. 134: b. Gabe Palmer/Corbis. 135: t.r. Stephen J. Boitano/ Stringer/Getty Images; r. Corel. 136-137: bkgd. MetaCreations/Kai Power Photos. 137: b.r. AP Photo/ The Herald-Dispatch, Jeff Gentner. 138: l. Allan Grant/Time Life Pictures/Getty Images. 138-139: bkgd. Corel. 139: t.r. Underwood & Underwood/ Corbis; c. MetaCreations/Kai Power Photos; b.r. Comstock. 140: b. Kathy Willens/AP/Wide World Photos; t.l. PhotoDisc, Inc. 140-141: bkgd. Corel. 142: l. AP Photo/New York Daily News, Susan Watts, Pool; b. AP Photo/Mike Segar, Pool. 143: t. Philip Gould/Corbis. 144: l. AP Photo/Aaron Favila. 145: t. AFP Photo/Beth Keiser/Corbis; 4. Corel. 146: t.l. Jacob August Riis/Corbis; b.r. Marion Post Wolcott/Corbis; b.l. Horace Bristol/Corbis; t.r. Underwood & Underwood/Corbis. 146-147: bkgd. PhotoDisc, Inc. 147: t.r. Frederic Lewis/Getty Images; t.l. Underwood & Underwood/Corbis; b.l. Bettmann/Corbis. 148: l. M. Peric/Lebrecht Music & Arts Photo Library; r. PhotoDisc, Inc. 150: t.l. Bettmann/Corbis. 150-151: b. Corbis. 152-153: bkgd. AP/Wide World Photos. 154: t.r. Scott Gries/Getty Images; bkgd. Corel. 155: t.r. "Song of Peace" by Briton Riviere, published by Old World Prints. 156: b. Lebrecht Music & Arts Photo Library. 157: c.r. Gabe Palmer/Corbis; t.l. AP Photo; b.l. Kathy Willens/AP Photo; b. Mike Segar, Pool/AP Photo. 158: c.l. America Sings!; b.l. Paramount/Kobal Collection. 158-159: bkgd. PhotoDisc, Inc. 159: t.r. Paramount/Kobal Collection; b.r. Everett Collection. 160: t.r. Bettmann/Corbis. 162: t.r. Jim and Mary Whitmer. 162-163: bkgd. PhotoDisc, Inc. 163: c.l. Jim and Mary Whitmer. 164: t.r. SuperStock. 164-165: bkgd. Corel. 165: b.r. Corbis. 166: t.l. PhotoDisc Blue/Getty Images; t.c., t.r., c.l. PhotoDisc, Inc.; c.r. Mark Wagoner; b.r. PhotoDisc Green/Getty Images. 166-167: bkgd. Corbis. 167: b.c. Corbis; c.l. PhotoDisc, Inc. 168: t.r. Corbis; b.r. Library of Congress. 168-169: bkgd. Kenneth Garrett. 169: t.r., b.l. Library of Congress; c.r. Library of Congress Photoduplication Services; b.r. James Gardner/ Library of Congress. 170: t.l. AP/Wide World Photos. 170-171: bkgd. Corbis; b. Michael S. Yamashita/ Corbis. 171: b., r. PhotoDisc, Inc. 172: b.l. Bettmann/ Corbis; c.r. PhotoDisc, Inc. 172-173: bkgd. Corel. 173: t.r. Bettmann/Corbis; t.l. Bernard Gotfryd/ Woodfin Camp & Associates; c.l. Chuck Savage/ Corbis; b.l. Photri/Microstock. 174: t.r. David Drapkin/ Getty Images; b. Leon Morris/Redferns Music Picture Library. 175: bkgd. AFP/Corbis; t.r. Reuters/NewMedia, Inc./Corbis. 176: b. Marilyn "Angel" Wynn/ Nativestock.com; bkgd. Corbis. 177: t.r. Photofest; b.l. Tony Freeman/PhotoEdit, Inc. 178: c.l. Bob Krist/ Corbis; b.r. Melissa Lubert; c.r. Everett Collection; b.l. Stuart Ramson/AP/Wide World Photos. 178-179: bkgd. Keith Sherman and Associates/AP/Wide World Photos. 179: b.l. Everett Collection; b.r. Eliot Elisofon/ Time Life Pictures/Getty Images; t.r. Beatriz Schiller/ Time Life Pictures/Getty Images. 180: b. Keith Sherman and Associates/AP/Wide World Photos; t.r. Vittoriano Rastelli/Corbis; c.r. Frank Micelotta/Getty Images Editorial; bkgd. PhotoDisc, Inc. 181: t.r. Robbie Jack/Corbis; t.l. AP/Wide World Photos. 182: b. Vittoriano Rastelli/Corbis; t.r. PhotoDisc, Inc.; bkgd. Corel. 183: t.l. Leon Morris/Redferns Music Picture Library; t.r. America Sings!; b. Michael S. Yamashita/ Corbis. 184: l. PhotoDisc, Inc.; b. Image Farm; b. Ariel Skelley/Corbis. 185: t. Alex Wong/Getty Images; t. Image Farm. 186: c. Wesley Frank/Woodfin Camp & Associates. 188: t. Getty Images. 189: bkgd. Corel. 190: b. ASAP, Ltd./Index Stock Imagery; b. Image Farm; l. PhotoDisc, Inc. 191: c., b. PhotoDisc, Inc. 192: b. Amy Sancetta/AP Photo. 192-193: bkgd. Getty Images. 193: t. The Granger Collection. 194: c. Getty Images. 194-195: bkgd. PhotoDisc, Inc. 195: b.r. Tim Mosenfelder/Corbis. 196: c.r. PhotoDisc, Inc. 196-197: bkgd. Kevin Fleming/Corbis. 197: t.r. Scott Gries/Getty Images Editorial; l., c. PhotoDisc, Inc. 198: b. Dick Loek/Toronto Star/Zuma Press; bkgd. Joe Carini/The Image Works. 198-199: bkgd. Corel. 199: r. PhotoDisc, Inc.; bkgd. Joe Carini/The Image Works. 200: b. PhotoDisc, Inc.; c. Sally Brown/Index Stock Imagery. 201: t.r. Gabe Palacio/Getty Images Editorial. 202-203: bkgd. Peter Adams/Alamy.com. 203: t.r. National Library of Canada. 204: c. Ivan Massar/Stock Photos. 205: r. PhotoDisc, Inc. 206: t.l. PhotoDisc, Inc.; b. Bob Adelman/Magnum Photos. 206-207: bkgd. MetaCreations/Kai Power Photos. 208: c. Redferns Music Picture Library; c., b. Image Farm. 209: t.l. Bob Adelman/Magnum Photos; c. ASAP, Ltd./Index Stock Imagery; t.r. Wesley Frank/Woodfin Camp & Associates; b.r. Dick Loek/Toronto Star/Zuma Press. 210: b. David and Peter Turnley/Corbis. 211: bkgd. Corel. 212: t.l. Roger Ressmeyer/Corbis; bkgd. Jim Richardson/Corbis. 213: t.r. Associated Press/AP/ Wide World Photos. 214-215: bkgd. Corel. 215: b. Louis Gubb/Corbis. 216: bkgd., b.r. PhotoDisc, Inc. 217: bkgd., c.r. PhotoDisc, Inc. 218: c.r. Roger Ressmeyer/Corbis; b. Brandon D. Cole/Corbis. 219: c. Corbis. 220: t.r. Clifford Keaney/Clifford Keaney Photography; bkgd. MetaCreations/Kai Power Photos. 221: bkgd. Corel; t.r. AP/Wide World Photos. 222: bkgd. Corbis. 223: t.r. Irene Young/Xenophile Records/Green Linnet Records, Inc.; bkgd. Corel. 224: b. AFP/Corbis. 226-227: bkgd. Corel. 228: l. Adam Rountree/Getty Images. 229: b.l. Miranda Meyer/ Associated Press, Iowa City Gazette/AP/Wide World Photos. 232: r. Bill Ross/Corbis; b.r. Mary Evans Picture Library; l. Roberto Otero/Stockphoto.com/ Stock Photos. 233: t.r. Hulton-Deutsch Collection/ Corbis; b. Beatriz Schiller/Getty Images Editorial. 234: t.r. Myrleen Ferguson Cate/PhotoEdit, Inc.; t.l. Bettmann/Corbis; b.l., b.c. NASA; bkgd. Corbis. 235: t.r. David and Peter Turnley/Corbis; t.l. Roger Ressmeyer/Corbis; b.c. Clifford Keaney/Clifford Keaney Photography. 236: r. Music Theatre International; b.l. PhotoDisc, Inc. 236-237: b.l. Corel. 238: t.r. PhotoDisc, Inc. 239: b. Music Theatre International; t.r. Corbis. 241: b.r. Image Club Graphics. 243: b.r. MetaCreations/Kai Power Photos. 245: b.r. PhotoDisc, Inc. 247: b.r. Music Theatre International. 249: b.c. Music Theatre International. 250: b.l., b.c., b.r. PhotoDisc, Inc. 251: b.l. Music Theatre International. 252: bkgd. Corbis; r. PhotoDisc, Inc. 254: l., b.l. Bettman Archive/Corbis. 255: t.l., b.r. PhotoDisc, Inc.; b.l. PhotoDisc Blue/Getty Images. 256: c.l., c.r. PhotoDisc, Inc.; b.r. Jules Frazier/ PhotoDisc, Inc./Getty Images. 257: t.l. PhotoDisc, Inc. 258: t.l., c.l. PhotoDisc, Inc. 259: t.l., t.r. PhotoDisc, Inc. 260: c.l., b.r. PhotoDisc, Inc.

All attempts have been made to provide complete and correct credits by the time of publication.

Classified Index

Folk and Traditional

Popular Songs

Songs from Broadway Musicals

Montages

Interviews

Music Index

Pronunciation Key

Simplified International Phonetic Alphabet

VOWELS

ɑ	father	o	obey	æ	cat	ɔ	paw
e	ape	u	moon	ɛ	pet	ʊ	put
i	bee	ʌ	up	ɩ	it	ə	ago

SPECIAL SOUNDS

β	say *b* without touching lips together; *Spanish* nueve, haba
ç	hue; *German* ich
ð	the; *Spanish* todo
ɬ	put tongue in position for *l* and say *sh*
n̩	sound *n* as individual syllable
ö	form [o] with lips and say [e]; *French* adieu, *German* schön
œ	form [ɔ] with lips and say [ɛ]; *French* coeur, *German* plötzlich
ɾ	flipped r; butter or r native to language
r̄	rolled r; *Spanish* perro
ǂ	click tongue on the ridge behind teeth; *Zulu* ngcwele
ü	form [u] with lips and say [i]; *French* tu, *German* grün
ʊ̈	form [ʊ] with lips and say [ɩ]
x	blow strong current of air with back of tongue up; *German* Bach, *Hebrew* Hanukkah, *Spanish* bajo
ʒ	pleasure
ʼ	glottal stop, as in the exclamation "uh oh!" [ˈʌˈo]
~	nasalized vowel, such as *French* bon [bõ]
˺	end consonants *k*, *p*, and *t* without puff of air, such as sky (no puff of air after *k*), as opposed to *k*ite (puff of air after *k*)

OTHER CONSONANTS PRONOUNCED SIMILAR TO ENGLISH

ch	cheese	ny	onion; *Spanish* niño
dy	adieu	sh	shine
g	go	sk	sky
ng	sing	th	think
nk	think	ts	boats